BRAVE
NEW
DIGITAL
CLASSROOM

BRAVE NEW DIGITAL CLASSROOM

TECHNOLOGY AND FOREIGN
LANGUAGE LEARNING
SECOND EDITION

ROBERT J.
BLAKE

GEORGETOWN UNIVERSITY PRESS

WASHINGTON, DC

Library of Congress Cataloging-in-Publication Data

Blake, Robert J., 1951–
Brave new digital classroom : technology and foreign language learning / Robert J. Blake. — Second edition.
p. cm.
Includes bibliographical references and index.
ISBN 978-1-58901-976-8 (pbk. : alk. paper)
1. Educational technology. 2. Computer-assisted instruction. 3. Language and languages—Study and teaching—Technological innovations. I. Title.
LB1028.3.B567 2013
418.00285—dc23

2012037461

∞ This book is printed on acid-free paper meeting the requirements of the American National Standard for Permanence in Paper for Printed Library Materials.

15 14 13   9 8 7 6 5 4 3 2 First printing

To Elizabeth, James, and Ian, with love

CONTENTS

ILLUSTRATIONS

Tables

Figures

FOREWORD

From Shakespeare to Aldous Huxley, the metaphor of a "brave new world" has always had ambiguous connotations—is technological progress always a good thing? Is technology threatening to replace humans? By contrast, *Brave New Digital Classroom*—a practical, useful, and seemingly modest introduction to the use of computer technology in the foreign language classroom—leaves no room for ambiguity. It states clearly and urgently what the stakes are: Either teachers embrace the new language learning technologies and integrate them in a new pedagogy or they will not only deprive themselves of the enormous benefits afforded by computer-assisted language learning (CALL), computer-mediated communication (CMC), distance learning, social networking, and language games, but they will be increasingly out of touch with their own students, who are by now wired, networked, and computer-savvy.

However, in every chapter, we are reminded that the technology is not a panacea in itself. It urgently needs the teacher to harness it properly if it is to help learners achieve the ultimate goal of foreign language learning: becoming bilingual. Again and again, we are shown how using the digital medium wisely can fulfill the implications of second language acquisition research, that is, facilitate interaction, foster the negotiation of meaning, help the autonomous search for knowledge, and help in the solving of communicative tasks. In addition, the digital medium can help implement the goals of intercultural competence, change the classroom from a teacher-centered to a student-directed environment, and provide a learning context where students can find their "third place." Ultimately, the digital classroom can meet the changing aspirations of future generations of students who are aching for more autonomy, agency, collaborative learning, and distributed creativity.

In this regard this book is by no means "modest." It shows how digital technology and the United States' digitally inclined students are putting increased pressure on their teachers to relinquish their exclusive control of the classroom and to espouse the student-centered pedagogy that applied linguistics has promoted in the last thirty years. It makes clear that the digital revolution is also a social revolution. The computer has ushered in not just a new technology but new ways of viewing knowledge, the acquisition and transmission of knowledge, and the very relation between teachers and their students and between the students themselves. It is in fact ironic that it is the advent of the computer and its irreducible presence today in all walks of life that is compelling educators to change the way they deliver foreign language (FL) education, with or without the aid of computers. Those language teachers who, by cultural tradition or personal preference, did not implement the tenets of communicative language teaching in the 1980s, nor change their classroom practice to meet the goals of intercultural communication in the 1990s, are now confronted with a digital culture in which students expect to be placed at the center of their learning. They no longer want to be passive recipients of grammar and vocabulary; they now demand to be given agency and autonomy in order to manipulate knowledge and to work collaboratively with others. The digital culture of the computer has become our students' way of learning, thinking, and communicating. Slowly but surely it has transformed what it means to learn a foreign language, what we mean when we talk of "communicating," "negotiating meaning," and, ultimately, "understanding the other."

After World War II, learning someone else's language was intended to facilitate the exchange of different worldviews; of different social, cultural, and political experiences; and of incompatible views of history—and in turn it was meant to help learners gain a deeper understanding of themselves and their own culture. Now, as globalization gives the illusion of worldwide peace, foreign language learners have a less urgent need to gain a deep understanding of history and its paradoxes. They seek connection, collaboration, and agency in the present. They cast a less metaphysical, more pragmatic view of the foreign other. Mostly they want to do things with others, and they seek the linguistic "resources" to do so. The challenges that this new way of thinking present for teachers, who may be of another generation or cultural tradition, are enormous. This book encourages teachers to face these challenges and to engage in an honest reappraisal of what they are in the business of doing when they teach their students the language of another through digital environments.

Claire Kramsch

PREFACE

No language instructor, professor, applied linguist, graduate student, or department chair would deny the importance of using new technologies to enhance the learning environment—and the subject area of foreign languages is no exception. But the rapidly changing parameters of the technological field have made the first-time entry into using technology in service of the FL curriculum a daunting, if not forbidding, task for many. My intent here is to explain the use of technology for language learning in a straightforward manner by maintaining a dogged focus on the pedagogy, whenever possible, rather than by concentrating on the dizzying array of tools and gadgets that assist us in this endeavor. Accordingly, this book is directed not only to all language teachers—whether from schools or the postsecondary level—who consider themselves technological neophytes or even troglodytes but still wish to plunge in and plug in. But the book is also intended to be read by experienced CALL practitioners who continue to evolve their CALL pedagogy so as to take maximum advantage of innovations. Chairs and administrators should also find ample food for thought with respect to revamping their institution's FL curriculum and evaluating those colleagues who work in the CALL field.

I do not advocate the use of new technologies as a mere replacement for equivalent functions that can be done well with more recognizable tools such as pencil and paper or chalk and board. Rather, as the title indicates, I envisage a radical change in language teaching to occur not solely because technology is involved but also as the result of teachers' rethinking what they do as they begin to incorporate new technologies into the syllabi along with their respective affordances. Clearly, I am tipping my hat to Jim Cummins's *Brave New Schools: Challenging Cultural Illiteracy through Global Learning Networks* (Cummins and Sayers 1995), which has led the way for so many teaching reforms in the fields of English as a second language and second language acquisition.

Undoubtedly, some of the technological tools reviewed here will have already been surpassed by other innovations by the time this book is published and lands in the hands of the reader; becoming outdated is a constant worry for those who work in the CALL field. In chapter 1 I squarely face this fear as well as deal with common misconceptions surrounding the use of new technologies that persist among some teachers and graduate students, despite the fact that the profession as a whole has reached a more sophisticated notion about technology in the postmodern era. Although newer generations of students may not suffer from all these misconceptions and worries, many classroom practitioners, both young and old, still shy away from using new technologies. Today's graduate preparation rarely includes as a required subject an exploration of the use of technology. My hope is that this text will provide a sound basis for professional training within the context of a single-author publication (although many edited volumes on CALL already exist; see Blake 2008). To assist in this endeavor, I place some concepts and terms in italics, and I draw the reader's attention to the glossary at the end of the book.

Without a doubt, the most ubiquitous entry point into new technologies is the internet, the focus of chapter 2, but discrete CALL application are still much alive in the field, as reviewed in chapter 3. In chapter 4 I examine CMC, especially synchronous chatting, the most exciting development in the CALL field in the last decade. In chapter 5 I summarize the first four chapters with an in-depth examination of how teachers must change their approach to language education if they wish to take full advantage of the benefits that new technologies can potentially offer. Chapters 6, 7, and 8 strike out in the newest directions of the CALL field. At the most radical end of the technological-use continuum is the idea of a completely online or virtual language course—distance language learning, the focus of chapter 6. In chapter 7 I present an overview of the rise of social networking, along with autonomous and tandem learning environments. Finally, I look into the future to determine what language gaming might contribute to the CALL field in the near future.

Woven among these chapters are ample references to CALL research, although the focus of this book is not about how to do research (a worthy goal in itself) but rather how to incorporate new technologies into the FL curriculum. Teachers should always remember that, in language learning, no particular technology is superior to any other tool; it is all in the way the activities are implemented so as to engage and foster the student's own sense of agency. Equally important for the brave new digital classroom is the constant reflection on intercultural themes. Too often, our colleagues from other disciplines forget that the language profession is charged with imparting much more than just the forms of the pluperfect subjunctive of the second language: We want students to discover and rediscover a new place along the bilingual continuum, a construct that includes cultural competence at its very heart.

Above all else, the language profession must move beyond a simple computer functional competence (knowing how to use the tools) toward both a critical competence (realizing what the tools are good for) and then, finally, to a rhetorical competence (understanding how these tools will help transform the learning environment). The word "rhetoric" normally implies skill in the effective use of speech. But in this case it refers to skill in the effective use of technology in service of learning a foreign language. This new rhetoric requires both students and teachers to put into action a new way of viewing the world, mediated by a new language and a new technologically assisted learning environment.

I wish to thank all the technological mentors who have patiently helped me along the way: most of all, María Victoria González Pagani, who showed me what content-based teaching supported by new technologies was all about. I owe a particular word of thanks to the University of Valladolid, Spain, whose scholarly exchange fellowship sponsored by Pilar Celma Valero during the summer of 2006 allowed me to complete the first edition draft of this book. I thank Gail Grella, my former editor at Georgetown University Press, whose constant expert advice and steadfast support encouraged me during the writing of the first edition, and David Nicholls, my current editor, who has guided me during the development of the present second edition. I also wish to thank the CALICO membership at large for always supporting each other and making what this language profession should always be: fun! Finally, I thank my wife and sons for putting up with all my computer fascination.

ABBREVIATIONS

ACMC	asynchronous computer-mediated communication
ACTFL	American Council on the Teaching of Foreign Languages
CALICO	Computer-Assisted Language Instruction Consortium
CALL	computer-assisted language learning
CGI	common gateway interface
CMC	computer-mediated communication
DL	distance learning
FL	foreign language
FonF	focus on form
HTML	hypertext markup language
HTTP	hypertext transfer protocol
ICC	intercultural communicative competence
IM	instant messaging
L1	first language—mother tongue
L2	second language
LCTLs	less commonly taught languages
MOO	multiuser dungeon/domain—object oriented
MUD	multiuser dungeon/domain
NNS	nonnative speaker
NS	native speaker
SCMC	synchronous computer-mediated communication
SLA	second language acquisition
URL	uniform resource locator
WYSIWYG	what you see is what you get

CHAPTER 1

Second Language Acquisition, Language Teaching, and Technology

Why Technology in the Second Language Curriculum?

Why should any foreign language (FL) educator or student in the process of learning a second language (L2) have any interest in technology, given that L2 learning is such a social, if not face-to-face, process? The answer lies in looking closely at the facts of second language acquisition (SLA) and the resources at hand.

SLA, the process of learning another language other than your mother tongue (i.e., your first language, or L1), is both an intensive and time-consuming activity.[1] The Foreign Service Institute (FSI) estimates that anywhere from 700 to 1,320 hours of full-time instruction are needed to reach a level of high fluency (Bialystok and Hakuta 1994, 34). More specifically, the time commitment for learning a Romance language minimally approaches 20 weeks of intensive, full-time study at 30 hours per week, for a grand total of 600 hours, whereas for other languages, such as Russian and Chinese, the ideal exposure can exceed 44 weeks at 30 hours per week, or 1,320 hours. In stark contrast to these calculations, most university students spend on average only 150 hours per academic year actively studying an L2 (10 weeks at 5 hours per week for three quarters = 150 total hours). Upon graduation from college, students of whatever L2 just barely reach the FSI's lowest-threshold requirements for achieving proficiency, that of the Romance languages. For students studying a non-Romance language at the university level, four years of L2 study are not sufficient to obtain functional proficiency, according to these FSI estimates.

For students who began studying an L2 in high school and continued at the university level, the picture still does not seem much brighter.

Many educators and public figures have expressed dismay that so much university language work appears to be remedial because much of the material taught was already covered in high school. But in light of the FSI statistics, this is not really the case; it simply takes from four to six years to reach functional proficiency in an L2—that is, L2 learning requires lots of time on task. Crucial to this L2 processing is the extent and nature of the input received—something all linguists and SLA researchers can agree on, even if their SLA models differ radically (see the SLA models discussed later in this chapter). In any event, university L2 learners, in terms of time on task, do not compare too unfavorably with children learning a first language during the first five years, with phonetic accuracy or accent perhaps being a notable exception (DeKeyser 2000).

How can this realistic, if not sobering, depiction of adult SLA be sped up and made more efficient? Increasing contact with the target language is the most obvious solution. In particular, traveling to the region(s) where the target language is spoken and immersing oneself in the society and culture clearly remains the preferred but most expensive method of acquiring linguistic competence in another language. However, Davidson (2007, 277) has shown that less than 3 percent of US university students go abroad on either academic or internship programs. What happens to the majority of the nation's L2 students who are unable or unwilling to take advantage of study abroad? Most SLA theorists agree, in some basic formulation of the issues, that formal L2 teaching is often unsuccessful because learners receive impoverished or insufficient input in the target language (Cummins 1998, 19). Technology, then, if used wisely, can play a major role in enhancing L2 learners' contact with the target language, especially in the absence of study abroad. Whether technology can actually fulfill this promise depends on how it is used in the curriculum. The principal focus of this book is to discuss how technology can best be employed in the FL curriculum in order to enhance and enrich the learners' contact with the target language and thereby assist L2 development.

A few words of caution, however, are in order at the outset. First, technology only provides a set of tools that are, for the most part, methodologically neutral. Selber (2004, 36) has called this attitude toward technology the tool metaphor: "From a functionalist design perspective, good tools become invisible once users understand their basic operation." In reality, all tools mediate our experiences in certain ways, which is to say that they are not totally value free. Applied linguists working within an ecological framework would say that new technologies provide certain affordances and, therefore, are not neutral (Zhao et al. 2005; Levy 2006, 13–15).

Despite this word of caution, how technological tools are used should largely be guided by a particular theoretical model and by recommendations from those who practice it. In this book I affirm the basic approach to SLA, which claims that an L2 is best learned and taught through interaction (for a similar endorsement, see Long 1991; and with reference to the computer learning environment, see Chapelle 2001). Pica, Kanagy, and Falodun (1993, 11) represent well the stance of those who hold to the interactionist theory (see the glossary for definitions of "interactionist theory" and other key terms used in the text) when they state, "Language learning is assisted through social interaction of learners and their interlocutors, particularly *when they negotiate toward mutual comprehension of each other's message meaning*" (emphasis added). The question examined in this book, then, is whether technology can offer the L2 curriculum certain benefits within this theoretical framework, and if so, how these technologically assisted activities should fit in with the FL curriculum.

At first blush this theoretical approach as applied to the field of computer-assisted language learning (CALL) might appear counterintuitive, ironic, or even futile. After all, computers are not human and cannot interact with anyone in the sense that two human beings can. Nevertheless, Reeves and Nass (1996, 5) have convincingly argued the following: "People's interactions with computers, television, and new media are fundamentally social and natural, just like interactions in real life." In their research they found that users are polite to computers and respond to the personality of both the interface and whatever computer agents or avatars that are present. In other words, computers are social actors as well, at least from the students' perspective, which is all that really matters (p. 28). Reeves and Nass's research further reinforces the notion that computers can make a significant contribution to the SLA process because the students themselves feel that they are interacting with the computer in a real social manner. The question of whether computer-mediated communication

(CMC) facilitates the L2 development acquisition process is examined in more depth in chapter 4.

The book's second disclaimer is that this is not a how-to manual: In the pages that follow, I am not instructing readers how to get connected to the internet, how to write fully functional Web pages, or how to program in Macromedia Director. There are plenty of technical guides or workshops designed to teach these hands-on skills. Rather, this book focuses on why certain technological tools should be integrated into the L2 curriculum and what potential contribution these tools stand to make to any given language program. My objectives are to stimulate technologically inexperienced readers to acquire the necessary hardware and technical skills to begin incorporating technology into their classrooms. For the language professional who already has some knowledge of technology, I promise to stimulate the imagination for what might be done with computers in the L2 classroom, now and in the near future. All language professionals need to become acquainted with the potential advantages of using technology in their programs. Without this knowledge, chairs, deans, and other decision-making bodies might fail to support new ways of teaching L2s with technology.

Nevertheless, it would be misleading to talk about technology as if it were just a single, homogeneous tool; different technologically based tools render different advantages for L2 learning. For instance, the internet is an ideal tool to use to allow students to gain access to authentic L2 materials; it might be the next best alternative to actually going abroad. L2 students can virtually "travel" to French-speaking Africa, Tokyo, or the Peruvian Incan ruins of Machu Picchu with just a click of the mouse. The Web gives all people a channel to express their voices, promote their self-images, and legitimize their goals. This sense of authenticity provides endless topics for cross-cultural analysis and discussions in any content-driven classroom.

The advantages for carrying out online discussions via computer have been well documented in the research literature (see chapter 4 in this volume). Researchers frequently cite the computer's usefulness as (1) a text-based medium that amplifies students' attention to linguistic form (Warschauer 1997a); (2) a stimulus for increased written L2 production (Kern 1995); (3) a less stressful environment for L2 practice (Chun 1998); (4) a more equitable and nonthreatening forum for L2 discussions, especially for women, minorities, and nonassertive personalities (Warschauer 1997a, 1997b; Sauro 2009); and (5) an expanded access channel with possibilities for creating global learning networks (Cummins and Sayers 1995; also see chapter 7 in this volume). Swaffar (1998, 1) has summarized the benefits derived from CMC as compared with classroom oral exchanges: "Networked exchanges seem to help all individuals in language classes engage more frequently, with greater confidence, and with greater enthusiasm in the communicative process than is characteristic for similar students in oral classrooms." Ironically, telling students that their responses will also be saved by the computer for research purposes does not seem to diminish their level of participation or their sense that the computer affords them a relatively anonymous, or at least protected, environment for their discussions (Pellettieri 2000).

Internet use among teenagers has exploded; Lenhart, Madden, and Hitlin (2005) reported in 2005 that 84 percent of teenagers today, who will be the college language learners of tomorrow, use the internet primarily as a tool for communications through instant messaging (IM) and text messaging. This figure has only increased since then. This means that CMC is not only a familiar activity to this new crop of university language learners but also the preferred tool, along with social networking (see chapter 7). Members of our profession need to harness students' disposition to chat online in order to maintain and even increase interest in FL learning.

Let us now return for a moment to the educational advantages of increased access, via the computer, to instruction and other learners outside the normal constraints of the classroom. Public schools, in particular, are faced with ever-increasing enrollment pressures, a veritable flood of baby-boomer children reaching college age; the US Department of Education reports that enrollments increased 25 percent, to 17.3 million students, from 1990 to 2004, along with projections for an additional 15 percent increase, to 19.9 million students by 2015 (National Center for Educational Statistics 2006). It is doubtful that all these students, or at least anyone who wants access to higher education, will find seats in a classroom setting as presently configured. Some L2 instruction in the future will have to take place at a distance or through what publishers call the home market. This does not diminish the on-campus/classroom experience; on the contrary, its value will appreciate even more, but access to that privileged learning format might not be available to everyone interested in language study. Likewise, as the United States slowly breaks out of its English-only delusions (i.e., that all the world will or should speak English), all kinds of learners will make known their interests in acquiring some type of L2 proficiency, whether to enter the global marketplace or, in the case of highly ethnically diverse states such as California or Florida, just to understand and get along better with their neighbors. This new demand will be met by an aggressive response either from the US language profession or by the more profit-minded publishing companies, or both. Most language professionals rightly feel that they should take the lead in determining the nature of instruction for this new and potentially significant audience. But will the language profession be ready to meet this challenge? Yes, but only if teachers start experimenting now with ways to enhance L2 development through technology.

Many of the examples cited above have dealt most closely with the beginning and intermediate levels, the lower-division language curriculum. Why should these courses be of concern to literature professors who typically do not teach a language—and sometimes do not even treat cultural issues in an explicit fashion? If incorporating technology into the curriculum can stimulate—and even improve—the overall language preparation of those majoring in a language, then literature professors also have a vital stake in promoting technology. In reality, all undergraduate courses—whether examining Cervantes's novels, reading French symbolist poetry, or dissecting Chinese cinema—are language courses at their most fundamental level. (Remember that it takes four to six years to develop high oral fluency in an L2, according to the FSI's findings, without taking into account the additional demands of advanced literacy or higher-order L2 reading and L2 writing skills.)[2]

Literature professors are often caught in a dilemma: Their language programs are too weak to prepare their students to read the original texts, but reading them in translation does nothing to further their students' L2 proficiency. The death knell of an FL literature program begins to sound when all the upper-division courses and their writing assignments are administered in English because the students are unable to cope with the more sophisticated forms of the L2 literary registers. The blame for this situation must be spread around, and literature professors solely concerned with teaching literary content bear their share. Pressure from the dean to fill those upper-division courses with students can also be a motivating factor in offering Chinese Poetry in Translation or any other subject. No doubt these courses in translation play an important role for students' general education within the undergraduate curriculum, but if the entire FL curriculum switches over to English as the medium of instruction, much will have been lost in the realm of cognitive development and humanities. There are significant cognitive benefits derived from learning an L2. Scholars such as Kramsch (1993) have made it abundantly clear that the process of learning another language involves much more than just skill-acquiring and skill-using faculties. Learning another language also presents an opportunity for a critical interrogation of the very notion of culture, which is an appropriate upper-division activity in the liberal arts context (also see Kramsch and Anderson 1999).

In all fairness, colleagues teaching languages with complex writing systems, such as Chinese or Japanese, justifiably express anxiety and frustration with respect to these upper-division courses. These writing systems impose a steep learning curve above and beyond the normal challenges of achieving oral proficiency. All upper-division language courses critically involve advanced levels of literary proficiency, in addition to oral proficiency, which is not always achieved by children in their native countries until early adolescence. It is unreasonable to expect university language students to gain advanced literacy in just four short years without active guidance from their professors. Knowing that these conditions result from the natural parameters imposed by the SLA process should assuage our colleagues' sense of disappointment and deflect the frequent cries of outrage over the issue of remedial language instruction; in other words, in the first four or five years of learning another language, nothing is remedial. Much cognitive processing is going on in students' brains as they participate in these upper-division language courses, even if the content's level of difficulty must be modified for the particular language and L2 students in question.

Less commonly taught languages (LCTLs) often suffer from another curricular dilemma: the lack of high-quality pedagogical materials at all levels, which typically is not addressed due to low commercial profit margins from the publishing houses' point of view. Publishers project small enrollments for these languages and, consequently, have little motivation to produce print materials for them. Fortunately, new technological advances for Web-based courses and development apps offer language professionals the opportunity to create their own L2 materials that respond to the specific needs of their students (see chapter 3). In short, a strong, technologically modernized language program will always be an advantage to all concerned in the department and will support a healthy major.

In addition, most institutions of higher education are affected by current student trends to gravitate toward courses that deal with either culture or language rather than just straight literature. By offering an L2 culture course supplemented by art or other forms of culture available in Web materials, language departments can rekindle student interest. Extended class discussions via e-mail, listservs, or chat programs can further augment student interest as well as student–student and student–instructor interactions. In fact, Gonglewski (1999) has already laid out in clear terms how using technology can satisfy the demands of a curriculum based on the national standards and the five Cs (ACTFL 1996): communication, cultures, comparisons, connections, and communities.

By the same token, it is important not to raise unrealistic expectations with respect to what technology can contribute to the L2 curriculum. Negative reactions to the introduction of technology into the L2 classroom feed off the failed promises of the audiolingual laboratory of the 1960s. Dashed expectations from that era have created a residual distrust of technology and account for many language teachers' reluctance to plunge into the implementation of any new technologies in the face of few demonstrable results (Roblyer 1988) and even fewer tangible career paybacks (Quinn 1990, 300; Garrett and Liddell 2004). To further compound these initial suspicions, many people have less than a clear notion of what technology means for L2 learning. Unfortunately, misconceptions about technology and language learning abound; some of these confusions are discussed in the next section.

Four Myths about Technology and L2 Acquisition

Four myths or misconceptions readily come to mind when the word "technology" is mentioned in language circles (also see Egbert, Paulus, and Nakamichi 2002; Lam 2000): In the first place, some language professionals refer to technology as if it were a monolithic concept. This myth might suggest that technology is either all good or all bad—that is to say, all technology is the same. Second, some teachers who are overly enthusiastic about technology tend to confuse the use of technology with some new and superior methodological approach to language teaching, although, in truth, new digital technologies only offer a new set of tools that can function in the service of a particular language curriculum. In other words, how these tools are used and to what principled ends define the scope of a methodology, but the mere use of technology by itself will not improve the curriculum. Third, all of us would like to believe (although we know better) that today's technology is sufficient for tomorrow's challenges. The fact that technology is constantly changing constitutes a frightening barrier for many language professionals who fear that they cannot possibly keep pace with new advances. Finally, the language profession suffers from the fear that technology will replace them. Let us look more carefully at these four misconceptions about using technology in the service of the FL curriculum.

Technology Is Monolithic—False

Have you noticed how people use the word "internet" in an almost mystical fashion? "Ah, the internet," they say, as if one word says it all. (A few years back, the magical term in our profession was CALL.) There is not *one* technology best suited for language study, but rather there exists an array of technological tools that can be harnessed, efficiently or otherwise, to the ends of learning an L2 or studying the SLA process. Moreover, these technological tools change very rapidly.

More specifically, there are three important technological platforms that provide tools to assist language learning, in order of increasing interactivity:[3] Web pages, Web-based apps, and network-based communication (i.e., e-mail, electronic mailing list, user groups, MOOs, chat programs, blogs, wikis, and social networking sites).

The Web offers a variety of authentic target-language resources—a virtual trip to Peru, a guided bicycle trip to Santiago de Compostela, a wine guide for La Rioja, and the murals of Orozco, to name only a few examples for Spanish—but materials for Chinese, French, Italian, Japanese, and Russian abound as well, along with an ever-increasingly sophisticated array of Web courses and self-tests. Teachers are now using Web pages, both original and adapted, to serve as the students' primary source materials, especially in content-based language courses. In this type of course, students work through the tasks and activities laid out before them and only gradually have recourse to learning the grammar (for a technologically supported, content-based approach, see Barson 1991; Debski 1997). The Web pages exist to provide content stimulation and a means for further inquiry. Given the richness of non-English Web materials, the members of the L2 class can move in new directions at any point or deepen their knowledge of any particular topic. For the experienced teacher who knows how to take advantage of these obvious communicative opportunities, a Web-based, content-driven approach is a dream come true—and the students will respond in kind. Web-based courses might eventually displace the notion of a static textbook, copyright problems notwithstanding.

The DVD platform and a new generation of Web apps were designed to deliver specific applications that take advantage of large amounts of sound, graphics, and video files. The publishing industry is heavily involved in producing high-quality DVDs because the marketplace demands it.[4] One of the jobs of today's language faculty and lab personnel is to keep track of this new generation of language DVDs and to know how to review them, which is a catch-22 in itself: Language professionals need to know something about interface design and computer pedagogy in order to be able to review software in the first place. Teachers must be trained to recognize well-grounded pedagogy when they see it, hear it, and read it on the screen. Many of today's DVDs have sophisticated visual interfaces, but one must be careful that the medium does not dominate the message, to borrow a phrase from Marshall McLuhan (1964). The benefits offered by these platforms are more fully examined in chapter 3.

Finally, CMC provides a third platform where L2 students can transcend the spatial and temporal confines of the classroom via the internet. E-mail or asynchronous (i.e., differed-time) communication and chat or synchronous (i.e., real-time) communication offers students the highest level of interactivity because they permit one-to-one, personal exchanges. SLA research has clearly demonstrated the importance of learning language through face-to-face exchanges that require the learners to negotiate meaning with other learners and/or native speakers (NSs) (Pica 1994; Long 1981, 1991; Gass 1997; Gass and Varonis 1994; Doughty 1998; Blake 2000, 2005a). When asked to negotiate meaning, L2 students are forced to notice what they do not know (i.e., the gaps in their L2 knowledge) and, subsequently, seek a resolution to their linguistic or cultural misunderstanding before resuming the free flow of dialogue. This process of mutual assistance, what many researchers refer to as scaffolding or interactionism, appears to be one of the principal ways in which students gradually liberate themselves from a seemingly interminable and ever-changing period of interlanguage, the interim stages of a learner's emerging L2 linguistic system, in pursuit of more advanced proficiency in the target language.

Students can carry off these negotiation events during regularly scheduled class time or lab sessions, but the benefits of negotiating meaning also obtain for tasks done through synchronous network-based communication (Pellettieri 2000; Blake 2000). This means that students can engage in negotiating meaning any time from home or the lab. This use of technology opens the door to an untapped potential for L2 language use. Again, theorists agree that increasing the amount and quality of the students' L2 input is crucial to SLA success. CMC has an enormous contribution to make to the L2 curriculum if teachers will become familiar enough with the technology to be able to incorporate it into the students' out-of-class assignments.

Technology Constitutes a Methodology—False

No SLA theory has anything to say directly about language teaching; the field's principal goals consist of studying the process of how languages are acquired, not how they are taught. Nevertheless, particular teaching methodologies (e.g., total physical response, the Natural Method, or the communicative classroom) necessarily attempt to make the leap between theory and practice by identifying the most favorable conditions for L2 learning. In an ideal world, then, a methodology should be informed by what is known about the nature of the SLA process.[5] Technology per se, however, has no stake in any particular theoretical model or teaching methodology: Technology is theoretically and methodologically neutral. But how technology is used in a particular community of practice is not neutral; it responds to what the practitioners understand or believe to be true about SLA. Teachers with little experience using technology often harbor the belief that merely transforming an activity into a Web or CALL format will guarantee its success for students. Again, any activity without adequate pedagogical planning—technologically enhanced or not—will produce unsatisfactory results with students, even if it is attractive from a multimedia point of view (e.g., colors, graphics, photos, video, sound).

Many teachers feel that the only curricular role for technology is to relieve the teacher of the more burdensome aspects of testing and rote drills, so that classroom time can be fully utilized for communication. For example, in the past the Spanish and Italian programs at the University of Illinois employed a Web-based program called Mallard to free up the maximum amount of classroom time for communicative activities and to justify the decrease in the course's seat time requirements from five to three hours a week (for more information and evaluation of this approach, see Arvan and Musumeci 2000; Echávez-Solano 2003; Epps 2004; Scida and Saury 2006; Walczynski 2002). Research has shown that there are no significant differences in final grades among the experimental (Mallard) group and the control group, with Scida and Saury's (2006) study registering slightly higher final grades for the group using Mallard. Researchers attributed much of the student success with the Mallard program to the students' ability to continue working on the exercises until reaching 100 percent accuracy. In essence, the availability of the tutorial CALL program appears to have allowed students to dedicate more time to making their control of the basic language structures more automatic. In other words, how the technology was used did have an impact, but there was nothing magical about the technology itself in producing this effect.

In practical terms only, tutorial computer programs allow teachers to handle more students with the same number of faculty/teaching assistant resources. Naturally, the administration is delighted with this increase in the student/teacher ratio. Likewise, some teachers are happy not to have to bother with morphologically based drills and tests during precious class time, which goes against the theoretical bent of the communicative classroom, and the students enjoy increased access for completing the language requirement. This appears to constitute a win-win situation for all concerned and an appropriate use of technology for these programs. Other institutions may wish to explore different solutions, depending on their respective expectations and theoretical orientations.

Today's Technology Is All We Need to Know—False

Constant change is a frightening phenomenon for most people, but that is the inherent nature of the technology field: New tools are being created all the time. As Hanson-Smith (2006, 301) observes: "One of the most significant problems facing computer-using teachers is that no education curriculum can prepare them for the swift and continuing changes that take place in the world of technology." To cope with the field's intrinsic flux, language programs need long-term institutional support, both from the campus information technology services that are delivered locally in the form of a designated language lab and through a college-wide humanities technology-resource person. But it should be patently obvious that technology rarely helps anyone save money. In most cases, it engenders more financial commitment, at least at the beginning. Nevertheless, new technologies allow an institution's human resources to work more efficiently and provide greater educational access for students, along with offering new channels for learning. New advances in technology allow an institution's personnel to do new things and, therefore, represent a catalyst for change, even reform.

Accordingly, working with technology requires constant updating and continuing education, which can be a very threatening concept for language professionals who are used to concentrating on teaching to established standards (i.e., keeping performance level constant) and achieving dominance of the more literary and prestigious registers of their respective world language. The often-repeated joke holds true for language faculty: "How many professors does it take to change a light bulb?" The faculty delivers the punch line: "Change?"

In all seriousness, this situation conjures up a natural conflict of interest from which language professionals are not immune. It should come as no surprise that the vertiginous pace of technological changes is responsible for considerable resistance to implementing technology into the L2 curriculum. "Who has the time for that kind of an investment?" some teachers might intone. Yet there are other, more powerful fears that stand in the way of using technology: "Will technology replace the teacher or the courses in the department?"

Technology Will Replace Teachers—Mostly False

Put bluntly, some in our profession fear that the use of technology will replace them and the courses they teach, especially when mention is made of implementing completely virtual online courses (i.e., distance language learning; see chapter 6 in this volume). Their fears are frequently fed by administrators who openly seek budgetary savings through downsizing the extremely labor-intensive language programs. In this mad rush, everyone seems to forget to answer the questions of who will teach those distance learning courses, write the curriculum, and train students to work within this format.

The technology platforms mentioned above—the Web, DVD applications, and CMC—do not pose a threat to language professionals but rather complement what can be done in the L2 classroom, if used wisely. Will technology expand in the future from this complementary role to replacing the teacher and the classroom venue completely? A rational response to this question might be that technology will not replace teachers in the future, but rather, teachers who use technology will probably replace teachers who do not (Clifford 1987, 13). Again, this implies hiring new faculty with at least a modicum of technological expertise, along with implementing training programs for the existing faculty so that they can come up to speed with new advances. Change, however, is never easy for the generation trained without the benefits of CALL.

What I am advocating by debunking these common misconceptions is a more realistic assessment of what technology might do for a particular institution's language curriculum. Nothing is achieved by promising the language profession a panacea for its financial and curricular woes, although many administrators would dearly like to downsize language departments by using technology as a replacement. Computer technology will be a key component to most everything accomplished in the twenty-first century. The language profession needs to capitalize on its advantages and strengths by using the best teaching practices, which, in turn, should be informed by SLA theory whenever possible. By resisting the temptation to believe in the four myths outlined above, language teachers and administrators open their minds to contemplating instances in which technology constitutes good teaching practice. Again, teaching practice should not be totally divorced from theory (although theorists may have no interest in practice).

Krashen's ←*i* + 1→ and Beyond: SLA Theories and Technology

No general discussion of technology within the context of language teaching would be complete without a brief overview of current SLA theories. Again, the process of how a language is acquired should be kept distinct from best practices for language teaching. But it would be an unnecessary fiction to maintain that methodologies are not informed, correctly or not, by SLA theories and models.

The intent here, then, is not to explain in detail the various SLA theories and their histories; there are a number of introductory books that already meet this need (e.g., Doughty and Long 2003a; Ellis 1994, 1997; Gass and Selinker 2001; Gass 1997; Larsen-Freeman and Long 1991; VanPatten 1996). But the various SLA theories suggest differing degrees of importance concerning the role of instruction/practice and, by implication, the use of technology in the classroom. Technology, as defined earlier, is a series of electronically based platforms and tools that support many language learning activities, from the most mechanical drill-and-kill exercises to fully communicative real-time conversations (i.e., chat). Language professionals need to have an adequate theoretical background in order to decide when a particular tool might assist the students' L2 development. Like the field of linguistics itself, SLA studies emanate from two distinct, but not necessarily incompatible, approaches: one that focuses attention on the psycholinguistic aspects of SLA and the other on the sociolinguistic aspects.

There is no denying that the recent interest and popularity of SLA studies owes much to Chomsky's psycholinguistic or mentalist inquiries into the nature of language, which has revolutionized the field of linguistics. Chomsky hypothesized that all children are innately predisposed, if not prewired, to learn language; the individual child only requires a sustained exposure (i.e., input) to one particular natural language in order to trigger the formation of an internal grammar or mental representation of linguistic competence that, in turn, governs language production or performance. According to Chomsky, this grammar-building process—known as the Language Acquisition Device (LAD), in his earlier theoretical formulation—is constrained by universal properties common to all languages (Chomsky 1986, 3). Through exposure to the rich linguistic input or positive evidence contained in the well-formed sentences of NSs in the environment, the child develops all the other language-specific constructions as well. In short, language performance is a rule-governed activity generated by the child's linguistic competence or internal grammar. The occasional slips of the tongue, false starts, and memory lapses, which are part and parcel of performance, are of little importance to Chomsky (1986) and other linguists from his generativist school, who seeks to discover the underlying structures and constraints that pertain to competence, the universal core of language that makes language acquisition possible in the first place, in his view.

Krashen (1982, 1985) embraced Chomsky's ideas and adapted them to the SLA field by highlighting the role of input. But at the same time, Krashen recognized that SLA is governed by special conditions different from first language acquisition—namely, L2 learners need input that is both challenging and assessable; they need *comprehensible input* that is within their grasp, input just slightly more complex than their current, still-emerging, mental representation of the target language, or what researchers have called their interlanguage (Gass and Selinker 2001, 11). Krashen symbolized comprehensible input and its scaffolding relationship to acquisition by means of a mathematical metaphor, where *i* stands for *interlanguage*:

<i + 1> designates input that pushes L2 learners to restructure their interlanguage without overwhelming them with data well beyond their present capabilities. Although the <i + 1> metaphor is now somewhat dated, given that other researchers have refined the notions of input considerably (see the discussion below), Krashen's impact on the FL teaching field has been definitive. The linguistic portion of most teaching credential examinations still tests Krashen's ideas almost exclusively. Likewise, most beginning FL textbooks make at least a cursory reference in their introductions to the need to present students with comprehensible input, an idea taken directly from Krashen. For this reason, I elaborate further on Krashen's model, although many SLA researchers would now consider his model somewhat out of date.

Similar to Chomsky's explicit distinction between competence and performance is Krashen's distinction between the process of acquisition and that of learning. He emphasizes the subconscious nature of acquisition (i.e., competence) in contrast to the students' more conscious attempts to manipulate and learn linguistic forms (i.e., performance). Conscious learning involves monitoring and practice, but acquisition entails a change in the internal representation or competence that eventually happens with enough exposure to <i + 1> input. For Krashen, learned or monitored knowledge has no relationship to acquired knowledge; they are separate systems of knowledge. Other researchers (McLaughlin 1987; Gregg 1984; Swain 1985; Salaberry 1997; Ellis 2002) have argued for interrelationship between controlled processing (i.e., learning or monitoring, in Krashen's terms) and the subsequent development of automatic processing, or automaticity (i.e., acquisition). In other words, after L2 learners have consciously practiced an item for a long time and no longer need to focus consciously on the structure to produce it, their responses become automatic—with the latter type of knowledge presupposing the former. With this new emphasis on more cognitive issues has also come a renewed interest in how L2 students make sense of new vocabulary, lexical chunks, and collocations in contrast to Chomsky's almost exclusive focus on formal syntactical representations as an independent and controlling module of the brain (Ellis 2002).

Krashen complements this central role assigned to comprehensible input with the sensible recognition that learning anxieties can block language acquisition for all intents and purposes. These anxieties erect an *affective filter* that reduces the students' ability to make use of comprehensible input and subsequently blocks interlanguage development. The implications he draws for the classroom should be obvious: Mechanized language drills might produce some learning of forms, but the real goal of acquisition is best fostered by a communicative environment rich in comprehensible input. The communicative classroom, in addition to providing much comprehensible input, should also create an inviting atmosphere with an eye to lowering the students' affective filters.

Krashen's SLA model, though neither uncontroversial nor unchallenged (see Gregg 1984; Lantolf and Frawley 1988; Gass and Selinker 2001, 148–52), has had an enormous impact on classroom practice, being most closely identified with what is known as the Natural Method (Krashen and Terrell 1983). In fact, today's varied communicative approaches to language teaching all have roots in Krashen's ideas. The implementation of Krashen's theory, however, places a heavy burden on teachers to provide large amounts of comprehensible input. In other words, the theory tends to reinforce a teacher-oriented classroom, albeit one in which much language communication is happening.

Setting aside for the moment the intractable—if not unsolvable— problem of determining just what constitutes comprehensible input (i.e., $i + 1$) for any particular L2 learner, let alone for a whole classroom of learners with many individual differences, the question arises as to who is to blame if the students fail to learn or progress too slowly. One interpretation would suggest that teachers have failed to provide a learning environment rich in $<i + 1>$ input. But it is equally plausible that the students were unable to process crucial segments of the comprehensible input because of short-term memory problems, failure to notice certain linguistic structures, or other as-yet-unexplained reasons.

This is precisely what other SLA researchers have pointed out: The existence of comprehensible input in any L2 learner's environment (classroom or otherwise) does not guarantee its usefulness for SLA. Unnoticed comprehensible input is as useless as input well beyond the learner's present level of competence or interlanguage. Only when L2 learners actually notice a particular unit of input—a process that Gass and Selinker (2001, 298) have dubbed *apperception*—and can also retain that information in their short-term memories, does it become *intake*, or internalized input that can be used to help restructure their interlanguage grammar in ways more like the L2 being studied.

The role of consciousness and negative evidence is crucial to this revised SLA input model. L2 learners must first notice the gap between the available input and their own interlanguage (i.e., apperception) before they can develop more target-like ways of communicating: "The first stage of input utilization is the recognition that there is something to be learned, that is, that there is a gap between what the learner already knows and what there is to know" (Gass 1997, 4). This implies that L2 learners must develop their own metalinguistic awareness—that is, a new sense that something is incorrect in their own knowledge of an L2—to stimulate a change in their interlanguage (Schmidt and Frota 1986, 306–19; Schmidt 1990).

The theoretical focus has now moved away from an examination of comprehensible input more in favor of a study of comprehended input, combined with an increased emphasis on the more social aspects of the SLA process. L2 learners discover these gaps in the course of normal communication, especially when miscommunications cause a breakdown in the conversational flow of information. In repairing these breakdowns through negotiations with NSs or other nonnative speakers (NNSs), L2 learners tend to focus on the gaps in their linguistic knowledge. This SLA approach constitutes an interactionist model because interactionists believe that an L2 is best learned—and by extension, best taught—through social interaction (Long 1981, 1991; Pica 1994; Gass 1997; Doughty 1998).

In contrast to the psycholinguistic approach, which highlights the role of positive evidence for SLA, the interactionist approach focuses on the importance of miscommunications and instances of negative evidence generated by the L2 learners' attempts to negotiate meaning with counterparts in their social (i.e., learning) environment. Miscommunications that lead to conversational negotiations, either of meaning or form, serve as a catalyst for change in L2 learners' linguistic knowledge, as described by Gass (1997, 87): "Through negotiation of meaning learners gain additional information about the language and focus their attention on particular parts of the language. This attention primes language for integration into a developing interlinguistic system."

Learners who are provided with information about incorrect forms are able to search for additional confirmatory or nonconfirmatory evidence. If negotiation as a form of negative evidence serves to initiate change, the factors that determine whether the initiated change results in a permanent restructuring of linguistic knowledge must be identified. As with any type of learning, there needs to be reinforcement of what is being learned. In other words, acquisition appears to be gradual and, simplistically, takes time and often requires numerous doses of evidence (Gass 1997, 144–45). The interactionists are careful not to claim that negotiations of meaning cause SLA to happen but rather that these interactions are a priming device that allows learners to focus their attention on areas on which they are working (p. 130).

A more practical instantiation of the interactionist approach is known as a *focus on form* (FonF; see Long and Robinson 1998), a task-based methodology that calls on L2 students to solve specific tasks. As students collaborate on these tasks with other L2 learners or other NSs, they focus on the source of their linguistic confusions (e.g., vocabulary, morphology, syntax); negotiate their incomplete understandings; and, consequently, analyze their own language.

In this approach, not only input, intake, and uptake but also output—forced output, to be precise—are important. Swain (1985, 2000) outlines three potential functions of output: (1) It provides the opportunity to meaningfully use one's linguistic resources, (2) it allows the learner to test hypotheses about the target language, and (3) it encourages the learner to move from semantic to syntactic processing. Swain argues that comprehension of input is a process driven by semantics; in other words, learners do not always need to parse the sentences they hear in order to arrive at the intended meaning. Production, conversely, requires the learner to utilize syntax in order to produce coherent, meaningful utterances. When a learner is pushed during output, he or she is encouraged to convey meaning in a precise and appropriate manner. This momentary "push" may be critical for language acquisition, because it promotes noticing (Swain 2000, 100): Learners may notice that they do not know how to express precisely the meaning they wish to convey at the very moment of attempting to produce it—they notice, so to speak, a "hole" in their interlanguage.

Finally, Krashen's exclusive emphasis on input led the FL profession to eschew any type of explicit teaching or linguistic explanations; for example, the Natural Method practitioners prefer to rely only on implicit forms of instruction. The FonF studies, along with other lines of inquiry, have reaffirmed the role that explicit instruction might play in the SLA process (MacWhinney 1997; Ellis 2002). This marks a significant change in attitude concerning the computer, a tool that can be used particularly well in support of explicit language instruction.

SLA Theory, Interactions, and the Computer

Most computer programs minimally do something in response to mouse clicks, data entry, or other keyboard actions: They beep, show a picture file, move to another screen, play digital sounds, or the like. These minimal computer reactions often constitute the sole basis for commercially labeling the program as "interactive." How does this sense of the word fare against the more social and interactionist definition described above? For the interactionists, L2 learners are motivated to learn new structures by being incited by other speakers to use the target language. In fact, for many language professionals technology might represent the antithesis of what learning an L2 should be all about: talking with and interacting with real *people* in the target language.

Nevertheless, the computer's obvious failings as a person (including Kubrick's infamous computer HAL in the film *2001: A Space Odyssey*) are relatively unimportant in the face of how people work with computers. As mentioned above, Reeves and Nass (1996, 5) have shown that people have a strong tendency to interact with computer machines in a fundamentally social manner, just as they do in their interactions in real life. These social scientists argue for the existence of a media equation where media can equal real-life experiences. For example, if a computer program addresses users in a polite fashion, then the users will respond politely as well, even though they know in purely intellectual terms that a machine has no feelings. According to Reeves and Nass, programs that capitalize on the media equation usually solicit more favorable reactions from computer users than programs that ignore the media equation. In other words, L2 learners conceive of the computer as their own personal helper rather as than the mindless, heartless tool that it really is. This inherent tendency to anthropomorphize our world—from our cars to our pets—persists and gives technology its potential to assist the SLA process. People think computers are trying to help them, and so they respond, as in any human relationship, by making a best-faith effort to cooperate.

Good interface design builds on this fiction. It is not necessary for computers to be human but only to simulate certain human qualities. Above all, people count on computers to follow basic Gricean principles (Pinker 1995, 228)—namely, that the information supplied is relevant, truthful, informative, clear, unambiguous, brief, and orderly. This is especially true if programs can be designed to intervene or provide feedback that is well suited or relevant to the particular user's needs. Fogg (2003, 38) calls this the *principle of tailoring*: "Information provided by computing technology will be more persuasive if it is tailored to the individual's needs, interests, personality, usage context, or other factors relevant to the individual." Fogg (2003, 69–70) also formulates two other principles of virtual rehearsals and rewards, which states that positive reinforcement or rewards received from computer programs can cause human beings to rehearse behavior with a carryover in attitudes and conduct to the real world. In a word, people expect good input from the computer, and therein lies its power to help students learn.

Quo Vadis?

We have come full circle from the outset of the chapter. Input, especially comprehended input, is one of the basic cornerstones of current SLA theories: Without input, SLA cannot occur; it is a necessary condition but not the only one—it is not a sufficient condition. Technology, then, if cleverly designed and properly incorporated into the curriculum, has a vital role to play in augmenting the opportunities for L2 learners to receive target-language input. Again, the extent of learners' contact with the L2 is the critical factor for the SLA process, which normally takes five to seven years under classroom conditions, as most FL professionals working in the trenches already know.

An increasingly multicultural world in both global and local contexts will put intense pressure on our profession to find the most efficient and readily accessible ways to learn another language. To this end, using technology is a challenge that language professionals must squarely face and to which they must endeavor to find pedagogically principled responses. Theory must be combined with practice, which will not happen without our colleagues' willingness to experiment with the newest modes of teaching with technology. Although FL teachers and students alike need to acquire a basic degree of functional computer literacy, they must also learn to exercise a critical literacy as consumers of technology and, eventually, a rhetorical literacy as future producers of technology (see Selber 2004; and see the further discussion in chapter 5). In other words, Dreamweaver, chat applications, blogs, wikis, JavaScript, or any other tricks of the trade are just a beginning that opens the doors to more student-directed activities and the L2 student's journey toward self-definition and identity as a multilingual/multicultural speaker, quite apart from whatever identity may be attributed to the ubiquitous but anonymous NS.[6]

Discussion Questions and Activities

1. What are researchers in SLA referring to when they speak of L2 competence versus L2 performance and L2 acquisition versus L2 learning? Can performance be separated from competence? Into which category would L2 pragmatics fall (i.e., the knowledge about the appropriate situational context for words, utterances, and meanings)?
2. Imagine that you have to convince your colleagues, who are mostly interested in literature, to make an investment in using technology for their FL curriculum. List five reasons why it is also in their interests to support your plan. Consider scientific as well as social reasons that provide an incentive for your department's investment in technology.
3. What would you say to your colleagues in order to ease their worries that investing in technology will eliminate language teaching jobs?
4. Discuss whether it is a problem or an advantage for language teachers that this generation of incoming students will most likely know more about using certain technological tools than their teachers do.

5. Conduct a Web search for the following theme: language teaching with technology. Share your results with a colleague or classmate.

6. Debate which aspects of Krashen's (1982, 1985) theories about SLA are well grounded and which are not supported given recent advances in the SLA field.

Notes

1. SLA theorists often make a distinction between foreign language acquisition, where instruction occurs in a place in which the target language is not spoken, and second language acquisition, where instruction occurs in a target-language speaking country. Throughout this book I use the term "second language acquisition (SLA)" to refer to both circumstances indiscriminately.

2. Cummins (personal communication) estimates that five to seven years are needed to reach academic proficiency on the English CALP exam, a figure quite consonant with the FSI's experience in teaching second languages.

3. *Interactive* is a loaded term. It has come to mean any program that includes user-responsiveness but, in fact, true interactivity supports reciprocal actions (Laurillard 2002, 107). Only CMC can truly be said to provide that level of interactivity.

4. See the special issue of the *CALICO Journal* 17, no. 2 (2000).

5. Our knowledge of SLA still remains quite modest, as Richard Schmidt has characterized in a recent talk at the Sixth Biennial Conference on Second Language Acquisition, sponsored by the University of California Consortium for Language Learning and Teaching, April 2011, in terms of "Fifty (Probably) True and (Possibly) Useful Findings from SLA" (see http://uccllt.ucdavis.edu).

6. Kramsch (2000) has argued persuasively against using the construct of a native speaker as the desired endpoint for the L2 learner.

CHAPTER 2

Web Pages in Service of L2 Learning

The Web in Non-English Languages

The growth of the World Wide Web (www, or more simply, the Web) in recent years has been nothing short of staggering. From 2000 to 2011, the number of internet users has increased by 482 percent (Internet World Stats 2006). More important for American educational circles, a 2005 survey by the Pew Foundation reports that nine out of ten teenage school-children, ages twelve through seventeen years, have online access (Lenhart, Madden, and Hitlin 2005, 2). These children predominantly use the internet to process e-mails (89 percent), browse for information about movies or public figures (84 percent), play games (81 percent), read the daily news (76 percent), send instant messages (75 percent), shop for colleges (57 percent), or buy merchandise online (43 percent). If FL instructors stop to contemplate the fact that these same children now populate their classes in the higher education system, the rationale and motivation to incorporate technology into the language curriculum becomes quite clear: It is a medium that our students understand, pay attention to, and like to use.[1] The same cannot be said about teachers; many language teachers resist investing in technology for the curriculum for a variety of reasons, including personal teaching philosophies, time-honored beliefs, additional time burdens, and the frightening pace of change in technology tools (Arnold and Ducate 2006).

Although English might seem to be the dominant language used on the internet at first blush, only 27 percent of the more than 2 billion internet users access the Web in English (see the statistics at www.internetworld stats.com/stats7.htm). Despite the commercial and scientific importance of English, the world's internet users clearly prefer to surf the Web in their native language, with Chinese (24 percent), Spanish (7.8 percent), Japanese (4.7 percent), Portuguese (3.9 percent), and German (3.6 percent) leading the way (Internet World Stats 2006). The growth rates in this last decade for Arabic (2,501 percent), Chinese (1,438 percent), and Russian (1,825 percent) have been spectacular, far outstripping the rate of increase for English users (301 percent) on the Web.

Fortunately, the advent of Unicode font standards has made displaying Web pages and typing in languages other than English relatively easy, as Godwin-Jones has so clearly explained for the FL profession (Godwin-Jones 2002). Both Macs and PCs allow the user to change the method of keyboard input on the fly, making the switch from English to Arabic, or any other language, a trivial matter as long as the writing program or browser supports Unicode.

There exists a series of important cultural explanations for why the Web will continue to be a place of multilingual and multicultural expression. Sociolinguistic research informs us that language always functions as an identity marker, in addition to fulfilling its role as a tool of communications and information transfer. Accordingly, people will always prefer to surf the Web in their native language, whether they are consuming or selling information or, more important, projecting a public self-image (for an illustration of how a Hawaiian community defines the terms of its own self-reference, see Warschauer and De Florio-Hansen 2003). In other words, the Web gives all people a relatively uncontrolled channel to project their own voice and promote their own particular view of reality. This helps to explain why non-English Web pages continue to grow despite the English language's dominant role in the world as a scientific and business lingua franca.

Kramsch (1993) has long made it clear to our profession that learning another language presents an opportunity for a critical interrogation of the very notion of culture (also see Lange et al. 2000). The Web directly provides primary source materials in pursuit of this intellectual inquiry, especially through searches commonly known as *webquests* (Godwin-Jones 2004; Chen 2006; also see http://webquest.org/), an inquiry-oriented activity based on Web sources. Dodge (2002) provides language teachers with a breakdown of the type of webquest tasks students might undertake: retellings, compilations, mystery hunts, journalistic reports, design projects, creative products, consensus building, persuasive discourses, self-knowledge searches, analyses, judgment tasks, and scientific inquiries.

This is not to say that the internet is a culturally neutral tool or that viewing multimedia materials on the Web reduces the need to interpret what we see and read, as Kramsch and Anderson (1999) have already pointed out in their study of students using online Quechua language pages. In other words, the use of the Web, far from diminishing the importance of the classroom experience and the role of the teacher, imbues classroom discussion with even more value, if the L2 teacher knows how to take advantage of the medium. Each L2 student needs to become a researcher on the Web, an interpreter of culture, a careful notetaker of cross-cultural differences along with any mediating effects induced by using this digital environment (Dubreil 2006, 252–56). This type of reflection closely parallels what students are asked to do with literary texts and explains why colleagues specializing in literature should also have a stake in promoting the use and best practices of a technologically assisted FL curriculum as part of the upper-division program in humanities.

In the following sections, I survey some of the basic technical constructs of the Web, introduce additional tools and extensions that enrich the internet's use, and, finally, discuss a number of recent pedagogical approaches to Web pages that are consonant with the established SLA theories already outlined in chapter 1.

Internet Basics

To get started in the use of the Web in service to the L2 curriculum, it is helpful to know where the internet came from and what it was originally designed to do. Regardless of whether one intends to produce Web pages, a few basic notions about the HTML programming language, which makes a Web page so attractive when viewed with a browser, are necessary before launching into more advanced Web page tricks or planning the design of sound Web lessons.

Roots of the Internet

In chapter 3 of *The Virtual Community*, Rheingold (2000) chronicles the development of the Web from its humble beginnings as ARPANET, a project funded in the 1960s and 1970s by the US Department of Defense's Advanced Research Projects Agency (DARPA). This project allowed a small group of unorthodox and visionary computer programmers and electronic engineers to redesign the way computers operated so that people could engage in interactive computing. Although two more decades of research and development passed before their ideas became a reality, this basic experiment laid the foundation for the computer network known today as the World Wide Web. In 1969, there were only a thousand ARPANET users, in contrast to the 2 billion plus Web surfers online in 2012.

In 1983 ARPANET split into ARPANET for research and MILNET for military operational use. Both systems provided a wide-area backbone network with high-speed access to communicate among their own backbone nodes in a completely distributed fashion. This structure provided the basis for an explosive growth of nodes and networks that expanded the original capacity and concept of ARPANET. In 1986 the National Science Foundation (NSF) initiated a network dubbed NSFNET that created a hub of interconnected supercomputer centers around the United States, which has evolved into the internet's main backbone. ARPANET was decommissioned in 1990, leaving the NSF's interconnected supercomputing centers as the sole public infrastructure for online communications or, more simply, the internet. This brief historical background explains why the internet is so often referred to as an electronic highway, made up of interconnecting roads of varying sizes and traffic. Anyone who has a connection to some road that leads into the system can use the internet.

The spirit and legacy of the original inventors of ARPANET and NSFNET lives on, too. From the security side, the decentralized packet-switching technology that made the internet function correctly also renders controlling or disabling this communication system almost impossible. The original inventors were worried about the effects of a massive nuclear attack. The digitized packet-switching technology permitted a network of routers to move information (i.e., text, sound, graphics, programs, and video) around the network, even when certain nodes had ceased to function. This feature democratized the Web so that no single individual could control it and dictate policy to anyone else. Even today, anyone can run a Web server and post Web pages for the entire world to see.

The other principal intent of the internet's creators was to empower humans to think better wherever they found themselves: on the road, at work, or at home. In other words, anytime/anywhere computing—a way of giving power to users. Accordingly, user autonomy became the norm and is still a key feature of today's internet. Restated in more educational terms, the very nature of the internet is designed to encourage student-centered learning rather than teacher-centered learning, which is also a principal focus of task-based or content-based instruction. Lai and Zhao (2005, 405) pointed out that the very hypertext nature of the Web affords L2 learners greater control over their own learning processes—that is, more flexible learning paths (hopefully, in more meaningful ways). In addition, this feature may lower students' affective filter, in Krashen's sense of the term.

Getting Started

Launching onto the Web for the first time is relatively easy. First, you need a wired or wireless internet connection via modem (which uses the telephone lines to reach a computer node), an internet service provider, or a T1 connection that links directly to a main network node. Second, you need a *browser* program such as Internet Explorer, Netscape, Firefox, Chrome, or Safari in order to read Web pages, which are written in compliance with an international standard for *hypertext transfer protocol* (*HTTP*) using a *hypertext markup language,* or *HTML* code. Finally, you need a Web page address, or a *uniform resource locator* (*URL*). Online manuals for getting started on the Web abound and can be found via internet search, using search words such as "guide to the internet" (e.g., www.learnthenet.com). Some years back, Blyth (1999) offered a comprehensible and friendly guide to the Web from an FL perspective, as did Fidelman (1995–96), and these guides continue to be useful for the beginner despite their relatively early publication dates, but a few basic concepts such as URLs and HTML coding deserve additional attention.

URLs, HTML, File Management, and the Language Lab

Composing Web pages oneself is obviously more complicated than view-ing them. In this section and the following section on advanced tools, I provide further details on what goes into making a Web page publicly vis-ible. Some technical descriptions may be more information than what a beginner might want to tackle initially. Very often novice Web composers simply drive into Web-page production by using blog software or appli-cations such as Google Sites (see chapter 3) with little need for techni-cal knowledge. Beginners can also count on expert help from the internet technology services or language lab personnel at their home institutions. The reader should feel free to skip over those details that seem unnecessary or too complicated. But it is always a good thing to know what is inside the black box, and this is what constitutes the rationale for the following two sections.

What Makes a Web Page Work?

Web pages can be viewed anywhere in the world by means of a Web browser if the user enters the correct URL. Web pages follow a protocol or scheme for delivering and retrieving multimedia information known as HTTP. Web pages are primarily written or coded in HTML, a standardized pro-gramming language for the Web, although more interactive enhancements can be added with JavaScripts and CGI scripts. URLs follow a particular syntax, as illustrated in table 2.1.

The first item of a URL entry begins by identifying HTTP as the pro-tocol in use so the browser can recognize and read it. The second item refers to the server or host name (e.g., "LooneyTunes") or a generic default such as "www" or "www4," followed by more specific location information such as the name of a university, a business, an organization, or a branch of government. The domain name indicates the type of entity that man-ages the Web page: *.edu* for an educational institution, *.com* for-profit busi-ness (.com), *.org* for a nonprofit organization, *.net* for a special network of people (mostly nonprofit), or *.mil* for the military network. Sometimes the

Table 2.1 URL Syntax

Protocol	Host Name	Domain	Directory Path	Filename
http://	LooneyTunes. ucdavis	.edu/	~Jones/	filename.html/
http://	www.learnthenet	.com/	english/	index.html/
http://	www.axis	.org/	usarios/	farocena
http://	www.asp	.net/	whitepaper/	whyaspnet. aspx?tabindex=0/
http://	www4.army	.mil/	outreach/	index2.html/
http://	national.gallery	.ca/		
		.gov/		

URL gives further information such as country of origin: *.ca* (Canada), *.mex* (Mexico), *.es* (Spain), *.fr* (France), *.de* (Germany).

The URL addresses examined up to this point constitute the bare minimum for a working URL, but the URL might also contain additional information related to the file's pathway (e.g., ~Jones, english, whitepaper, outreach, usarios), often followed by the exact file name for a particular Web page (e.g., filename.html, index.html, whyaspnet.aspx?tabindex=0). Most file names carry the extension *.html* or *.htm* to confirm that the page is coded in a standard fashion. The tilde (~) identifies a pathway that belongs to a specific individual rather than a group. A URL address is always case sensitive; for example, the word *filename* is not the same entry as *Filename*.

HTTP is not the only protocol that is used on the internet. Here is a list of some of the other common protocols:

- ftp: indicates a resource that can be retrieved using *FTP* (*file transfer protocol*); an FTP file cannot be read by a Web browser—a separate FTP program is needed to move it to the desktop or to a server
- gopher: signals a distributed document search of Gopher servers, a system used early on, especially by libraries; but this system has been largely supplanted by other protocols
- mailto: initiates a mail command to an electronic mail address

- news: refers to a newsgroup or an article in Usenet news
- telnet: starts an interactive session via the telnet protocol

The FTP protocol is particularly important for L2 teachers because they can use these addresses to send and receive files from a computer's desktop to a public Web server—especially large, multimedia files with graphics, audio, and video. To move files to and from a server requires a different program from that of a browser: an FTP program such as Fetch, Fugu, Ipwitch, Core, or WS_FTP—just to name a few options—can be downloaded for free from the Web.

More recently, the hosting function and the posting of resources on a server has largely been taken over by both private and public virtual servers called clouds, such as Dropbox.com and iCloud. As long as you have internet access, the cloud provides the user with shared documents, pictures, videos, and any other type of file.

The process of composing a Web page has become relatively easy with the advent of *what-you-see-is-what-you-get* (*WYSIWYG*) Web-editing programs such as Adobe's Dreamweaver, Komo Edit, Microsoft's Expression Web, WordPress.org, CoffeeCup HTML Editor, Mozilla's SeaMonkey, BlueGriffon, RapidWeaver, and Coda 2—to name a few—and new options are being developed all the time for users at all levels and budgets. Even Microsoft Word allows users to save a document in HTML source code. Despite the ease of using one of these, L2 teachers should have a minimum understanding of the syntax that makes HTML source code turn into attractive Web pages when viewed with a browser application.

HTML code consists of a series of tags that tell the browser what to do with the materials nested inside them. Every tag comes in pairs: opening with <the beginning of the tag> and closing with </the end of the tag>. The first and most necessary pair of tags for a source code simply states that what follows is written in HTML: for example, <HTML> . . .</HTML>. Everything in the middle of this pair of tags should be interpreted according to the HTTP protocol. Consider the following sample of HTML source code written to produce a very simple Web page, as adapted from Arocena's (2006, http://ldc.usb.ve/~vtheok/webmaestro/) HTML tutorials written in Spanish.

```
<HTML>
<HEAD>
<TITLE> My Web Page—lesson 4 </TITLE>
</HEAD>
<BODY>
<CENTER>
<H1> My Web Page </H1>
</CENTER>
<HR>
This is my Web page. It's rather simple, but I hope you like it.
<P> <A HREF="hobbies.html"> <IMG SRC="man.gif"> </A> My
hobbies
<P> <A HREF="favorites.html"> <IMG SRC="house.gif"> </A> My
favorite pages
<CENTER>
<H3> The ideal place for a vacation </H3>
<IMG SRC="island.gif" ALT="island">
</CENTER>
</BODY>
</HTML>
```

This source code has a separate section enclosed by <HEAD> . . . </HEAD> and, later, another section called <BODY> . . .</BODY>. The title of the Web page (which appears in the title bar of the browser) is nested within the HEAD tags; the main information of the Web page is inserted between the BODY tags. The actual text of the Web page can be formatted for size by different header tags (<H1> or <H3>), with additional tags added for alignment (<CENTER>), for spacing (<P>), and for other style features. Remember that all text and/or multimedia files must be nested between a beginning tag and an ending tag.

The ANCHOR tag (<A>) found in the sample code is used to create hyperlinks: for example, <A HREF="hobbies.html"> <IMG SRC="man. gif"> </A>. In this case, the ANCHOR tag (<A>) allows the Web user to click on a picture or image source (IMG SRC = man.gif) and link it to a different Web page named *hobbies.html*. The same sort of hyperreferencing

(<A HREF =. . . >) or hyperlinking could also be anchored to a single word or series of words, for example, <A HREF="hobbies.html"> Click on this sentence to see a list of my hobbies </A>. When viewed with a browser, then, this source code displays the words "Click on this sentence to see a list of my hobbies" in a special color (usually blue, to indicate a hyperlink), and clicking on it takes you to the other Web page named *hobbies.html*. In other words, the ANCHOR tags specify both a link (i.e., reference) and an anchor point.

Source code can be copied from existing Web pages (within a browser application, select SOURCE under the VIEW menu, or right click and select PROPERTIES and then SOURCE), and then pasted into an HTML editor, modified, saved as an HTML document, and subsequently viewed locally as a Web page by a browser program. If the same HTML file is transferred via an FTP program to a server on the Web, it becomes public and anyone with the corresponding URL can view the same page. But a word of caution is in order: In the sample source code given above, reference is made to three graphics files in gif format (man.gif, house.gif, island.gif) and two additional text files (hobbies.html, favorites.html). These five files must all be transferred to and reside on the same server and in the same area or folder as the main Web page. If that is not the case, the links in the Web page will *break*, or not display properly.

Creating functional and inviting Web pages, then, is like putting together an intricate salad: All the ingredients must be present, moved around or tossed, and served according to the correct protocol if internet users are going to be able to consume it. Figure 2.1 is meant to capture the creation process for a Web page, including the notion of proper file management.

For the novice Web creator, managing the different pieces of multimedia can be challenging, even frustrating, despite the transparency of the process as outlined in figure 2.1. Likewise, producing audio clips, video clips, and animated files that make Web pages so interesting and interactive requires additional knowledge of other multimedia tools. Using multimedia files often requires an additional download and installation of a plug-in or Web extension program in order to make everything execute properly (e.g., Flash, QuickTime, RealPlayer, Shockwave, Java).

Ideally, all L2 teachers using technology should be supported and trained by the staff in a language lab or university computer lab. The language lab, much like the library, constitutes an intimate part of an institution's infrastructure. The International Association for Language Learning Technology (www.iallt.org) has published a detailed description of the professional responsibilities and services that language lab personnel should provide. Even an advanced Web page user or producer will need assistance from time to time; this is just the nature of digital technologies—they are constantly changing (remember myth 3 from chapter 1: *Technology will not change.*).

Similarly, institutions should provide their teachers with space where Web pages can be *hosted* or placed on a public Web server. Space becomes

Figure 2.1 The Creation of a Published Web Page

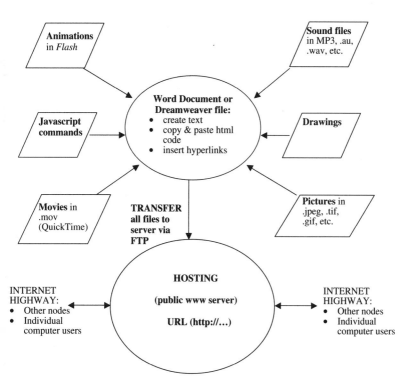

crucial, especially if large amounts of digitized audio and/or video are included in the Web curriculum. Hosting should be considered part of the general infrastructure of any educational enterprise. Nevertheless, some schools or school districts cannot afford to maintain a server for their instructors. In that case, individuals can purchase hosting privileges for relatively modest prices by shopping around on the internet or by posting files and Web pages in an internet cloud or through Google Docs or Google Sites (see chapter 3).

FL Dictionaries, Links, and Search Engines

When FL teachers were just beginning to exploit the Web in the service of the FL curriculum, much energy went into developing long lists of URLs without much thought as to how they might be used. In addition to not providing a pedagogical framework for using the Web, these efforts ran into problems from *link rot*—that is, inactive, moved, or defunct links—a phenomenon that occurs with great frequency on the Web because the network is constantly changing.

As with any new print materials included in the FL curriculum, teachers should ask themselves what they want students to do with these internet resources. But teachers should realize that link rot can render even the most pedagogically well-designed Web materials useless if key hyperlinks are broken. To get around this problem, many L2 teachers ask their students to carry out their own searches for FL materials, usually guided by a list of key words that the instructors provide. Obviously, the teacher should test those key words beforehand to make sure that they produce a variety of acceptable results for the task at hand.

Today's students are quite familiar with performing Web searches via a search engine such as Google, Yahoo! Search, Bing, or MSN Search. By using these tools or similar ones, students can retrieve primary source information in the target language. Likewise, online FL dictionaries and digital newspapers are available for most of the world's languages. The FLTEACH listserv (http://web.cortland.edu/flteach/flteach-res.html) offers a particularly comprehensive list of materials and resources, as well as many other professional development uses (LeLoup and Ponterio 2004).

Enhancing Web Interactivity: Advanced Tools

Without wrapping a pedagogy around them, the instructor who assigns the reading of Web pages creates a relatively static educational activity. Fortunately, certain advanced Web programming tricks can increase a Web page's level of (inter)activity, although these more sophisticated techniques are not for beginner Web users. FL instructors new to the Web should develop a help network or have access to a *cyberguru* who is cognizant of what these advanced techniques can provide to L2 students. By default, the most obvious cyberguru for the L2 teacher should be the staff at the language lab or the university computer center. But teachers should not discount the knowledge of other colleagues or students who have acquired sophisticated Web knowledge through experience. Two excellent sources of advanced tips are the "On the Net" and "Emerging Technologies" columns written for the online journal *Language, Learning, and Technology* (http://llt.msu.edu/). Many Web-page enhancements are realized by creating Java applets, adding CGI scripts, inserting JavaScript into the standard HTML source code, or writing pages in dynamic HTML or DHTML coding. I will treat each of these topics separately in the following sections, with appreciation for Godwin-Jones's (1998) expert explanations.

I have already mentioned the use of miniprograms called *plug-ins* that allow for animation extensions derived from programs produced by Flash and Shockwave. In a similar fashion, Java, a full-fledged programming language from Sun, Inc., can be used to create miniprograms that can be fully integrated with Web pages to perform sophisticated functions such as chat programs with sound, interactive quizzes, and questionnaires, just to name a few applications.

JavaScript refers to a scripting language that shares a syntactic structure similar to Java but only operates within a Web browser. Clearly, JavaScript lacks the power and independence that Java offers, but it is much easier to learn and to use. The JavaScript commands can be embedded directly into the regular HTML source code in order to perform functions such as quiz self-corrections and responses to mouse clicks or cursor movements. Godwin-Jones (1998) also highlights JavaScript's ability to work with form elements on a Web page such as radio buttons, check boxes, or text fields without having to send the data to a Web server. All the interaction is carried out locally within the user's Web browser, which makes it execute instructions very fast. JavaScript is not a compiled program; it can be inserted into other HTML code with any text or Web editor. As with any Web page source code, JavaScript can also be copied and pasted into other Web pages. WYSIWYG page editors now facilitate adding JavaScript to your Web page by means of drop-down menus that automatically add the necessary code.

An older (and, perhaps, less secure) method of extracting data from a Web form involves writing *CGI script* (*common gateway interface*) in PERL, a programming language, and then placing it on a Web server. When the Web forms are submitted, the CGI script takes the data from the form, analyzes it, stores it in a database, and then sends feedback to the user in the form of another Web page or e-mail message. Only an experienced cyberguru with network training or a lab technician would be capable of setting up this type of CGI script, but once installed only the address for the CGI scripts is needed to use the FORM command provided by a WYSIWYG editor.

Combining HTML, JavaScript, and other coding conventions, also referred to as dynamic HTML, allows certain features of the Web page to be changed according to user choices entered in on the fly. Godwin-Jones (1998, 10) extols the benefits of DHTML: "With DHTML the goal is to make virtually everything on the Web page able to be changed in reaction to user actions. This includes the possibility of knowing where on the page a user has clicked. By making everything on a Web page both *hot* and changeable, a dynamic environment is being created with functionality similar to what is possible with traditional multimedia authoring systems. Typeface, color, size, visibility, position, and other attributes can all be manipulated on the fly or in response to users' actions."

Toward a Pedagogy for Web-Based Language Learning

The technical information imparted in the previous sections is a prerequisite for both consumers and producers of FL Web pages but is not sufficient for the L2 teacher who wishes to implement technology in service of an L2 curriculum. Without a clear pedagogy for Web-based language learning, the best applications of technology will be for naught (remember myth 2,

Technology [by itself] constitutes a methodology) and abandons the student to nothing more than a series of navigable resources (URLs) accompanied by fill-in-the-blank exercises. Having already examined in previous sections some of the Web's distinct advantages—especially those of information access in FLs and the possibilities for learner control—I now reflect on how teachers must integrate these materials into the FL curriculum to gain the maximum benefits; again, teachers remain the most crucial link in creating a successful Web-based language curriculum. Unfortunately, teachers tend to focus on the Web exclusively to solve the eternal problem of how to teach grammar.

The problem can be illustrated by analyzing a typical title from a paper given at a recent national conference on language teaching: "Using Authentic Web-Based Materials to Teach Grammar in Context."[2] Likewise, many publishing houses accompany their language textbooks with websites that promise to teach grammar in context. At first, this approach sounds reasonable and representative of what many teachers wish to accomplish with their own Web pages: to teach grammar in context. The basic idea is that Web pages can be adapted to all FLs with only a few minor adjustments. Web materials of this ilk are usually produced following a predictable algorithm: (1) Identify a Web reading or Web video clip in the target language that contains a particular linguistic structure to be practiced (e.g., the Spanish subjunctive, the French *passé simple*, the German passive voice); (2) link photos and graphics from the Web; (3) add sound files recorded by NSs; and (4) ask the students to fill in the blanks with the correct form of the verb. This type of Web page reflects a grammar-driven pedagogy that assumes that technology can best help L2 students practice grammar online in order to free up more time for conversation in class (for a critique of the grammar-driven uses of technology, see Garrett 1988; for additional examples of grammar-driven pages, see LeLoup and Ponterio 2003). This formula for producing Web pages assumes that everything is better if accompanied by multimedia or presented via technology (i.e., myth 2).

Every FL teacher has encountered written exercises like this at one time or another, whether on paper or in Web form, but the disconnect with the true goals of FL education should be self-evident—students need practice in engaging in real-life interactions, not just discrete grammar exercises (for a more in-depth critique, see Brandl 2002). Although contextualized exercises of this type may be superior to the decontextualized ones used by the translation method, this approach still falls short of taking proper advantage of the Web's access to authentic materials and the possibilities for fostering both student autonomy and collaboration. In other words, exercises of this type present students with a more elegant type of drill-and-kill computer exercise that is still not very different in function from the dominant form of exercises common in the early stages of the CALL field (Garrett 1986, 1988).

Arguably, there is nothing intrinsically wrong with incorporating grammar exercises into the curriculum, even the drill-and-kill type, especially in the beginning stages of learning a new language where new morphology and syntactic structures present so many challenges to the L2 learner. But drill-and-kill should not constitute the driving concept behind a Web-based L2 curriculum. Best practices would dictate that teachers should try to adapt their Web lessons into a framework such as the one suggested by FonF (see chapter 1), which puts the negotiation of meaning at the center of its implementation.

To avoid the curricular pitfall described above, I turn now to more basic educational notions by asking, "What are FL teachers trying to achieve?" Laurillard (2002, 23), of the British Open University, identifies the general goals of university teaching: "Teaching is essentially a rhetorical activity, seeking to persuade students to change the way they experience the world through an understanding of the insights of others. It has to create the environment that enables students to embrace the twin poles of experiential and formal knowledge." If applied to language teaching, Laurillard's goals highlight two important concepts only briefly touched on above: (1) Language learning (or teaching) is a mediated or negotiated process, an endeavor best carried out within an interactionist framework (see chapter 1); and (2) learning an L2 involves the development of a new sense of identity that blends insights from both L1 and L2. The latter refers to the desire for L2 students to develop a sense of the other without losing their own sense of self—what Kramsch, A'Ness, and Lam (2000) have dubbed the tension between authenticity (from the Web) and authorship (from the L2 learner).

Formal knowledge gained from the classroom, such as grammar and the like, remains important but needs to be taught in a manner that Laurillard

(2002, 13–16) describes as *situated knowledge*, knowledge that deals with real-world activities. In other words, the curriculum should not treat the body of conceptual knowledge to be learned as separate from the situation in which it is to be used. Accordingly, this educational philosophy nudges the FL teacher to rethink how to incorporate authentic materials along with the activities that students are asked to perform with them in order to bring the students' potential contributions into the learning equation.

All learning environments afford certain benefits and also incur disadvantages for learning—the Web-based environment being no exception (for a less optimistic view of using the Web, see Vogel 2001). The Web's multimedia environment allows teachers to focus on authentic texts in wondrous ways. Teachers can fashion reading assignments supported by multimedia glosses (sound, video, text) that are simply unavailable in print form (Chun and Plass 1997).[3] A reading task delivered in a Web format can also provide attractive cultural sidebars and background information that focus the students' attention and stimulate reading as well as more explorations of the L2 culture (Osuna and Meskill 1998). Textbooks attempt to do the same with elaborate color layouts and design, but the Web environment offers an organic, ever-changing medium with palpable and proven ways of capturing students' attention.

For instance, Web pages can include sound files that harness a sensorial channel that is lacking in books. Sound files increase the prospects of building lasting mental associations for words and phrases in a phonological, semantic, and even aesthetic context. While reading the Web version of a Lorca poem, to cite one example of many, the L2 student can simultaneously hear the poetry recited aloud so that the words come alive. Clearly, these types of affordances affect one's perception of the poem. The same can be said of Web texts of a more prosaic nature: interviews, commercials, recipes, and business slogans. Likewise, a similar supporting role can be invented for visual imagery, another one of the Web's strong points.

But none of these Web affordances relieves the teacher from preparing a pathway for students to engage with Web readings accompanied by the appropriate battery of prereading strategies such as an advance organizer, extensive and intensive reading activities, cognate study, and a follow-up application (Phillips 1984). Chun (2006, 81) reports that background knowledge of an authentic reading accounts for nearly 28 percent of the variance in student comprehension rates, especially for intermediate readers. Salaberry (2001, 51) claims, "The success of a technology-driven activity will likely depend as much or more on the successful accomplishment of pre- and post-activities than on the technology activity itself." Accordingly, only by means of a well-constructed lesson can L2 students progress from being passive consumers of authentic source materials (on the Web or in print) to active authors/owners of the material in the sense discussed by Kramsch, A'Ness, and Lam (2000). In addition, Laurillard (2002, 112) warns that the Web's nonlinear nature demands that teachers map out a learning pathway so that students do not become lost in constructing their own narrative line.

Some techniques for helping students construct meaning in a Web environment undoubtedly require more interactive or communicative tools that go beyond simple reading strategies performed in isolation. To accomplish this online, teachers must resort to a dialogic or conversational framework (see Laurillard 2002), on which I elaborate in chapter 4 with respect to CMC and describe its potential for transforming the student's online experience.

Now I return to the topic of Web pages and to every FL teacher's nagging worry, the same worry lurking beneath the sample conference title: How can you teach the L2 grammar (pronunciation, vocabulary, and syntax) with Web pages? Can technology really help us carry out this task in a way that improves on sterile, decontextualized exercises and supersedes even the more contextualized Web-mediated fill-in-the-blank exercises offered along with most commercial language textbooks? Yes, it is possible, especially if the curriculum has been shaped by the practice of task-based language teaching (TBLT; see Ellis 2003) or content-based instruction (CBI; see Stryker and Leaver 1997). It is a matter of linking and engaging the students' (pre)conceptions with their contact with new experiences and getting them to put their newly acquired knowledge into action. As Laurillard (2002, 23) phrases it, the teacher's job is to mediate between the poles of experiential and formal knowledge.

Task-Based Instruction and the Teaching of Grammar

Task-based or content-based instruction (commonly known as task-based language teaching, or TBLT), in its essence, recommends a top-down constructivist approach based on Vygotsky's (1986) ideas, whereby teachers and classmates facilitate involvement in real-world task analysis, problem generation, and assessment grounded in real-world activities (Laurillard 2002, 67; Ellis 2003; Willis and Willis 2009).[4] This cooperative approach to learning extends each person's zone of proximal development, meaning that two or more heads (i.e., teamwork) will be better than one with respect to L2 learning. The TBLT/CBI approach supports learning activities that have a primary focus on making meaning by engaging with real-world authentic language use with communication-based learning outcomes (Ellis 2003, 9–10). Above all, a TBLT curriculum strives for language activities that are student centered rather than teacher centered (for examples of well-designed technology-mediated tasks, see Brandl 2002; Warschauer 1995; Lomicka and Cooke-Plagwitz 2004; and Thomas and Reinders 2010) and offers an alternative to the piecemeal, bottom-up approaches that are common to most grammar-driven curricula (Stryker and Leaver 1997, 3). The target language largely serves as the vehicle through which subject matter content is learned rather than as the immediate object of study (Brinton, Snow, and Wesche 1989, 5; Crandall and Tucker 1990, 187). Genesee (1994, 3) further suggests that content in a TBLT or CBI curriculum need not be strictly academic (i.e., only dealing with traditional subjects such as mathematics, history, science, geography, and the arts); it can include any topic, theme, or nonlanguage issue of interest or importance to the L2 learner. Accordingly, this focus on content first promotes negotiation of meaning, which is known to enhance language acquisition (Lightbrown and Spada 1993), in part because the tasks are intrinsically interesting, self-motivating, and cognitively engaging (Byrnes 2000; Brown 2001). Historically, the TBLT or CBI approach formed the cornerstone methodology for the Canadian immersion programs of the 1960s (Stryker and Leaver 1997, 15).

In this approach, developing Web-based grammar tutorials is not so much about finding a Web text with lots of target-language subjunctive, passive voice, past tenses, or any other specific linguistic structure but rather about asking students to engage with the L2 materials in a meaningful way that will involve those grammatical structures. In practical terms, this means that instructors might present learners with authentic materials that contain grammatical structures not seen before or well beyond their present capacity, as opposed to using graded language texts. Stryker and Leaver (1997, 8–9) offer the following suggestions for dealing with the linguistic difficulties that authentic materials might engender when the CBI approach is followed:

> CBI teachers can find themselves routinely working with materials that are, in the traditional view, far beyond the current linguistic expertise of their students. In such a case, the important issue is not so much what those texts are but what the teacher does with them. If the teacher carefully selects the content, students will study topics for which they already possess schemata (i.e., the relevant linguistic, content, and cultural background knowledge): for example, geography, the arts, history, society, and literature. Using content and context together to understand messages, students develop coping mechanisms for dealing with unknown language in other context, ultimately fostering the development of foreign language proficiency.

Yet teachers sometimes feel intimidated when giving materials prepared for NSs to students who are at proficiency levels of 2 or lower. A typical teacher reaction is, "This material is too advanced for my students!" In this situation, the challenge to the teacher is to create a linguistically simple but cognitively challenging task that is at once realistic and interesting to the students (Stryker and Leaver 1997, 297).

Teachers trained in this method, then, do not set out to find Web materials with a high frequency of certain linguistic structures—which is the goal of the grammar-in-context approach—but rather try to identify topics that allow L2 learners to reflect on their L1 and L2 knowledge base (i.e., existing schemata) in new and illuminating ways. What would be an algorithm for creating a TBLT/CBI lesson? The following procedures might be one way to get started within a Web-supported learning environment:

- Identify a topic of interest from the perspective of both the goals of the curriculum and the present knowledge of the L2 learners.
- Find a brief Web passage dealing with that topic (copyright laws must be observed!).
- Add sound and glosses to the text.
- Provide brainstorming activities to activate semantic notions (i.e., schemata) about the topic in such a way as to bridge students' knowledge base to the new concepts found in the target culture.
- Design reading strategies and prereading tasks that address the difficulties associated with the selected reading passage.
- Instruct students to read and/or listen to the passage.
- Prepare comprehension questions.
- Design grammar tasks that ask students to do something with materials and the text, with the difficulty level sensitive to the class's present linguistic level (the same reading passage can be repurposed for different levels): for example, (1) find nouns marked for feminine gender, (2) search for cognates, (3) change spoken citation or first-person verbs into indirect discourse, (4) rewrite the narrative using the past tense (i.e., using indirect discourse instead of direct discourse).
- Provide supplementary grammar explanations as needed to support the assigned grammar task(s).
- Direct students to work in pairs to accomplish a real-world task related to the topic and grammar at hand.
- Incorporate the resources available on the Web.
- Give students key words (pretested for successful results) to facilitate their carrying out additional Web searches related to the process of their collaborative task.
- Guide students to write an essay that summarizes the results of their collaborative work.
- Instruct students how to make a presentation in class based on the results of their collaborative work.

Clearly, this is a generic, but not exhaustive, formula for creating TBLT/CBI language materials supported by technology (also see, on the project-oriented classroom, Leaver and Willis 2004 and Jeon-Ellis, Debski, and Wigglesworth 2005; on student-determined lessons, Brandl 2002; and on a global simulation German course, Levine and Morse 2004). Nor do proponents of this method advocate a fixed approach (Stryker and Leaver 1997, 3); each reading, video, or sound recording demands a fresh approach that depends on a unique interaction among the teacher, the students, and the authentic materials (what Meskill 2005 has called a triadic scaffold). Crucially, this approach favors student control while allowing the instructor to establish a learning pathway so that students will not get lost.

Schaumann and Green (2004) have taken the idea of student control to heart and have developed an upper-division literature course for German in which their students create a Web curriculum as a class project. Their students, like all L2 literature students, must first grapple with the difficulties presented by primary literature texts, then provide glosses, annotations, cultural and grammatical explanations, and background materials as an articulated set of Web pages from which future classes can benefit. Selber (2004) calls this type of student-driven activity the cultivation of rhetorical computer literacy, a topic to which I return in chapter 5.

Also notice that these suggestions—with the exception of doing Web searches, playing Web sound, and setting up pop-up textual glosses—can also be implemented in more traditional ways. The instructor needs only to find appropriate Web materials (URLs); the rest of the lesson has to do with constructing a sound pedagogy on the basis of these materials, which is what teaching should be about. Some of the activities are done individually on the Web outside class as preparation (e.g., prereading activities, intensive reading, searching), and other tasks are carried out working in conjunction with a partner face to face. This is not to deny the attraction of putting all parts of the lesson on the Web to take full advantage of the medium if the instructor has the knowledge, time, and patience to persevere. In chapter 4 I illustrate how collaborative tasks such as those discussed here can be done online using CMC tools.

Discussion Questions and Activities

1. Find a Web page in the language that you teach that you predict will help your students learn something important about the L2 language

and culture. Create a lesson plan around this Web page that can be carried out in a classroom setting. Include a set of learning objectives for your lesson and try to make your accompanying activities as student centered as possible. Consider ways in which your students would benefit from previewing guidance; what would they need to do to appreciate your selection? Share your Web page with your colleagues and ask for reactions.

2. Revisit your lesson plan from question 1 and consider what you would have to include in the way of online materials (e.g., text, images, sound, video, explanations, instructions) if students were to accomplish the stated learning objectives by working outside class time, either by themselves or in groups.

3. Can pragmatics be taught online? Review *Dancing with Words: Strategies for Learning Pragmatics in Spanish* (Cohen and Sykes 2006) at www.carla.umn.edu/speechacts/sp_pragmatics/home.html. Is the overall presentation and design helpful for teaching pragmatics? Discuss how your students would react to using these Web pages. If your language is one other than Spanish, imagine the effect that similar Web pages in your language would have on your students. How could this approach be adapted to the language and the level that you teach?

4. Use Microsoft Word to produce a simple Web page for your students (perhaps a presentation of the rationale or goals for taking one of your courses). Be sure to save it by choosing the option <Save as Web page>. View your page with your favorite browser and share the results with a colleague or your class for comments and suggestions.

5. According to Laurillard (2002, 93), Web pages such as the ones you researched in connection with question 1 are best suited for presenting and working with narratives. If that is true, discuss how you could adapt these pages using a CBI approach in order to teach points about grammar, vocabulary, or L2 culture.

Notes

1. The authors of the Pew report also caution that 13 percent of American teenagers (3 million), characterized by their lower levels of income and/or African American ethnicity, still do not use the internet. This could potentially feed a digital divide with insidious effects for our society (for a different perspective on this topic, see Warschauer 2002; Warschauer, Knobel, and Stone 2004; Crump and McIlroy 2003).

2. For a more critical look at using Web pages to teach FLs, see Yagüe 2007.

3. Ironically, Chun also reported at the CALICO 2002 conference that when students were free to choose, they preferred simple English-translation glosses without video or sound. Chun found (personal communication) that these different strategies were not correlated with academic performance. The data from Karp's (2002) unpublished dissertation also demonstrated learner preference for English-translation glosses over multimedia ones.

4. I include under this rubric content-based instruction, project-based instruction, and inquiry-based learning as well, although each name is intended to highlight special procedural features. A top-down method puts meaning first, in contrast to a bottom-up method, which begins by decoding morphemes, words, phrases, sentences, and so on.

CHAPTER 3

CALL and Its Evaluation

Programs and Apps

A History of CALL

As discussed in chapter 2, the impact of the internet is the central focus of CALL today because of its prominent role in the modern FL classroom and, moreover, in the lives of the students. However, the first applications of computer technology in the field of FL teaching were implemented in the 1960s on mainframe computers within a Skinnerian behaviorist framework where learning a language meant memorizing a body of well-choreographed responses that included frequent vocabulary items, clichés, and phrases used at appropriate moments in a conversation. Accordingly, language teaching was viewed as a type of conditioning, as getting students to produce a series of responses in reaction to particular stimuli (i.e., stimulus/response theory). Not surprising, given the political reaction caused by the Sputnik launch, the first computer language programs developed at Stanford University, Dartmouth College, and the University of Essex exclusively dealt with Russian language instruction (Beatty 2003, 17–18). These mainframe programs were linear in nature and patterned after the activities typically found in language workbooks. This approach is often referred to as *computer-assisted language instruction* (*CALI*, or language CAI), in contrast to *computer-assisted language learning* (*CALL*), where the latter term implies an approach more in line with the notions of communicative competence and the negotiation of meaning in a non-behaviorist framework. The Computer-Assisted Language Instruction Consortium (CALICO), the name of the main professional organization dedicated to studying technology and language teaching, still bears the original CALI acronym.

The most extreme form of language CAI is derogatorily labeled as *drill-and-kill*. This is not to say that the CAI approach of programmed instruction has no value for language learning or that it does not produce any positive student outcomes. Rather, this approach assumes that the mastery of any given subject matter results directly from a cumulative investment of time and practice applied to a learning object that can be broken into subunits and arranged in a linear fashion (Lai and Biggs 1994, 13). Many SLA theorists would argue that perfect mastery (i.e., speaking like a native speaker) is not a realistic or even desirable goal for L2 learners (Bley-Vroman 1990; Kramsch 2009). Certainly, the idea that language can be reduced to a collection of linearly organized subunits (i.e., learn *a*, then *b*, then *c*, etc.) is linguistically an insufficient descriptive framework. However, the fact that drill-and-kill exercises are still widely used proves, at the very least, that some in the FL profession, along with the students themselves, still believe them to be of value for L2 learners in certain circumstances, especially for learning heavily inflected verb morphology systems such as Russian.

Alternately, Delcloque (2001, 69) referred to the 1960s and 1970s as the text phase in the history of CALL, where "much of the pioneering work . . . involved the manipulation of text on screen." There was also a preoccupation with making foreign-character fonts work on the computer, a topic that has been completely surpassed by the advent of Unicode, a universal protocol for assigning ASCII values to the letters found in more than 250 of the world's languages.[1]

This period also encompassed the groundbreaking efforts carried out in the 1960s at the University of Illinois with the PLATO project (Programmed Logic/Learning for Automated Teaching Operations; Beatty 2003, 18). Despite its reliance on a grammar translation approach—and again, Russian dominated the early focus of the PLATO project—this pre-DOS CAI program offered students an amazing variety of computer language activities dealing with vocabulary, grammar, and translations that took more than seventy hours for students to complete. These materials also provided students both corrective and diagnostic feedback, spell checkers, and grammar checkers.

The 1980s marked the introduction of a new groundbreaking platform, Macintosh (released in 1984), along with its *GUI*, or *graphical user interface*, and a general switch from mainframe computers to microcomputers. Macintosh's HyperCard application also introduced the new concept of hypertext, a nonlinear way of organizing multimedia materials, information, and activities that broke the CAI linear mold and launched a new generation of computer programs that now could be referred to as CALL (Delcloque 2001, 69). Microcomputers were also driving (i.e., "giving instructions to") laserdisc players and, in time, the more compact and convenient media of CD-ROMs and DVDs, all of which have a large capacity for multimedia (e.g., video, audio, graphics, images, and text) that could be accessed randomly using digital technology. The earliest nonlinear programs developed at Brigham Young University (BYU)—Macario, Montevidisco, and Dígame (Gale 1989)—used laserdisc technology to simulate adventures in a Spanish-speaking country and force students to become involved in the storyline by making choices that branched off in different directions. The descriptor *interactive* truly seemed to apply to this type of software.

Following fast on BYU's footsteps, a group of researchers at the Massachusetts Institute of Technology (MIT) embarked on the Athena Language Learning Project (ALLP) and produced three laserdisc simulations of exceptional quality, mimicking real-world tasks based on meaning and authentic materials: *À la rencontre de Phillippe, Dans le Quartier Saint-Gervais*, and *No Recuerdo* (Murray, Morgenstern, and Furstenberg 1989). These simulations provided multiple protagonists, multiple plots, knowledge-based choices, surprises, multimedia presentations, and an intrinsic motivation to complete the materials.[2] These stimulations were originally programmed for the UNIX platform, which never translated gracefully to the microcomputer environment with CD-ROMs (instead of laserdiscs) so as to be widely used by the FL profession. Nor did the authoring tools of the time (i.e., HyperCard) provide the necessary robustness to duplicate the original performance afforded by the UNIX system. Despite these drawbacks, these programs still stand as a pillar of CALL creativity because they emphasized meaning over endless repetition of forms.

In both the BYU and MIT cases, the programming and video production costs for these projects required a sizable institutional investment along with additional governmental support. Few individual teachers or CALL developers found themselves in such favorable circumstances. In the meantime, in the classroom trenches, many more modest efforts to produce in-house CALL programs for the microcomputing environment were being pursued by language teachers using relatively transparent authoring tools such as HyperCard (Mac), Tool Book (PC), Libra (Mac/PC), and WinCalis (PC), just to name a few. These technical advances coincided with what Delcloque (2001, 70) has dubbed the CD-ROM and authoring tool phases of CALL. The ability to produce do-it-yourself programs generated considerable interest in CALL from among the rank and file, which was a very positive outcome for the profession.

Commercial entities also began to produce what Levy (1997, 178–214) has called *tutorial CALL* programs (with or without CD-ROMs) for consumption in this new microcomputing world. Tutorial CALL is a more friendly way to refer to language CAI programmed instruction, where the computer guides the learner and, hopefully, offers feedback along the way. The *CALICO Review* is an excellent source for evaluating existing commercial language software, as is the FLTEACH website.[3] Publishing houses began to invest in multimedia programs, as well, usually delivered on CD-ROMs and intended as a complement to help sell their books (see Jones 1999).

Feedback and artificial intelligence also became a new focus for what was called *iCALL* (i.e., intelligent CALL). Previously, the behaviorist model had viewed students as a blank slate that needed stimulation to make them produce correct answers by using a very controlled sequencing of the learning materials. But what should a computer program do when the learner fails to reach the expected outcome, despite the controlled stimuli of the programmed instruction? Inevitably, students are going to make mistakes along the way—lots of mistakes. What feedback or directions will they receive from the CALL program at these junctures? The iCALL approach uses a database to track learners' responses and, ultimately, provide feedback with commonly asked questions and mistakes.

In contrast to the CALI phase, the new CALL paradigm assumes that students bring certain schemata to the learning process. Consequently, a well-designed CALL program should engage learners in problem-solving activities or constructivism in order to make use of each learner's previous learning experiences. To accomplish this, the program must guide students by giving feedback. This is easier said than done if the feedback must be customized for each learner, the obvious ideal. Providing error correction is a more complex programming proposition than just signaling that the answer is right or wrong and the student should try again.

To begin with, computer scientists have hotly debated what constitutes computer intelligence. Alan Turing (1950) argued in the early 1950s that if you cannot discern that you are interacting with a machine, then the program is intelligent. To add fuel to this debate, Weizenbaum (1966) wrote a simple *chatterbot* program in 1966 called Eliza that mimicked through textual exchanges the behavior of a psychiatrist. The program gives the appearance of being a sympathetic listener who prods the user with follow-up questions such as "How are you feeling?" "Why are you feeling tired? "Tell me more about last night." In actual fact, the program matches key phrases, nouns, adjectives, verbs, and adverbs—recognized only as character strings (i.e., not as fully parsed linguistic structures)—and then matches these strings with clichéd responses that give the impression of a normal, give-and-take conversation. The basic programming was later adapted for German (PSYCHIATER and SCION) and Spanish (FAMILIA; see Underwood 1984, 75–79, and Underwood 1989; for online examples, see Fryer and Carpenter 2006).[4] Eliza and other chatterbot programs are amusing to students in the short run but hardly what they need in the long run in order to develop their L2 competence.

For most CALL practitioners and language learners, the level of feedback is closely tied to the program's level of interactivity and its ability to allow the learner to enjoy more autonomy to direct the discovery process. Kern and Warschauer (2000) use the word "agency" to describe this educational goal. They argue that the ideal CALL activity is one that encourages the L2 learner to become an agent in the learning process. Accordingly, they analyze CALL history in terms of pedagogical advances rather than technological innovations such as those described above (i.e., mainframe computers, microcomputers, laserdiscs, CD-ROMs, the Web), as illustrated in table 3.1. Integrative CALL, the third phase, includes activities in which people interact with other people via the computer—that is, computer-mediated communication (CMC)—which is the topic of the next chapter. In turn, the study of CMC motivates the need to discuss issues concerning

Table 3.1 The Three Stages of CALL

Stage	1970s–1980s: Structural CALL	1980s–1990s: Communicative CALL	Twenty-First Century: Integrative CALL
Technology	Mainframe	PCs	Multimedia and internet
Teaching paradigm	Grammar translation and audiolingual	Communicative language teaching	Content-based instruction
View of language	Structural (a formal structural system)	Cognitive (a mentally constructed system)	Sociocognitive (developed in social interaction)
Principal use of computers	Drill and practice	Communicative exercises	Authentic discourse
Principal objective	Accuracy	Fluency	Agency

Source: Adapted from Kern and Warschauer (2000).

sociocultural or intercultural competences, which are also covered in the next chapter.

Tutorial CALL

Although social computing appears to have completely captured students' interest, tutorial CALL remains an important component of any technologically assisted curriculum. These are stand-alone programs, in the traditional sense, that students carry out on their own, hopefully with some form of feedback in response to the students' actions. In this section only a few exemplars are examined closely, with the intent of sparking the reader's interest in exploring the tutorial CALL options and authoring tools for any given L2 under study.

Pedagogical Background

Levy (1997) as well as Hubbard and Bradin Siskin (2004) distinguished between the computer as tutor and the computer as tool in support of human interactions and CMC activities. In the former case, the computer controls the learning and automatically evaluates the students' responses while the instructor seemingly has little or no role. Hubbard and Bradin Siskin suggested that this conception of CALL harkens back to the old type of CALL, what I have labeled the CAI phase. They questioned whether or not this separation between old versus new CALL continues to be a useful distinction. In other words, a FL digitally assisted curriculum should employ both types of CALL to advantage. Clearly, students with relatively low levels of linguistic competence in L2 need more guidance, such as might be offered by a tutorial CALL program (Bertin 2001). In chapter 6 I explore the topic of distance language learning where both tutorial CALL and the computer as tool are employed to advance different purposes at different times in the online course. Below, I focus on one specific usage of tutorial CALL that everyone accepts and even expects from CALL materials: vocabulary glossing.

Apps for L2 Reading and Vocabulary Development

Recent advances in Web 2.0 tools have led to a proliferation of useful *apps* or programs that run on the internet and can be accessed by an iPad or iPhone. This growth in computer apps has dwarfed the more traditional server–client approach that was common to many previously designed CALL programs. Web apps to assist vocabulary development, in particular, have sprung up to help L2 learners handle what Nation (2001) and others refer to as *the learning burden*: namely, L2 reading is next to impossible without a critical mass of vocabulary items (Cobb 2007; Nation and Waring 1997; Nation 2001). Fully independent reading requires knowledge of close to 3,000 of the target language's most frequent words, while the ability to guess words in context demands that the student knows approximately 95 to 98 percent of the words contained in a particular text (Nation 2001). Most first-year courses optimistically expect students to learn approximately 1,000 of the most frequent words, although when dealing with category III (e.g., Russian, Filipino) and IV languages (e.g., Chinese, Arabic), that figure might be unrealistically high. Subsequently, the jump to second-year language courses saddles students with drastically increased vocabulary demands in order to ramp up to the increased lexical load demanded by the reading and listening materials. This is where vocabulary apps have an important role to play.

The FL profession needs no convincing with respect to the importance of reading authentic materials in order to stimulate L2 development. Krashen (2004) considered reading to be of fundamental importance for moving ahead with advanced proficiency and academic language skills; he routinely campaigns in the schools in favor of setting aside time during class for free voluntary reading. But for the L2 student, the lack of both vocabulary breadth and depth remains a formidable obstacle to reading authentic materials, especially because most unfamiliar words, excluding the high-frequency functors (i.e., words with a grammatical function but little referential meaning), are used only once or twice in a given passage (Knight 1994).

An online program such as WordChamp.com (for a review, see LeLoup and Ponterio 2005) presents one software solution to this problem by allowing users to paste the L2 texts or enter the URLs into the WordChamp interface (NB: This service was previously free but requires a small annual fee for service).[5] WordChamp then analyzes the passage and highlights the words it has in its database, allowing the user to roll the cursor over a word and receive a gloss and, if available, an audio recording of its pronunciation. WordChamp offers an option to add new words to the user's customized flash card list to be practiced at another session. WordChamp offers this service in an amazing number of languages, but not every language database has extensive audio recordings to accompany the word definitions. Ultralingua.net (LeLoup and Ponterio 2005) is a similar software program that uses pop-up windows instead of the rollover cursor, but it only covers the major European languages.

Other avenues to confront the learning burden presented by the L2 lexicon are offered by products that send out a word of the day to the learner's e-mail address. For Spanish, two social networking sites, Elcastellano.org and SpanishDict.com, offer both online and e-mailed vocabulary information for Spanish. Web-based flashcard apps exist for almost all languages and have become a regular feature of most language social network sites (see chapter 7).

With respect to research on vocabulary learning, multimedia glossing has been the focus of much CALL research (for an excellent overview, see

Chun 2006). According to Chun (2006, 78), L2 vocabulary is best remembered when learners look up picture or video glosses in addition to receiving translations of unfamiliar words. A vocabulary app such as *EyeVocab. com* is a perfect illustration of learning vocabulary with the support of pictures, sound, and textual clues.

However, if given the choice, L2 learners tended to choose only simple translations so as to speed up their ability to finish the reading assignment (Chun 2006, 82). Chun's study also showed that lexical knowledge was significantly related to both reading and listening comprehension, while grammatical knowledge was not. Following Grabe's work (2004), Chun correctly pointed out two separate aspects of lexical knowledge that have an impact on reading comprehension: the learning of vocabulary and the fluency (i.e., automaticity) of word recognition. In general, the research has shown that explicit instruction, including tutorial CALL (see Lafford, Lafford, and Sykes 2007), has a significant impact on vocabulary acquisition, but reading comprehension is affected by a number of complicated factors, including prior or background knowledge of the material to be read. As was suggested in chapter 2 with respect to preparing Web activities, Chun (2006, 92) counseled teachers to include a large battery of prereading activities in order to prime students for what they will encounter.

Note that glossing programs such as WordChamp combine both user and computer control in ways that blur the distinctions between tutorial CALL and tool CALL. The user is fully in control of which words are looked up, but the size and complexity of the database determine what stimuli the reader has available and in what form, multimedia or not. Fukkink, Hulstijn, and Simis (2005) have demonstrated that L2 students will retrieve faster and with less variation the unfamiliar words on which they have trained in contrast to those on which they have not trained. Research of this kind indicates obvious areas where tutorial CALL and explicit instruction can make a difference in L2 development.

Langbot (www.amherst.edu/aboutamherst/news/faculty/node /144997) represents another type of interactive vocabulary app still in development by Scott Payne at Amherst College. Langbot helps students increase their vocabulary both in terms of breadth (i.e., more words) and depth (i.e., a better semantic network with more connotations) by providing a vocabulary *buddy* via their iPhone, iPad, and/or computer. Langbot can be accessed through any IM program (e.g., Instant Messenger, iChat, etc.) and then questioned for word translations in Spanish, Chinese, or German. The Spanish version of Langbot returns a translation for each query and then prompts the user to see the word in context as provided by a selection from Wikipedia. Students can also ask to see the word of the day selected from a list of the most frequent 3,000 words in Spanish, following Spanish word-frequency guidelines given by M. Davies (2006). Langbot adjusts the difficulty level on the basis of each learner's respective linguistic level. Langbot keeps a record of each student's requests that is also available for the instructor to see. Whenever the student asks for a pop quiz on vocabulary, Langbot retrieves the student's search history and customizes the exam to that student's particular needs.

Arispe (2012) tested three groups of L2 Spanish learners—novice high, intermediate low, and intermediate high—who used Langbot for one quarter. She predicted that those students using Langbot would experience more vocabulary growth than those who had no access to this vocabulary app. She measured vocabulary breadth and depth before and after the treatment with an instrument adapted from Meara's protocols for gaging vocabulary growth (Read and Nation 2009). The results were quite striking, as shown in tables 3.2 and 3.3, and demonstrated that all three groups using Langbot added significantly more words to their vocabulary than did those without access to this app. But with respect to vocabulary depth, only the intermediate high students were able to restructure their semantic nets in more meaningful ways as a result of the extra practice afforded by Langbot. Similarly, the amount of Langbot usage (i.e., sending messages and receiving queries) correlated with significant increases in their vocabulary breadth, an observation that, once again, speaks to the importance of time on task with respect to L2 development.

Authoring Tools

Using a template to develop CALL activities enormously simplifies the development phase, but it also tends to constrain the creator to a predetermined set of formats—multiple choice, fill in the blank, drag and drop, click text/

Table 3.2 Analysis of Variance for Access to LangBot Across Levels According to Vocabulary Breadth

Vocabulary Breadth	Treatment		df
	Access $\mu \pm$ SE	No Access $\mu \pm$ SE	
Beginner	1.36 ± .74[*]	0.23 ± 0.49	1
	N = 25	N = 32	
Inter-low	3.40 ± .44[*]	2.27 ± 0.57	1
	N = 20	N = 22	
Inter-high	2.48 ± 0.39[*]	0.29 ± 0.49	1
	N = 25	N = 18	

[*] = $p < .05$ within rows.

image on screen, and the like. In general, the student feedback produced by these authoring tools is also limited to string recognition. Nevertheless, the ease in the development phase of software creation makes the authoring tool approach attractive to all. When several templates or functions are bundled into one seamless development package, along with more advanced multimedia capabilities, then one can speak of an authoring system.

At the height of the CALL platform wars (Mac vs. PC) that took place in the 1980s, the CALL field was searching for the perfect authoring template, a program that would allow nonprogrammers, which is the condition of most FL teachers, the ability to create CALL exercises with relative

Table 3.3 Analysis of Variance for Access to LangBot Across Intermediate Levels According to Vocabulary Depth

Vocabulary Depth	Treatment		df
	Access $\mu \pm$ SE	No Access $\mu \pm$ SE	
Inter-low	2.45 ± 1	4.3 ± 1	1
	N = 20	N = 22	
Inter-high	4.62 ± 0.92*	1.47 ± 0.79	1
	N = 25	N = 18	

* = $p < .05$ within rows.

ease (Garrett 1991). M. Davies (2006, module 2.5) provided a partial list of authoring tools from that period that have vied for the distinction of the ideal CALL template—although few from this list have survived into the twenty-first century:

> TES/T, Pilot, COMET, CAN, WatCAN, CALIS, WinCALIS, Dasher, Edutext, Microtext, Tutor, TenCore, Course of Action, Storyboard, CopyWrite, Quartext, WordPlay, TextPlay, Developing Tray, Question Mark, ClozeWrite, Clozemaster, UNIT, Gapfil, Speedread, ToolBook, HyperCard, HyperStudio, MediaLink, QuestNet, IconAuthor, CBT Express, Course Builder, Guide, HyperShell, Linkway, BonAccord, Partner Tools, Learning Space, Authorware, Director.

Delcloque (2001, 71) added a few more authoring tools from the 1980s and 1990s to this list: LAVAC, Libra, MacLang, SuperMacLang, Speaker, and SuperCard. At the turn of the century, another group of platform-specific authoring tools cropped up, all with different pricing schemes and affordances: Author Plus (PC), Authoring Suite/Wida Software (PC, includes Storyboard), BlueGLAS (PC), and MaxAuthor (PC). Increasingly so, authoring tools have shifted to Web-based applications, avoiding the pesky issues of cross-platform compatibility altogether—for example, Interactive Language Learning Authoring Package (Web-based), ExTemplate (Web-based), Swarthmore Makers (Web-based), Marmo Marmo's JavaScript templates (Web-based), Yale's Center for Language Study Comet templates (Web-based), and CLEAR's SMILE templates (Web-based).[6] This generalization extends to learning/class management systems (*LMS/CMS*) such as WebCT, Blackboard, and Moodle.

In the 1990s the University of Victoria sponsored the development of a set of templates that came to be known as Hot Potatoes that is now distributed free as version 6.0 for educators by Half-Baked Software.[7] Hot Potatoes provides an interface for both Mac and Windows operating systems that can be exported to the Web and is free for educators. The Hot Potatoes software consists of a suite of six cross-platform templates (for Mac OS X, Windows, Linux, or any computer running a Java Virtual Machine) that has stood the test of time and heavy use by language teachers. The different templates allow FL teachers to create multiple choice exercises, word-entry exercises (single word, phrase, string, or open-ended), crossword puzzles, cloze (fill-in) exercises, jumble-word exercises, and mix-and-match exercises (Winke and MacGregor 2001). All types of activities can be published as a stand-alone PC or Mac application or as a Web document. Both interface and some of the feedback routines can be customized along with adding a common gateway interface hook to store the results or scores in a designated server available to the course instructors. The current versions are fully Unicode compliant.

New Web-authoring tools are popping up constantly that allow instructors to create sophisticated online materials quickly and efficiently without excessive amounts of help from professional programmers. Some authoring systems require significantly more programming experience and have steep learning curves. In general, the more powerful the tool, the longer the learning curve to learn how to use it. Teachers are well served to seek out technical support with these more complicated authoring systems from their respective institutions. Nevertheless, with the right technical support, authoring systems help to produce CALL programs that are sophisticated even at the commercial level. Here is a selected list of current authoring systems, along with their most prominent features (also see the review at http://elearnmag.acm.org/archive.cfm?aid=2221186):

- Adobe Captivate (www.adobe.com): a powerful authoring system for Mac and Windows much like Adobe Presenter with a high learning curve that forms part of the Adobe eLearning Suite (i.e., Dreamweaver, Photoshop, Flash, Captivate, Presenter).
- Softchalk (www.softchalk.com): an easy-to-use authoring system for Mac and Windows that supports a variety of exercises and interactions packaged as Web-based or stand-alone apps; Softchalk will release soon a new Flash-independent version that will provide mobile friendly (HTML-5) activities that can be displayed on iPhones and iPads.
- Camtasia (www.camtasia.com): a screen-sharing and video-editing tool for Mac and Windows that is easy to use, but strictly for video; it provides no interaction activities.

- Articulate (www.articulate.com): an expensive suite of tools for Windows only that facilitates the production of sophisticated content materials. This system has just added Articulate Storyline, a promising tool for developing complex content.
- Lectora (www.trivantis.com): an expensive, Windows-only, powerful authoring system with a very steep learning curve.

Following the current trend to make everything Web-based, LMSs such as WebCT, Blackboard, and Moodle (Brandl 2005) also offer a template-based system already built into their course framework. Godwin-Jones (2003b, 18) extolled the virtues of LMSs for distance learning, because "an LMS can supply crucial communication and management tools, as well as assessment builders and grade book functionality." Again, Godwin-Jones correctly states that "LMS excel at course and user management but they are not strong in content creation." This fact sometimes forces the teacher to develop the content outside the LMS and then link these materials to the LMS shell. But both Blackboard and WebCT are beginning to open up their proprietary systems to accommodate plug-ins and add-ons in order to extend the functionality while retaining the familiar LMS user interface.

Google Apps for Education

Google has created a number of useful apps, especially with educators in mind and with the philosophy that Google will supply teachers with one-stop shopping for all their technological needs. In this section I review many of them, but a more complete review can be found on Google's own training pages: http://edutraining.googleapps.com/ (for an educator's take on these tools, see Nicole Naditz's blog for language educators at http://3rs4teachers.wordpress.com/). First and foremost on the list would be Google Docs, an app that allows anyone to create text files and share them with others at any level of privileges. In a Google Doc, the text itself is being saved as you add to it, which allows users to share their work much as if it were a wiki by giving everyone in the group the same privileges to create and edit at will. Groups of students in the same locale or in different locations (or countries) can collaborate on a Google Doc and write a project together either in deferred time at each person's convenience or in real time, for all intents and purposes, as the program saves any changes on the fly. For instance, while two or more people are carrying on a phone conversation or a Skype session (for more on CMC tools, see chapter 4), they can also be taking notes together and adding separately to the same Google Doc. When the editing process has been completed, a copy can be printed, downloaded, posted to the Web, or e-mailed to other participants or the instructor. Google Docs are fully Unicode compliant, which means, again, that writing in languages such as Arabic, Chinese, or Japanese presents no problems. Google Docs allows users to create text files, presentations (a doc similar to a PowerPoint file), spreadsheets, tables, drawings, and forms.

Google Forms are a very special type of Google Doc that can be used to create exams or surveys that students can complete online at their convenience. Each Google Form is uniquely associated with a spreadsheet that keeps track of the questions/field created in the form. When students take the test or fill out the survey online, their respective responses flow into the linked spreadsheet item by item so as to create a new entry in the spreadsheet. The instructor submits answers, too—the correct ones, which normally are recorded in the first line of the spreadsheet. From the *Insert* menu > *Script* menu, the instructor installs Flubaroo.com and lets this set of scripts automatically grade the assignment based on the designated correct answers. Answers are limited, of course, to multiple choice options or discrete words listed in fill in the blanks, but for some quizzes or assignments this is entirely appropriate. Flubaroo calculates the class averages and automatically provides a summary report of the quiz results.

Google Maps provide another wonderful Google tool to explore the cities and streets of the target country. Instructors can customize routes from a given location as well as add videos, voiceovers, and textual explanations. Students can annotate their own favorite walking routes in a given city and explore the plethora of pictures, videos, and sound recordings that other people have already posted on any given Google map. An option also exists to focus in on the street level with Google's 360-degree camera, which gives students a real feel for the city life of the target country. The instructor can invent a series of task-based activities that require using commands, directions, and all kinds of useful vocabulary dealing with navigations.

Google Sites is a powerful app that any teacher or student can use to publish a project or blog on the internet. Google has made everything about Web design very transparent and easy to use. Accordingly, this Web 2.0 tool truly turns the student into an active agent or producer of Web materials. Teachers are increasingly using Google Sites as a mechanism for managing their classes as well as a medium for publishing materials customized for their own students' benefit. Google provides an excellent online training module for Google Sites at http://edutraining.googleapps.com /Training-Home/module-5-sites/module-5-chapter-2.

Google Moderator permits instructors to create a feedback channel for use during their classroom presentations by creating what is called a *series*. A series can be about anything of interest to the class, and the instructor can open it up for people to enter *submissions* (i.e., questions, ideas, or suggestions). Anyone can come to the site and submit a question, idea, or vote, and anyone can vote. Google Moderator shows you a Featured Question in the box with the blue background. Instructors can also break up a series into small units or topics in order to better manage the discussions. The idea is to increase participation in class and manage discussion for large groups.

The final Google app of interest to language teachers is Google Talk and its companion, Hangout. Google Talk (www.google.com/talk) offers a Web plug-in that can be used to carry on live video/audio/text conversations over the Web. I give a full presentation of this app in chapter 4 on CMC tools.

Feedback, iCALL, and Automatic Speech Recognition (ASR)

One of the key concerns about tutorial CALL revolves around the notion of interactivity: How responsive and adaptive (or rather, effective) can computers be to students' needs at the discursive level? Laurillard (2002, 118) is right to caution us about the limits of providing discursive feedback:

The responsiveness of the interactive medium is limited, however. Hypermedia environments, enhanced or otherwise, are not truly adaptive to the student's needs at either the discursive or the interactive level. It would not be possible for the student to tell if they had made an inappropriate interpretation of the resources, as the system remains neutral and unvarying with respect to anything they do. There is no way for the student to test whether their interpretation is correct, except by comparing it with the various expert views made available in the form of model answers.

In the earlier days of CALL, feedback focused more on the grammatical or sentence level. CALL feedback was limited to spellcheckers, grammar checkers, and discrete string or keyword matching. Unfortunately, most spellcheckers assume that the users are already competent speakers of that language. Few programs are designed with L2 learners in mind; L2 learners exhibit an emerging linguistic competence referred to as interlanguage (for an example of this problem, see Burston's 1998 review of a French spellchecker). Spellcheckers do well at catching single-letter violations but often fail to analyze learners' more competence-based errors (Heift and Schulze 2007, 166–67).

Although string-matching routines, such as what is available from Hot Potatoes, are far better than simple right/wrong responses, this approach still falls short of providing students with CALL materials that can truly be labeled as interactive. As the CALL field has moved away from the model of drill-and-kill tutorials, the field has demanded CALL applications that react to student input in ways that appeared to be more context-sensitive. As early as the 1980s, Underwood (1989) described what the ideal intelligent tutoring system (ITS) should be able to do: act as a real tutor or guardian for L2 students, leading them by the hand to discover more and more about the target language with each response and prescribing the appropriate exercises and metalinguistic explanations about the language that are needed to advance. An ITS, then, involves an expert (usually, some type of grammatical parser, a program capable of separating utterances into phrases, words, parts of speech, and limited semantic interpretations), a student, and a teacher module, frequently circumscribed in a highly defined semantic microworld, or domain, in order to minimize potential ambiguities and confusion. At the time, artificial intelligence (AI), a subfield of computer science, held great promise that something like Underwood's forward-looking description of an expert tutor could actually come to pass.

Gradually the term ITS, or *expert system*, was supplanted by the term *iCALL*, or intelligent CALL, but as Schulze (2001) explained, a more accurate name would be *parser-based CALL*. This later term makes it clear that natural language parsers are used to evaluate students' syntactic and sometimes semantic input. Although Schulze (2001, 117) openly acknowledges that a parser-based CALL cannot account for the full complexity of natural human languages, "it does not mean that interesting fragments or aspects of a given language cannot be captured by a formal linguistic theory and hence implemented in a CALL application." Obviously, a parser-based approach places an inordinate emphasis on morpho-syntactic errors—not a bad thing seeing that these types of errors appear to constitute the most frequently occurring mistakes that students make in freely produced texts (Schulze 2001, 121; Juozulynas 1994). However, the parser approach also produces its share of false acceptances and false alarms. The more constrained the semantic domain is, the more successful the parser will be at diagnosing errors.

Much more serious for the iCALL field has been the fact that despite a great deal of work in AI over the years, there still exist only two operational Web-based iCALL programs: E-Tutor for German (Heift 2002; Heift and Schulze 2007), and Robo-Sensei for Japanese (formerly called Banzai; Nagata 1993, 1995, 2002; for a review, see Ushida 2007).[8] A third system, Tagarela for Portuguese, was recently introduced at Ohio State University. The goal of all these programs is to provide error-specific feedback and flexibility in handling student textual input.

In the case of the E-Tutor, a natural language parser for German is combined with a student module that tracks each student's errors and proficiency level, controlling the type of feedback that will be delivered—namely, for beginners and intermediates, rich metalinguistic feedback messages and remedial exercises (e.g., dictation, build a phrase, which word is different, word order practice, build a sentence) but something much less explicit for advanced users who need only light guidance.

Heift (2001) acknowledges that building this type of parser-based CALL is very labor and time intensive and requires close cooperation among computer programmers, linguists, and pedagogues. However, error analysis of this ilk can also be very accurate in providing the type of feedback and interactivity that is helpful to the learner, even if it does not meet the lofty ideals that Underwood (1989) originally imagined. And students really pay attention to well-crafted feedback. Heift (2002) discovered that most students (85 percent) using E-Tutor revised their sentences without peeking at the answers, with the weaker performers tending to also be the more frequent peekers. Heift (2004) has also shown that the more explicit and metalinguistic in nature the feedback is, the more it helps the L2 learners successfully complete their L2 tasks.

Why, then, has iCALL not gained more notice in the CALL field? Perhaps what has distracted the field from the slow but sure advances in parser-based error analysis has been the meteoric surge of interest in CMC and sociocultural/intercultural research, the subject of chapters 4, 6, and 7. In short, CALL practitioners are looking at human communication as the true source of interactivity. However, much learning still occurs when individuals are alone, working by themselves in isolation at odd times and places. In these self-study times, iCALL has proven superior to using static workbooks alone (Nagata 1996). When one considers that classroom teachers infrequently correct phonological and grammatical errors but rather concentrate on discourse, content, and lexical errors (Ellis 1994, 585), iCALL could have an honored niche in the L2 learner's individual study time. As more parser-based systems become available for a large array of languages, iCALL still holds considerable promise as a useful tool for L2 learning.

Feedback to textual input is not the only kind of response of which the computer is capable. Although iCALL has concentrated on syntax and text production, researchers working on *automatic speech recognition* (ASR) have looked to applying their results to teach pronunciation. As in the case of parsers, ASR applications "perform best when designed to operate in clearly circumscribed linguistic sub-domains" (Ehsani and Knodt 1998, 56), in pursuit of executing specific tasks—for example, individual sound practice, word recognition, and short sentence repetition.

Ehsani and Knodt (1998, 56) suggested that the most common approach to implementing ASR involves developing (1) an acoustic signal analyzer that computes a spectral representation of incoming speech; (2) a set of sound or phonemic models based on sophisticated probabilistic computations called hidden Markov modeling and, then, further trained by a large corpus of actual speech; (3) a lexicon for converting phones into words; (4) a statistically based grammar that defines legitimate word combinations at the sentence level; and (5) a decoder that makes the best match between the sound and a corresponding word string. Building such a system requires a large amount of speech data from speakers of different accents and conditions (i.e., while reading or producing spontaneous speech). Adapting it for L2 learners requires additional training of the system using large corpora of nonnative speech data from learners of varying degrees of proficiency.

Ehsani and Knodt (1998, 60) cautioned that delimiting the performance domain or task remains one of the most important steps in designing a successful ASR application. Although ASR software is good at recognizing short utterances (words, phrases, or short sentences), continuous spoken language input with open responses and multiturn dialogues poses almost insurmountable challenges without access to powerful computers and lots of memory. In addition, the input must be clear and noise free, which often depends on a good microphone and noise-cancellation baffle.

Despite these obstacles, commercial software does exist that provides specific exercises dealing with mastering linguistic forms at the word or sentence level as opposed to simulating real communicative exchanges. For instance, Tell Me More Pro (Auralog; for a review of the Spanish version, see Lafford 2004) tracks and visually displays the waveform and pitch contours from speech input in nine languages and compares them with those patterned after NS; the program then scores the learner's efforts on a scale from 1 to 7.[9] The learner can zero in and practice particular phones in isolation, if so desired. Tell Me More also provides a 3-D animation that demonstrates how the lips and tongue should move to produce the target sound.

With the Auralog sentence exercises, L2 learners choose to speak one of several closed responses with ready-made vocabulary and syntax, which greatly simplifies the speech recognition algorithm but prohibits learners from actively constructing their own utterances (Eskenazi 1999, 64). As Eskenazi (1999, 64–65) observes, "To our knowledge, current speech-interactive language tutors do not let learners freely create their own utterances because underlying speech recognizers require a high degree of predictability to perform reliably." Eskenazi (1999) and Eskenazi and Brown (2006) report on some successful research efforts (i.e., the FLUENCY project and the Sphinx-2 project at Carnegie Mellon University) to construct a production task that uses carefully constrained elicitation techniques (patterned after the MLA's audiolingual method) to guide the L2 learners into speaking only the specifically targeted speech data.

ASR technology, as in the case of parser-based iCALL, may have a significant impact on CALL development in the near future, but what the field needs now is an authoring tool that makes incorporating ASR simple for nonengineers. Undoubtedly this will be forthcoming soon, but more serious obstacles to implementing ASR in any given language will be the existence of and access to large corpora of native and nonnative speech data, in both written and conversational formats.

CALL Evaluation

Understandably, not every language teacher will actively wish to launch into the creation of technologically based materials for their students, but everyone should be interested in evaluating CALL materials in the service of the FL curriculum. Just as with the myriad textbook choices in the FL marketplace, teachers have a professional responsibility to seek out and select what they consider to be the best set of CALL learning materials for their students. But evaluating CALL software is no longer the straightforward endeavor that it might have been in the 1960s, as Levy and Stockwell (2006, chap. 3) took pains to point out (also see Bickerton, Stenton, and Temmerman 2001). Current techniques range from using checklists to more complicated longitudinal evaluation studies involving the collection of both qualitative and quantitative data (Levy and Stockwell 2006, 40).

In the first place, the CALL field has expanded to include not only tutorial CAI programs but also Web pages, CD-ROMs, DVDs, and computer-mediated activities such as chat. The variety of CALL programs and activities cannot all be evaluated in the same way, because they have different purposes and ask students to achieve different goals. Likewise, software evaluation needs to be considered separately from the more general SLA research questions dealing with the effects and/or effectiveness of CALL (for more on research issues, see Burston 2006). Typically, CALL software evaluation emphasizes design issues, activity procedures, or theoretical and/or methodological approaches.

Checklists and surveys, usually based on a Likert scale (i.e., numerical ratings from 1 to 5, with 1 being "strongly disagree" and 5 being "strongly agree"), with room for additional comments, overwhelmingly focus on design issues and probably constitute the most widely used method for evaluating CALL materials. The Information and Communications Technology for Language Teachers Project (ICT4LT; see M. Davies 2006), sponsored by the Commission of the European Communities and the EUROCALL organization, provides a handy CALL evaluation checklist that is downloadable from their website.[10] This checklist offers a series of queries dealing with the L2 language level, the user interface and navigational issues, the use of multimedia (e.g., video, photos, graphics, animation, sound), the provision of help and/or feedback, the level of interactivity, and the availability of performance scoring. Checklists are a good place to start but often restrict the evaluation process to technical and design factors.

The *CALICO Journal* provides a more elaborated evaluation framework that asks their reviewers to examine the critical properties of the CALL materials in question, focusing on pedagogical validity, adaptability to different learning environments, efficiency, effectiveness (as judged by student outcomes), and innovation.[11] Instead of checklists or surveys, the *CALICO Journal* advocates using a set of eclectic criteria that combine the best of Hubbard's (2006) methodological approach and Chapelle's (2001) interactionist SLA framework (see Burston 2003).

In Hubbard's (1996, 2006) evaluation process, the principal concern is finding the right fit of the CALL software to the teacher's instructional approach. Hubbard (1996) highlights factors such as the teacher fit (methodological approach), the learner fit (as a function of the individual learner profiles, interests, and computer infrastructure), and the operational/procedural fit (interface features and activities types). Both Burston and Hubbard's concerns dictate the following guide to software evaluation, which is the basic format for all the *CALICO Journal* reviews:

1. technical preview
2. operational description (activities and procedures)
3. learner fit
4. teacher fit.

The reviewer must then decide what implementation schemes will be needed to integrate the reviewed CALL materials into the curriculum and, finally, make appropriateness judgments as to whether or not there is a good match between learner fit and teacher fit.

Chapelle (2001) interpreted the concept of teacher fit more in the sense of what the teacher assumes about how language is learned. Accordingly, her model provides an evaluation framework that is more driven by SLA theory. The central concept in her model is the language-learning potential or the extent to which the CALL materials under review produce FonF and meaningful language negotiation, the very foundation of the interactionist theory reviewed briefly in chapter 1. Chapelle judges all CALL materials as if they were activities or tasks with a positive or negative potential to stimulate learners to engage in language negotiations. For Chapelle, *appropriateness* judgments deal with six factors: language-learning potential, learner fit, meaning focus, authenticity, positive impact (i.e., the effect on developing learning strategies, pragmatic abilities, and cultural awareness), and, finally, practicality. Given Chapelle's emphasis on FonF, it is not immediately obvious how to use this framework to evaluate CALL materials that focus solely on pronunciation, vocabulary, or discourse. Likewise, Levy and Stockwell (2006, 76) correctly noted that too much is being grouped under the rather vague heading of positive impact ("the positive effects of the CALL activity on those who participate in it"). Linking an evaluation framework to a specific SLA theory is something of a doubled-edged sword: It increases specificity, which is good, but limits what will be looked at and, subsequently, valued.

In summary, CALL evaluation may examine design, procedures, approaches, or a combination of all of these factors. Clearly, the evaluation process has been complicated by the changing nature of what constitutes CALL materials. Although general frameworks such as Hubbard's and Chapelle's stimulate important avenues for evaluation, the specific goals of how an institution is using a given CALL program may require formulating a series of criteria based on the local learning environments and concerns. In a word, CALL evaluation is and should always be sensitive to local context.

CALL and the Profession

Academics working in CALL have only gradually experienced professional acceptance and recognition of their efforts. In general, applied fields always seem to struggle in academia for validation when compared with entrenched notions of what constitutes real academic work, and the case of CALL is no different. Fortunately, professional organizations such as CALICO, the Modern Language Association (MLA), and EUROCALL agree quite closely on what constitutes the field of CALL and what academic value this type of work should have in terms of career advancement. It is noteworthy that the American Association for Applied Linguistics, which hosts one of the premier SLA annual conferences, regularly includes a strand dealing with language and technology. In other words, the CALL field is considered part of SLA studies, with all the privileges and responsibilities to do sound research (Chapelle 2005). Unfortunately, applied linguistics often suffers from a lack of respect from theoretical linguists, which carries over to researchers in the CALL field as well.

Nevertheless, CALICO and EUROCALL issued a joint statement in 1999 on CALL research that carefully situates the field within an SLA context.[12] These organizations stipulate that CALL work can include research, development, and/or practice. Although carefully distinguishing among these three aspects of CALL work, the CALICO and EUROCALL statement also stresses that they often overlap.

Research may be separate from development, in that a researcher may explore the effects of using technology-based tools or materials developed by others (e.g., formative evaluations), or may focus entirely on theory development. In CALL the progression often begins with pedagogical practice or learner needs driving the development of technology-based materials, techniques, or environments. This development effort may then later lead to research, which in turn may or may not be used to generate theoretical implications. Nonetheless, in establishing criteria for evaluating CALL work for purposes of academic recognition and reward, it is important that the distinctions between these activities be clearly articulated.

The MLA's policy statement on CALL research focuses more on the contractual issues surrounding someone engaged in CALL development:

In other words, will they be judged fairly in their careers by their colleagues in the humanities? The MLA policy suggests that academics doing CALL research, development, and practice should negotiate and validate these activities at the time of employment so that misunderstandings will not arise later in the personnel process. The MLA statement also acknowledges the changing nature of this field and the need to temper traditional perceptions about scholarship, especially when based on research only done in literature: "Academic work in digital media should be evaluated in the light of these rapidly changing institutional and professional contexts, and departments should recognize that some traditional notions of scholarship, teaching, and service are being redefined."[13] Clearly, academics doing CALL work need to be reviewed by their peers, other academics involved in the CALL field, especially given the abrupt changes or phases outlined above that have occurred in a relatively short time period.

Summary

Like the technology and the tools themselves, the notion of CALL has changed rapidly since its Sputnik-inspired beginnings with the PLATO system in the 1960s. The field has evolved from notions such as tutorial programs and technology used as tools to accomplish learning tasks to a more integrated phase that emphasizes discursive and intercultural competence. Earlier concerns about how to type international fonts and drill morphology have fallen away to reveal a more sophisticated preoccupation with how to get students to develop a new and more bilingual sense of L2 cultural competence. Learning morphology and grammar has not disappeared, but rather teachers are endeavoring to put this learning in its proper place within the overall L2 curriculum. Accordingly, each type of CALL program and activity has its own place and time, as should be revealed by any thoughtful CALL evaluation process. Language teachers should be fully involved in evaluating CALL materials, even if they do not produce them—it is part of their profession.

Recently the CALL field has experienced a surge of interest in CMC, whether in real or deferred time. This social activity is immensely appealing to students and teachers alike as soon as they have enough vocabulary and structure to carry this off, which is the topic of the next chapter. CMC research and practice have also been stimulated by a heightened awareness of the properties of discursive language and the need for students to develop intercultural competence.

Discussion Questions and Activities

1. Make a list of the pros and cons of using drill-and-kill types of CALL exercises.
2. Write a definition for what the word *agency* means in relation to CALL.
3. Describe what the word *interactive* means to you in the context of CALL.
4. Review a CALL lesson produced by a colleague, classmate, or company and use the criteria of "learner fit" and "teacher fit" to critique it.
5. Write a review of some commercially available software that deals with the language you teach, following the CALICO guides (https://calico.org/page.php?id=523).
6. Discuss the ultimate goals of L2 instruction. Is it possible to reach mastery of an L2 through classroom language instruction alone? Bley-Vroman (1990) and others would argue that it is not possible. Discuss whether their findings invalidate the goals of the language programs at the high school and university levels. Give reasons why not. What role does CALL play?
7. Conduct a survey of your colleagues and students to determine how much feedback (i.e., error correction) and of what type they would like to have available in a CALL program. Discuss whether their requests are practical given today's state of technology and the cost of producing CALL programs.

Notes

1. See http://unicode.org.
2. In the commercial realm, *Who Is Oscar Lake?* (http://whoisoscarlake.com/) provided simulations similar to the Athena project that used a video game/mystery approach to CALL.

3. For *CALICO Review*, see https://calico.org/page.php?id=523; for FLTEACH, see http://web.cortland.edu/flteach/flteach-res.html.

4. See also www-ai.ijs.si/eliza/eliza.html.

5. See www.wordchamp.com/lingua2/Home.do.

6. For Yale's Center for Language Study Comet templates, see http://comet.cls.yale.edu/; for CLEAR's SMILE templates, see http://clear.msu.edu/clear/store/products.php?product_category=online.

7. See www.halfbakedsoftware.com/index.php.

8. For E-Tutor, see www.e-tutor.org; for Robo-Sensei, see http://usf.usfca.edu/japanese/RSdemo/preRSfiles/Robo-Sensei.htm; for Tagarela, see http://sifnos.sfs.uni-tuebingen.de/tagarela/index.py/main.

9. See http://en.tellmemore.com/.

10. This is available from www.ict4lt.org. Also see "Software and Website Evaluation Forms," www.ict4lt.org/en/index.htm.

11. See https://calico.org/page.php?id=523.

12. See www.eurocall-languages.org/research/research_policy.html.

13. The MLA policy statement is at www.mla.org/guidelines_evaluation_digital.

CHAPTER 4

Computer-Mediated Communication

Background

From the brief survey of SLA theories presented in chapter 1, it should be clear that best practices in FL teaching need to be firmly grounded in interactionist notions of one flavor or another; for example, the proximal zone of development, negotiation of meaning, focus-on-form (FonF), task-based learning, project-based learning, or pair collaboration. These constructs, whether simple or complex, rely on the power of human interactions to stimulate the process of SLA (O'Rourke 2005, 436–37). Although cooperative exchanges—whether between learners or with mixed groups of native speakers and learners (see Blake and Zyzik 2003)—cannot be said to be a direct cause of SLA, they most certainly get students ready to learn, as Gass (1997, 130) has explained, by focusing attention on unfamiliar structures (i.e., "noticing," in Schmidt's 1990 term) and by providing the necessary scaffolding in the learning environment (Bruner 1996).

Not surprisingly, talented classroom teachers actively seek to provide opportunities for their students to engage in collaborative interactions and the same should be true for digital learning environments. Teachers can create the similar opportunities for interactions within the context of *computer-mediated communication* (*CMC*), whether in real time (*synchronous, SCMC*) or deferred time (*asynchronous, ACMC*). Kern and Warschauer (2000) have labeled this communication in the service of language learning as network-based language teaching (NBLT), which includes e-mail, discussion forums or electronic bulletin boards, blogs, wikis, and chatting with or without sound/video. The potential benefits of collaborative exchanges, whether set in the classroom or managed online, depend more on the sound pedagogical design of the tasks the participants are asked to accomplish than on the actual medium of the learning event. This chapter reviews both asynchronous and synchronous CMC tools, and it also closely examines the discourse that students produce when they engage in online communication.[1] Finally, the Cultura project developed at the Massachusetts Institute of Technology is showcased as an ideal way to use technology in the service of developing *intercultural communicative competence*, the ultimate goal of L2 language study for all those in pursuit of becoming bilingual.

Asynchronous CMC

Godwin-Jones (2003a, 12) makes a distinction between first- and second-generation tools for the internet, the former being widely familiar to most internet users and the latter being built on an updated code protocol known as XML (extensible markup language), as opposed to HTML (see chapter 2).

First-Generation CMC Tools

First-generation CMC tools include e-mail, electronic mailing lists, and discussion forums, also known as threaded bulletin boards. Most e-mail clients (e.g., Outlook, Thunderbird, Eudora) support formatted text (i.e., not just ASCII text), non-Roman fonts, and the capacity to attach photos, graphics, and even sound/video. The same is true of Web-based e-mail programs such as Microsoft's Hotmail.com or Yahoo.com, the only difference being that the Web-based programs can be accessed directly using a Web browser without downloading a separate client or special e-mail program. When all else fails, e-mail is the lowest common denominator for exchanging information and ideas with students from the same class or from around the world. E-mail is the default technology used by tandem learning, an organization that pairs two people who wish to learn each other's language and focuses in pedagogical terms on the principles of reciprocity and learner autonomy (O'Rourke 2005, 434).[2]

Despite new technological advances, e-mail has not lost any of its usefulness within the internet landscape, especially as everyone is so willing to engage in e-mail exchanges and because this platform is supported with minimal access to the internet via either the superhighway (i.e., broadband, internet II) or back alleys (i.e., low bandwidth providers).

Electronic mailing lists (listservs) made up of a group of e-mail users are another frequently used tool in both commerce and education. A message sent to a listserv goes out to everyone registered in the group. Many universities or course management systems automatically provide their instructors with class listservs linked to their respective courses and student enrollments. Listserv participants need only remember that when wishing to respond to a single individual rather than the whole group, they must replace the general listserv address with the individual's unique e-mail address—otherwise, everyone in the group will read what might be a personal message. This error might seem obvious to the reader, but it is repeated on a daily basis, much to the embarrassment of some and the irritation of others from the listserv.

Teachers often use listservs to their advantage as the best medium for posting general class announcements because the ubiquitous medium of e-mail/listserv guarantees that everyone in the class will receive the pertinent information. Although students do not always log on to a course management system, they almost always check their e-mail. But for most interactive exchanges, discussion forums or electronic bulletin boards are preferred. With the advent of social networking sites such as Facebook (see chapter 7), the look and feel of the discussion forums has been more completely modernized to include graphics, photos, videos, and sound files. Nevertheless, these modes are all instances of digital forums.

In their more basic form, discussion forums automatically maintain a record of all messages in a threaded or hierarchical structure. Each topic represents one thread to which others in the forum can respond. The instructor usually determines who can begin new threads or topics—only instructors or everyone in the class. Forums, like listservs, are semipublic writing areas, as opposed to e-mail, which is a private and more informal CMC medium. Forums are a pervasive feature of course management systems such as WebCT, Blackboard, and Moodle and have been considered a cardinal tool for asynchronous distance learning for a long time (see chapter 5).

Godwin-Jones (2003a) considers discussion forums as an equalizing tool where universal participation is encouraged as opposed to the more complicated dynamics found in face-to-face dialogues, where certain individuals can dominate the flow of the discourse by force of personality. However, Payne (2004, 159) cautions that participating in asynchronous discussion forums is not the same as doing a writing assignment; rather, it is more like a protracted conversation that takes place over time. Teachers need to think about structuring interaction in online learning much more than in the classroom because online activities such as forums cannot be fine-tuned on the fly in the same way as discussions in the classroom context. Students carry out these activities by themselves on their own time, away from the eyes of the instructor. Clear instructions, goals, and learning objectives are imperative if the tasks are going to succeed.

Second-Generation CMC Tools

Blogs and wikis are examples of second-generation asynchronous internet tools. Blogs can be described as online hypertext journals that others read and react to. The reactions are logged and posted chronologically and become part of the blog. Most blogs are personal or journalistic in nature (Godwin-Jones 2003a; Ducate and Lomicka 2005) and, as such, allow students to exercise their own voice with a freedom that cannot be experienced in moderated discussion forums. In truth, a blogging tool such as Blogger.com empowers students to become their own agents and real producers of multimedia materials. By the same token, blogs demand more personal responsibility from students than forums, because only one student is ultimately responsible for publishing an online diary. Obviously, blogs also afford the student the possibility of reaching a public beyond the confines of the classroom through publishing a record of the student's thought. A blog requires no special knowledge of HTML; the interface offers a WYSIWYG editing palette where students can choose how they wish to format text or insert graphics or other multimedia objects.[3] Reynard (2007) maintains that blogs can be used effectively to develop each student's individual learning voice but only if they are intentionally designed into the course and are clearly valued throughout the course to ensure student motivation and participation. She contends that blogs used as a mere assignment add-on will have little reflection value for the student.

Wikis (*wiki* is Hawaiian for "quick") are similar to blogs but are the product of a group rather than the initiative of one individual. Wikis share the blog's WYSIWYG editing environment that makes adding to or modifying content extremely easy. Wikis, however, are not simply chronologically oriented but rather allow the group to reorganize content as they see fit. Any participant can add, modify, rearrange, or even destroy text, images, and other multimedia objects from earlier contributions. The wiki keeps a record of all modifications and allows any participant to regress to a previous content state. Any change or regression affects everyone working on the wiki. Consequently, working together on a wiki has the potential to be counterproductive if the participants enter into a constant revisionist war over content and form. Conversely, a wiki provides the ideal tool with which to carry out collaborative writing and project-based work. The goal of a wiki site is to become a shared repository of knowledge, with the knowledge base growing over time. Unlike chat rooms, wiki content is expected to have some degree of seriousness and permanence. For instance, Moodle allows users to create multiple wikis with full Unicode compliance. Students of Arabic, for instance, can work on their Arabic writing and ask each other questions, alternating between Arabic and English, through the wiki. In essence, Google Docs (see chapter 3) function just like a wiki but also provide the ability to publish or post the final product.

Synchronous CMC (SCMC)

Early attempts at using SCMC programs for language teaching were carried out in chat rooms where large groups or even a whole class would log on and chat at once, usually from the same language lab. Daedalus Interchange was one of the first programs to be used in this way, especially by English composition teachers. Kern (1995) reported that L2 students of French using Daedalus wrote much more and produced more turns than students talking face to face in the classroom (an average of 12.5 vs. 5.3 turns) but frequently with less linguistic accuracy than teachers would normally demand from a written medium such as a formal composition assignment. Similarly, Chun (1994) found that the use of chat rooms promoted increased morphological complexity for fourth-semester L2 students of German.

Gradually the profession has begun to recognize that writing in a chat room is different from writing a formal composition at home as an assignment. Chat room discourse consists of language that is much closer to oral discourse than to written discourse (Sotillo 2000). Asynchronous chat has even been adapted from the computer gaming world, such as *MUDs* (*multiuser dungeon/domain*) and *MOOs* (*MUD object oriented*), to the needs of teaching FLs (Thorne and Payne 2005, 379).

SCMC with Voice/Video Tools

Recently, more and more language teachers have begun to employ SCMC in pairs or small groups with the idea of fostering as much task-based interaction as possible, sometimes with the addition of voice tools as well. Lafford and Lafford (2005) have reviewed a number of text-based chat programs intended for small group use and have classified them under the label of IM tools. IM tools consist of a client program that participants first download to their respective computers and then log on to a particular system—for example, ICQ, MSN Messenger, Yahoo! Messenger, AOL's Instant Messenger (AIM), PalTalk, and iVisit (for another review of these tools, see Cziko and Park 2003). In order for students in any given class to connect to other users, they must create a buddy list using e-mail addresses, account numbers, or screen names. Learning management systems such as Blackboard, WebCT, and Moodle offer their own internal chat programs within a more controlled learning environment where all students are automatically enrolled in a chat room.

Written chat comes in two different modes: one in which written entries are posted by means of a carriage return, and another in which participants share a text field and a single cursor placed in a field with immediate display-style chat that updates the window character by character (i.e., IRC-style chat). Each modality has its advantages and disadvantages. With the immediate display-style chat, participants can see the thought process of their partners evolving on the screen, but a protocol for who gets to write at any one time must be clearly worked out among participants. Otherwise, the chat partners could spend their time arguing over who has the stylus, with one person or the other endlessly rewriting previous contributions.

The carriage-return modality allows anyone to post a message at any time, which empowers less assertive or inherently shy students (see Sauro 2009). No one can stop someone else from posting ideas. Conversely, this modality produces long pauses while one's partner is typing. Frequently, questions go unanswered for several turns until the participants catch up with previous postings. This lag effect is disconcerting and even disruptive to the natural flow of any dialogue and takes some getting used to, but the affordances of SCMC are also very attractive. Payne (2004, 159) has identified the benefits of written SCMC:

- SCMC reduces the pace of discussion.
- Textual exchanges are posted and are therefore not ephemeral but rather ever present on the screen for students to consult and continue processing.
- Students have more time for linguistic processing to prepare their own contributions.
- Students' affective filters are lower in SCMC because no one is looking over their shoulder, as is the case in face-to-face exchanges.

Smith (2009) observed that having to type within the medium of textual chat itself often forced learners to notice their mistakes, much like Swain's idea of forced output (see chapter 1). Students tend to undertake self-initiated self-repairs that are not usually captured by the written transcripts but do show up when researchers employ methods of video screen capture.

Wildner-Bassett (2005, 636–37) focuses, in particular, on SCMC's spatial independence from the immediate face-to-face context to stress out-of-body experiences, a metaphor for increased opportunities for students engaging in CMC to step back and contemplate new identities and voices that move students beyond preestablished categories. She envisages using SCMC to establish a particular learning ecology where "learners cooperate in their ways of knowing and of being together by revealing their processes of naming and critically viewing their own identities" (p. 646). Wildner-Bassett warned the profession, as I did earlier in this chapter in connection to assigning asynchronous CMC tasks, that conscious stewardship by the teacher is necessary for this critical social-constructivist viewpoint to emerge.

Ultimately, both teachers and students are charged with creating a class-room climate where all voices can be heard and all participants are willing to listen (p. 654).

Other benefits of a more controversial nature include claims that SCMC levels hierarchical differences originating from ethnicity, age, gender, and shyness (Thorne 2003; Sauro 2009). But much depends on the tasks, teachers, and idiosyncratic characteristics of the students themselves. What is clear is that students like to chat, so by assigning CMC tasks teachers can harness more of the students' time outside class for L2 learning. After all, chatting is an activity that students know how to do and do frequently on a daily basis.

A variety of synchronous SCMC tools are commercially available (and the list is changing all the time)—such as AdobeConnect.com, BlackboardCollaborate.com (which has bought out both Eluminate.com and Wimba.com), Google+ Hangout, and BigBlueButton.org, to name only a few. Increasingly, these CMC tools provide the exchange of video, sound, text, whiteboards, and even screen sharing (an operation that is very bandwidth-intensive) packaged in user-friendly interfaces with differing pricing options that depends on the level of desired service. These SCMC tools handle the audio feature either as half-duplex (i.e., walkie-talkie-type sound exchanges) or as full-duplex (*voice-over IP*, *VoIP*) or telephonic sound exchanges.

Another free voice chat program that also uses a Flash communication server is YackPack.com. Its free, Web-based Walkie Talkie widget can be inserted into any Web, blog, or wiki to allow all users the ability to exchange telephonic voice on the fly (i.e., VoIP). When the user sets up a Walkie Talkie widget, YackPack provides the code for its instantiation that can be copied and inserted into any Web page. As long as the other users also have the Flash plug-in installed, this tool—a product of B. J. Fogg's Persuasive Technology Lab at Stanford University (Fogg 2003)—works seamlessly with no additional setup or installation of a separate client.[4]

In the interactionist literature, there are numerous studies that illustrate the benefits of face-to-face negotiations carried out between native and nonnative speakers (Lomicka 2006, 213; Sauro 2011). Students can enhance cultural awareness, motivate themselves to engage in real interactions, increase the quantity of their oral production, explore stereotypes, and establish a personal connection with the target language or culture. Similar benefits, including a heightened focus on form, have also been demonstrated for pairs engaging in SCMC (Blake 2000) and include native speakers chatting with nonnative speakers, NS/NNS; heritage speakers chatting with nonnative speakers, HS/NNS (Blake and Zyzik 2003); and nonnative speakers chatting with nonnative speakers, NNS/NNS. In the following sections I discuss the NNS/NNS context and describe the ideal conditions for its use, and I provide a case study of a bimodal SCMC tool that allows the exchange of both text and audio chat.

Intracultural CMC

Proponents of the interactionist hypothesis (e.g., among many others, Ellis 1997, 2003; Gass 1997; Gass, Mackey, and Pica 1998; Long and Robinson 1998) have established that face-to-face classroom negotiations play a fundamental role in SLA, although their results are highly sensitive to the type of tasks that the participants are asked to carry out (Pica, Kanagy, and Falodun 1993). Among the benefits cited, these negotiations tend to increase input comprehensibility through language modifications—such as simplifications, elaborations, confirmation and comprehension checks, clarification requests, or recasts—which end up providing the L2 learner with the type of negative evidence deemed necessary by certain SLA theories for continued language development. This type of negotiation has also been described in the literature as focus-on-form (FonF) and is defined by Long (1991, 45–46): "Focus on form . . . overtly draws students' attention to linguistic elements as they arise incidentally in lessons whose overriding focus is on meaning or communication."

With respect to tasks, Pica, Kanagy, and Falodun (1993) classified tasks as either one-way or two-way exchanges, with the participants either reaching a single solution or not (± convergence). Jigsaw tasks provide each of two partners with only half the information needed to solve the communication task; the partners must share their respective parts equally (i.e., two-way task) and then try to converge on a single outcome. Information-gap tasks assume that only one person holds the pertinent information, which the other partner must solicit (i.e., this constitutes a one-way task, but the task can be repeated with the roles reversed in order to form a two-way task), whether or not a unique outcome is predictable. Pica, Kanagy, and Falodun predicted that jigsaw and information-gap tasks would promote more of these negotiations than other task stimuli. They also observed that negotiations took the discursive form of a trigger (the occurrence of a particular linguistic feature that causes a misunderstanding), an indicator (explicit notice that a misunderstanding has occurred), a response (an effort to repair the misunderstanding), and a reaction (an acknowledgment that the repair was successful). The benefits of negotiations of meaning were first demonstrated for learner–native speaker oral discussions (Hatch 1978; Holliday 1995; Long 1981), but further investigations registered the same benefits for learner–learner oral discussions as well (Varonis and Gass 1985; Gass and Varonis 1994).

Other researchers (Blake 2000, 2006; Pellettieri 2000; Sotillo 2000; Smith 2003) have documented how SCMC negotiations of meaning obtain similar benefits to those found in face-to-face exchanges, although Smith (2003) felt it necessary to add two additional functions—confirmations and reconfirmations—to the CMC discourse paradigm in order to compensate for the delayed nature of the communication that is endemic to chat.

Abrams (2006) has christened task-based learner–learner CMC as intracultural communication and attests to its wide use in college-level L2 classrooms. Both Blake (2000) and Smith (2003) claim that the majority of spontaneous negotiations in online intracultural communication deal with lexical confusions or misunderstandings. However, Pellettieri (2000) reports that carefully designed tasks can yield similar benefits for morphological and syntactic topics as well. Sotillo's (2000, 470–71) study of written SCMC discourse showed that whereas written SCMC was similar to face-to-face communication in terms of discourse functions and syntactic complexity, ACMC writing promoted more sustained interactions and greater syntactic complexity.

Doughty and Long (2003b) have approached SCMC with the aim of establishing the most propitious psycholinguistic environment for its implementation. They suggested ten methodological principles (MPs), or language teacher universals, that instructors should follow when implementing SCMC tasks, with an eye to stimulating negotiations and L2 language development:

- Use tasks, not texts, as the unit of analysis; it is the process that makes the difference in SLA.
- Promote learning by doing.
- Elaborate input through negotiations of meaning (do not simplify the linguistic material; do not rely solely on authentic texts).
- Provide rich (not impoverished) input in terms of quality, quantity, variety, genuineness, and relevance.
- Encourage inductive ("chunk") learning through implicit instruction.
- Focus on form through meaning-focused tasks that allow L2 students to notice their linguistic gaps (via input flooding, input elaboration, input enhancement, corrective feedback on errors, or input processing).
- Provide negative feedback (e.g., recasts) in order to induce noticing.
- Respect "learner syllabuses"/developmental processes by providing input that is attuned to the learner's current processing capabilities.
- Promote cooperative/collaborative learning.
- Individualize instruction (according to communicative and psycholinguistic needs).

Many of Doughty and Long's MPs are intuitively applicable to the SCMC or ACMC context. In the SCMC exchange analyzed in the next section between a Spanish instructor and a first-year learner, the reader will recognize the instructor's attempts to follow some of these MPs by elaborating input, providing rich input, supplying negative feedback for errors, using implicit instruction, stimulating collaborative learning, and individualizing the instruction to fit the learner's need at any particular moment. The teacher also uses sound and text to carry out the lesson plan, but applying these principles is not always as easy as it may seem at first. Sometimes an instructor misses the target. Fortunately, students are most forgiving of this in an SCMC collaborative environment because of an overarching concern to communicate effectively in L2.

Case Study of Bimodal SCMC

To date, few researchers have tried to analyze bimodal SCMC, or chatting that includes the capacity to exchange both text and audio messages (Blake 2005a; Yanguas 2010). The SCMC examples examined here come from a regularly scheduled virtual office hour that an instructor of Spanish hosted every week with first-year students enrolled in a distance learning introductory Spanish class. The chat tool was home grown but relied on a Flash communication server, just like the commercial product available from Adobe Connect. This particular conversation between one adult student of beginning Spanish and her NS instructor represents the ideal SCMC situation of pair work. The potential for discursive confusions and management problems naturally escalates in direct proportion to the number of participants involved in a chat session.

Understandably, any protracted silences in a bimodal chat environment are routinely interpreted as signs that the other party failed to hear the previous utterance. In actual fact, the partner's silence might be due to thinking, slow typing, or utter confusion caused by the original question, some unknown linguistic form, or an interruption from life. In face-to-face conversations, these potential sources of breakdowns are mitigated by body language and phatic communication (e.g., "o k . . . right . . . , " "let's see . . . , " "right, " "like . . . u h-hu h . . . , " "oh . . . ," "ah . . . ," "you don't say, " "wait just a minute"). This time-lag effect is unavoidable in chat and often prompts participants to resort to using the voice channel, if available, to establish some phatic contact, much like the cell phone advertisement where the salesman runs around everywhere saying, "Can you hear me now?"

The following seven examples come from a first-year Spanish L2 student of low verbal ability, as judged by the instructor. Adjusting for different levels of proficiency, this student is representative of the types of exchanges that are possible with bimodal chatting, a technique that is not as easy to use as one initially might think. Both students and instructors can freely use both channels (i.e., sound and text) separately or more or less in tandem. It takes instructors a while to get used to using the textual mode as a support or backup to what students are practicing in the voice channel.

For the instructor it is a bit like using the blackboard in the classroom to record what is being said or to offer other pertinent information without interrupting the flow of sound conversation.

With respect to the following transcripts, the time stamp is provided at the end of each exchange to document the flow of the conversation and the alternations between the text and voice modalities. Sound exchanges are all in capital letters, and code-switching between languages is shown in italics. Certain portions of the text are highlighted in bold to draw attention to a particular grammatical or discursive point under question.

Notice in example (1) how the instructor insists that the student practice orally as well as textually so that the instructor will be able to evaluate the student's responses for pronunciation and syntactic accuracy. In this fashion, the instructor can then provide the appropriate feedback with both oral and textual reinforcements and hints. The instructor also indulges in frequent repetitions and recasts of a highly didactic nature, much like the discourse often heard within the walls of a typical language classroom. Lee (2004) has described this type of exchange as linguistic scaffolding on the part of the more experienced partner. As discussed above, the instructor interprets the student's slowness to respond as a sign that she did not previously hear the instructor's helpful responses. The truth is that the student heard them but did not understand, which caused a complete breakdown in the conversation and the need for negotiation or repair in order to get the exchange flowing again:

(1) Making Students Practice via the Oral Channel

STUDENT: Que "trajajaste"? 20:37:19 [What [is] *trabajaste*?]
INSTRUCTOR: Did you work? 20:37:26
INSTRUCTOR: YA ESTOY AQUÍ CON MICROFONO. YA HE ARREGLADO EL PROBLEMA. EH . . . ¿**TRABAJASTE** HOY EN TU ESPANOL, NANCY? 20:37:40 [I'm here with the microphone. I've solved the problem. Did you work today on your Spanish?]
STUDENT: ¿OTRA VEZ? 20:37:44 [Again?]
INSTRUCTOR: ¿ME PUEDES OIR? 20:38:3 [Can you hear me?]

STUDENT: **Trabajaste?** 20:38:08 [*Trabajaste?* [What's that mean?]]
INSTRUCTOR: ¿Me escuchas? 20:38:12 [Can you hear me?]
INSTRUCTOR: SI ¿TRABAJASTE? ***DID YOU WORK?***
¿TRABAJASTE? SÍ, TRABAJÉ. 20:38:18 [Yes, did you work?
Did you work? Did you work? Yes, I worked.]
STUDENT: No comprendo. 20:38:25 [I don't understand.]
INSTRUCTOR: Háblame por favor. 20:38:34. [Please talk to me.]

As a follow-up comment on (1), note that the instructor's introduction of a verb in the preterit, an unfamiliar tense at this point in a first-year course, precipitates the breakdown here. The same would be true for the classroom environment: New grammatical material causes a disruption in the communicative flow of the discourse that can only be resolved through intense efforts to negotiate the meaning of the past tense. The instructor uses the voice channel in order to model what the student should reply to the original question: "Did you work?" But the student is totally confused by this new verb form and falls silent. Then she wonders if *trabajé* ('I worked') is a third-person form in the present tense. The instructor finally realizes her misstep, as shown in example (2); the negotiation process has made apparent to both individuals the root of the problem:

(2) Breakdown, Negotiation, and Repair

STUDENT: That is the entire question? 20:38:48
INSTRUCTOR: ¿A QUÉ TE REFIERES? *THAT'S THE ENTIRE
QUESTION.* ¿QUÉ PREGUNTAS? ¿TRABAJASTE? SI.
TRABAJÉ, TRABAJÉ EN MI ESPAÑOL. 20:38:59 [What are
you referring to? *That's the entire question.* What are you asking?
Did you work? Yes, I worked. I worked on my Spanish.]
INSTRUCTOR: ¿PUEDES REPETIR, NANCY? 20:39:21 [Could
you repeat, Nancy?]
STUDENT: *Trabajé* **is third person word**. 20:39:35
STUDENT: Pero trabajaste? 20:39:52 [But what about *trabajaste*?]
INSTRUCTOR: No, trabajé es la primera persona pero es pasado.
20:39:53 [No, *trabajé* is the first person but it's the past.]

INSTRUCTOR: EH ... NANCY, NO. TRABAJÉ ES PRIMERA PERSONA. PERO ES PASADO. *YOU DIDN'T STUDY PASADO YET*. ¿DE ACUERDO? 20:39:57 [Nancy, no. *Trabajé* is first person but it's the past. You didn't [*sic*] study past yet. Ok?]

As in face-to-face interactions, one of the most important benefits of SCMC chat centers on what Swain (2000) has called *forced output*. For Swain, forced output means that students monitor their own interlanguage much more closely precisely because they must use L2 syntax to formulate their responses—they have no other choice. The results from this type of output create a feedback loop that creates new input for the learner and a second chance to get it right—in other words, forced output feeds self-initiated self-corrections and, in time, structural integration, as can be seen in oral exchanges in example (3). Not only does this L2 student finally retrieve the correct word in Spanish for *since*, but also she corrects her first incorrect attempt at translating "in the afternoon (P.M.)," which was based on an English calque. The final sound transmission gets it all correct, undoubtedly, to the student's great sense of personal relief and satisfaction:

(3) Self-Correction as a Result of Forced Output

STUDENT: ¿PROFESORA? ¿DÓNDE ESTÁ CINDY? 20:24:45 [Professor? Where is Cindy?]
INSTRUCTOR: NO SE, NO SÉ DONDE ESTÁ. ¿TÚ ESTÁS ALLÍ DESDE LAS OCHO? 20:24:5 [I don't know; I don't know where she is. You've been there since eight?]
INSTRUCTOR: TÚ TE CONECTASTE A LAS OCHO Y CINDY NO ESTABA, ¿CIERTO? 20:24:9 [You connected at eight and Cindy wasn't there, right?]
INSTRUCTOR: PERFECTO, NANCY, PERFECTO. TENEMOS OTRO ESTUDIANTE QUE SE LLAMA "ED" PERO NO ESTÁ TAMPOCO. NO SE, A LO MEJOR TIENE PROBLEMAS CON LA CONEXIÓN, ¿COMPRENDES? 20:25:11 [Perfect, Nancy, perfect. We have another student named Ed but he's not online either. I don't know . . . maybe he

has connection problems, do you understand?]
STUDENT: Uh . . . TENGO . . . UH . . . TENGO . . . UH. LO
. . . (NO, THAT'S WRONG), TENGO...OCHO EN TARDE.
20:25:32 [Uh, I have, uh, I have, uh, the . . . (No, that's wrong),
I have . . . eight in evening.]
STUDENT: LO SIENTO. NO COMPRENDO. 20:25:8 [I'm
sorry. I don't understand.]
INSTRUCTOR: ¿TRABAJASTE CON EL? 20:25:53 [Do you work
with him?]
STUDENT: NO CINDY *SINCE* **OCHO EN TARDE**. 20:26:28
[No Cindy since eight in evening.]
STUDENT: DESDE . . . NO CINDY **DESDE LAS OCHO EN
TARDE ... DE LA TARDE**. 20:26:42 [Since . . . no Cindy . . .
since eight in evening . . . in the evening.]
STUDENT: NO CINDY DESDE LAS OCHO DE LA TARDE.
20:26:58 [No Cindy [has been here] since eight in the evening.]

Another advantage often associated with chatting stems from the ease
with which students can direct their own linguistic progress. As in example
(4), the student can stop the flow of conversation with the instructor at any
time, demand immediate answers to linguistic problems or miscommunications, and subsequently try out new responses for accuracy. This particular student has had little experience with the common verbal expression
to *like* (*gustar*), which in Spanish behaves syntactically as an unaccusative
verb where the logical object becomes the surface subject (i.e., "It pleases
[likes] me . . ."). In experimenting with *gustar* the student gets in over
her head and uses a superlative adverb incorrectly—or so it appears. The
instructor corrects her, but that is not what the student had in mind; the
student quickly asks for a translation of the adverbial expression *too much*.
The student chooses to use only the written chat interface, as opposed to
the voice channel, because it gives her more of an equal footing with the
instructor to direct the path of conversation and to solve her own communication difficulties

(4) Student-Directed Learning and Error Correction

STUDENT: Voy a escribir. 20:45:21 [I'm going to write.]
INSTRUCTOR: Dime (tell me). ¿Qué te gusta comer? 20:45:42.
[Tell me. What do you like to eat?]
INSTRUCTOR: A mí me gusta comer patatas fritas y huevo. ¿y a ti?
20:46:10 [Me, I like to eat french fries and eggs. And you?]
INSTRUCTOR: What do you like to eat? 20:46:21
STUDENT: Es ortro tiempo? 20:46:23 [Is that another tense?]
INSTRUCTOR: Es presente. 20:46:34 [It's the present tense.]
INSTRUCTOR: Pero es la expresión de gustar. **Me gusta, te gusta,
le gusta** . . . 20:46:58 [But it's the expression *GUSTAR*. I like,
you like, s/he likes.]
STUDENT: Me gusta spaghetti y italiano. 20:47:29 [I like spaghetti
and Italian.]
STUDENT: Me gusta chocolate. 20:47:41 [I like chocolate.]
STUDENT: **Me gusta muy mucho**. 20:47:54 [I like it muchly
much.]
INSTRUCTOR: Me gusta muchísimo. **Es incorrecto decir [muy
mucho]** 20:48:19 [I like it very much. It's incorrect to say
"muchly much."]
INSTRUCTOR: ¿Te gusta comer espaguetis? 20:48:38 [Do you like
to eat spaghetti?]
STUDENT: How do you say "too much"? 20:48:44 [How do you
say "too much"?]
INSTRUCTOR: demasiado. 20:48:55.140316 [too much]
STUDENT: Me gusta demasiado. 20:49:16 [I like it too much.]
INSTRUCTOR: How do you say: Cómo se dice. 20:49:25.
STUDENT: No/ **Me gusta comir damasiado**. 20:49:35 [No . . .
I like to eat too much.]
STUDENT: Como se dice? 20:49:49 [How do you say?]
STUDENT: Sí. 20:49:54 [Yes.]

Despite the student's initial success with *gustar*, the real syntactic difficulty for the L2 learner revolves around choosing the correct indirect object

that signals who experiences this sensation of pleasure (i.e., liking). An additional complication arises from the requirement to make *gustar* agree with what is the surface subject, but in reality is the semantic object or theme noun, for example, "*Me gusta eso*" (That likes me). To complicate matters more, the indirect object clitic is often accompanied by a full coreferential NP introduced by the personal *a*: "*A mi esposo le gusta la carne*" (My husband, he likes meat).[5] The instructor successfully leads the student to grasp this last point by offering the student a series of recasts that model the proper response, but as she tries to echo what the instructor has provided as a model, she neglects to change the narrative point of view. For example, the instructor says "Do you like it?" and the student replies incorrectly "Yes, **you** like it," instead of "**I** like it."

The instructor ignores the relatively minor spelling mistakes and uses a textual response to resolve these misunderstandings, much to the student's relief (e.g., Whew 21:02:41). In general, faulty spelling is less problematic in written chat than faulty pronunciation is for face-to-face negotiations or voice chat exchanges (O'Rourke 2005, 459):

(5) Noticing the Gap

STUDENT: Mi esposo te gusta patatas fritas. 20:55:59 [My husband, you like french fries (← My husband, french fries is pleasing to you).]
INSTRUCTOR: A mí esposo le gustan las patatas fritas. 20:56:16 [My husband, he likeS french fries.]
STUDENT: Y carne. 20:56:29 [And meat.]
INSTRUCTOR: Ah! Tu esposo no es vegetariano, ¿verdad? 20:56:43 [Ah, your husband isn't a vegetarian, right?]
STUDENT: Mi esposo le gustan las patatas fritas y carne. 20:56:51 [My husband, he likes french fries and meat.]
STUDENT: No es vegetariano. 20:57:08 [He's not a vegetarian.]
INSTRUCTOR: A mí esposo también le gusta la carne y las patatas fritas. 20:57:16 [My husband, he also likes meat and french fries.]
INSTRUCTOR: ¿Tú eres vegetariana? 20:57:27 [Are you a vegetarian?]

STUDENT: No, pero ensaldas y frutas. 20:57:47 [No, but salads and fruits.]

INSTRUCTOR: No, pero te gusta comer ensaladas y frutas. 20:58:03 [No, but you like to eat salads and fruits.]

STUDENT: No, pero te gusta comer ensaladas y frutas. 20:58:15 [No, but you like to eat salads and fruits.]

INSTRUCTOR: A mí también me gusta comer ensaladas y frutas. 20:58:28 [Me, I also like to eat salads and fruits.]

INSTRUCTOR: *me*, **when you talk about you as I like;** *te*, **when you talk about you, you like.** 20:59:24 [I (when you ...) YOU (when you . . .).]

INSTRUCTOR: Otra vez. 20:59:36 [Come again?]

INSTRUCTOR: Qué TE gusta comer? 20:59:48 [What do YOU like to eat?]

INSTRUCTOR: Otra vez (again). 21:00:01 [Again?]

STUDENT: Me gusta comer ensaladas y frutas. 21:00:25 [I like to eat salads and fruits.]

STUDENT: Correcto? 21:00:47. [Is that correct?]

INSTRUCTOR: Sí, es correcto. Y a tu esposo, ¿Qué le gusta comer a él? 21:00:58 [Yes, that's correct. And your husband, what does he like to eat?]

STUDENT: A mi esposo te gusta comer patatas fritas y carne. 21:01:37 [My husband, you like to eat french fries and meat.]

STUDENT: Corrector? 21:01:50 [Correct?]

STUDENT: Correcto? 21:01:55 [Correct?]

STUDENT: Lo siento. 21:02:01 [Sorry (for the misspelling).]

INSTRUCTOR: No. A mi esposo **le gusta**. 21:02:04 [No. My husband, he likes.]

STUDENT: A mi esposa le guasta comer patatas fritas y carne. 21:02:25 [My husband, he likes to eat french fries and meat.]

STUDENT: gusta. 21:02:30 [likes.]

INSTRUCTOR: Ahora sí. 21:02:33 [Now it's correct.]

STUDENT: Whew. 21:02:41

The true test of success, however, comes when the instructor shifts the focus to a different third party, Michelle, the student's daughter. By now the student has had sufficient written practice in producing *gustar*-type constructions so that changing the reference to the new person presents few problems, as seen in example (6); only the personal *a* is still missing, but that error is extremely common with L2 students right up into the third year of Spanish language study (Montrul 2004). At such a time when the student finally drops the redundant *a Michelle* altogether or puts it after the verb (rather than following the typical English subject–verb–object syntactic pattern), a more proficient level of language competence will have been achieved:

(6) Explicit Correction and Practice Make Perfect

INSTRUCTOR: Qué le gusta a tu hija Michelle? 21:02:49 [What does your daughter Michelle like?]
STUDENT: Michelle le gusta comer ensaladas y margaritas. 21:03:13 [Michelle, she likes to eat salads and margaritas.]

Notice from examples (5) and (6) that both the student and instructor depend heavily on textual clues to raise the student's metalinguistic awareness. But do these explicit discussions transfer into acceptable oral production as well? At the right moment in the exchange, the instructor switches to the sound mode and peppers the student with a series of oral questions until the student finally responds in kind—the final test of whether the *gustar* construction is beginning to sink in. Both the written production and the oral utterance of "*A mi gato le gusta comer* . . ." (21:07:20) constitutes convincing evidence that the student is gaining considerable control over this new syntactic structure:

(7) Switching into "Overdrive"—the Oral Mode

INSTRUCTOR: Y a tu gato? 21:04:43 [And your cat?]
INSTRUCTOR: NANCY, ¿QUE LE GUSTA COMER A TU GATO? 21:05:12 [Nancy, what does your cat like to eat?]

STUDENT: A mi gato le gusta comer (too much)? 21:05:55 [My cat, he likes to eat (too much).]

STUDENT: desmaisdos? 21:06:16 [Too much?]

INSTRUCTOR: NANCY, ¿QUE TE GUSTA A TI COMER? ¿QUE TE GUSTA? 21:06:34 [Nancy, what do you like to eat? What do you like?]

INSTRUCTOR: **DEMASIADO. TOO MUCH IS DEMASIADO**. 21:06:40 [Too much. Too much is demasiado.]

STUDENT: A MI GATO LE GUSTA COMER *AND I WAS LOOKING FOR THE WORD "TOO MUCH" B UT I CAN'T FIND IT*. 21:07:20 [My cat, he likes to eat and I was looking for the word "too much" but I can't find it.]

INSTRUCTOR: ¿QUE TE GUSTA COMER? ¿A MI? A MI ME GUSTA COMER PATATAS FRITAS. ME GUSTA COMER PATATAS FRITAS. Y A TI, ¿QUE TE GUSTA? 21:07:22 [What do you like to eat? Me? Me, I like to eat French fries. Me, I like to eat French fries. And you, what do you like (to eat)?]

Despite the time/turn lag so typical of networked exchanges, the student finally responds to the teacher's more personalized question, "What do YOU like to eat?" (21:6:34), in an appropriate way, setting aside for the moment ungrammatical use of a noun in subject position unaccompanied by an article (e.g., *ensalada* [salad] without the article, instead of *la ensalada*): "A MI ME GUSTA ENSALADA." (21:9:36) [Me, I like salad].

What should be obvious from the analysis of these networked exchanges is that they parallel very closely how people carry out their face-to-face interactions and provide evidence for the small but steady steps forward in the SLA process, with allowances being made for the typical time lags that result from overlapping or delayed turn taking in written SCMC. In fact, except for this delay effect, it would be difficult to distinguish the language and discourse routines displayed in examples (1) through (7) from other transcriptions derived from face-to-face learner/instructor talk taking place in the classroom. The sound channel for these SCMC exchanges plays an important role in providing confirmations that give both students and teachers a sense of accomplishment and successful collaboration.

Weekly sessions such as the one examined in examples (1) through (7) provide L2 students with the opportunity to bring alive the language they are studying either in the classroom or in the distance learning format (see chapter 6). Despite the highly entertaining nature of multimedia materials delivered via the Web, nothing can replace human interaction. Online students need the give-and-take that occurs in SCMC exchanges in order to try out new hypotheses and receive immediate feedback, even if that feedback comes from other, less expert L2 learners (i.e., intracultural CMC). Ironically, with rising enrollment pressures, CMC exchanges such as those examined above might give the student more opportunities to interact than can normally be supported in face-to-face conversations due to crowded classrooms.

What the interactionist model does not overtly stress, however, is the learning of culture and the notion of *intercultural communicative competence* (ICC), a corollary of Hymes's concept of communicative competence. Sociocultural theory (Lantolf 2000) tries to address the issue of L2 students' learning ICC and is the focus of the next section.

Intercultural CMC: Telecollaborations

Another group of sociocultural researchers (Byram 1997; Belz 2002, 2003; Belz and Thorne 2006; Thorne 2003; O'Dowd 2003, 2005, 2006; Lomicka 2006; Kern, Ware, and Warschauer 2004; Warschauer 2004) disfavors the purely interactionist SCMC paradigm outlined above because CMC is portrayed only from the standpoint of a particular tradition of information processing that separates the environment from its users. For sociocultural theorists, negotiation of meaning is often reduced in the classroom to nothing more than getting students to manage transactions that are devoid of real L2 cultural import. The implicit assumption they reject is that transactional routines are somehow culture free, the same the world over, which is patently false.

Sociocultural researchers contrast intracultural CMC with intercultural CMC or intercultural communication for FL learning (see Thorne and Payne 2005) to "draw attention to the complex nature of humans as sociocultural actors and technological setting as artifact and as mediators, rather than determiners of action and interaction" (O'Rourke 2005, 435).

These ideas draw heavily on Byram (1997), who defines intercultural competence as "an ability to evaluate, critically and on the basis of explicit criteria, perspectives, practices and products in one's own and other cultures and countries" (Byram, Gribkova, and Starkey 2002, 9). In other words, the goals of the L2 student should be to become flexible and open to other cultures and ideas so as to be able to change one's own values and attitudes as a function of contact with the world. In essence, then, the L2 learner should be viewed as an emerging bilingual, someone who uses both L1 and L2, no matter how limited, to evaluate new experiences with the world. Kramsch (1993, 2000, 2009) describes this process in terms of the L2 learner trying to find a psychological third place somewhere between the native-like mindset of L1 and the evolving sense of the L2 language and culture.

With respect to a working definition of ICC, Lomicka (2006, 213) very astutely recognizes the commonality among (1) Kramsch's (1993, 2000) notion of the L2 learner's locating himself or herself in a third place somewhere between native-like competence in L1 and the target language; (2) Byram's call for critical cultural awareness; and (3) Freinet (1994) and Cummins and Sayers's (1995) "recul," or distancing, that must take place as the L2 learner moves toward any meaningful kind of bilingualism. To be sure, the conceptualization of the target culture in a sociocultural framework has little to do with the idea of transferring "one complete *essence* or *reality* about the target culture" (O'Dowd 2006, 18), if that could ever be said to exist with either high culture or popular culture. For the sociocultural theorist, ICC deals with a more interactive and dialogic process that connects the learner, the home culture, and the target culture.

The intercultural approach to SCMC has also been called *telecollaboration* (Warschauer 1997a; Belz 2002). O'Dowd and Ritter (2006, 623) describe telecollaboration as "online communication used to bring together language learners in different countries in order to carry out collaborative projects or undertake intercultural exchanges." As such, telecollaboration is not a necessary feature of a distance learning language course but rather a component that can be added to any language course taught at a distance or not. O'Rourke (2005, 434) envisages telecollaboration as a socially and culturally situated activity engaged in by learners as agents who co-construct not only shared meanings but also their own roles. In chapter 3 I employ the term *agency* in reference to Kern and Warschauer's (2000) description of the current stage of CALL development. This new research paradigm explicitly endorses a shift in pedagogical concerns to view the student as an actor who directly shapes and reshapes his or her universe.

One welcome result of this paradigmatic shift has been a heightened emphasis on intercultural pragmatics, an area mostly ignored in the FL curriculum but that often lies at the heart of so many communicative breakdowns for the L2 learner. Many of the sociocultural CMC studies report on the frequent and serious communicative breakdowns that occur when teachers fail to alert their students to the intercultural differences (for CALL lessons on Spanish pragmatics, see Cohen and Sykes 2006).

Lomicka (2006, 218) and Thorne and Payne (2005, 376) correctly point out that current ideas about ICC have their beginnings in Freinet's movement in France in the 1920s to establish intercultural learning networks, work that continues even today.[6] Cummins and Sayers (1995) adapted Freinet's model to the computer world by using e-mail as the medium of intercultural exchange. *Tandem language learning* (also see chapter 7), an arrangement where two native speakers of different languages communicate regularly with one another, each with the purpose of learning the other's language, is almost aimed at creating networks (O'Rourke 2005, 434), although ICC has not been particularly highlighted by its proponents (O'Rourke and Schwienhorst 2003).

How do teachers implement an effective ICC experience via CMC, especially in light of the well-documented failures that have occurred? The Cultura project offers teachers a highly structured curriculum designed to foster an intercultural learning network using CMC tools. In the following sections I showcase Cultura as one of the ideal ways to move students toward a new sense of ICC.

The Cultura Project: Intercultural Learning at Its Best

The Cultura project was developed at the Massachusetts Institute of Technology in the late 1990s to allow L2 learners from two different cultures to improve their ICC and their linguistic base (Furstenberg et al. 2001; Levet and Waryn 2006; Bauer et al. 2006).[7] Students of the two respective countries (NB: The authors started with France and the United States) complete online questionnaires related to their cultural values and associations. These questionnaires can be based on word associations (e.g., What words do you associate with the word *freedom*?), sentence completions (e.g., A good citizen is someone who . . .), or reactions to situations (e.g., You see a mother hitting her child in the supermarket. How do you feel?). Other key topics include work, leisure, nature, race, gender, family, identity, education, government, citizenship, politeness, authority, and individualism.

Each group fills out the questionnaire in their native language so as to be able to express themselves fully. The results from both sets of students are then compiled and presented online. In addition to the questionnaires, learners are also supplied with online resources such as opinion polls and press articles from the two cultures that can support them in their investigation and understanding of their partner class's responses. Responses from previous classes are also archived online for further research and consultation. The respective teachers then guide their students in class to analyze the two lists side by side in order to find differences and similarities between the two groups' responses and identify the implied values, with the goal of showing students that "understanding the other culture requires more than a list" and "is grounded in developing a curiosity toward the culture of *otherness*" (Furstenberg et al. 2001). The challenge of the Cultura project is to make the L2 cultural values visible, accessible, and understandable. In the process, linguistic difficulties are analyzed, and grammar is introduced as needed.

Following this analysis, students from both countries exchange thoughts through ACMC sessions to discuss their findings, pose queries, request clarification from their counterparts, analyze the semantic networks implicit in the questionnaire material, and begin to develop a better understanding of their respective cultural differences by delving into the cultural assumptions that lie beneath stated beliefs. In other words, both sets of students have to step back and reflect on their own cultural values and those of others. So begins the dynamic and never-ending process of students' finding their own third place. Afterward, both groups of students continue to deepen their new insights by studying films, newspaper articles, and selected texts from anthropology, history, literature, or philosophy that deal with cross-cultural perspectives. Videoconferences and/or SCMC sessions can be optionally added to heighten motivation and increase the personal relationships between the groups, if logistics are favorable (i.e., time differences and available equipment permitting).

Finally, students present their ideas and analyses orally in class in the L2, continue discussing, and then turn in a series of written compositions dealing with their respective and collective observations. They also post the final observations in L1 online, which become fodder for further discussion between the two groups. Furstenberg and colleagues (2001, 79) describe the process: "Students are therefore listening and reading mostly in the target language, although not exclusively, as we will see later. Speech and writing are produced in both languages. The interaction between a *foreign* language and a *mother tongue* leads to an effective integration of conceptual differences." Hence the first step in the process of cultural literacy comes about through this constant interaction between languages.

This Cultura guide states that although the model is very flexible, there are five fundamental principles for this method:

- The students from the two schools involved should be similar in age and life experiences.
- Students should use L2 during class time and to write their essays but L1 to complete the questionnaires and the discussion forums.
- The discussion forums should always be asynchronous in order to nurture reflection and analysis.
- Cultura needs to be completely integrated into the classroom curriculum (or students will not take the work seriously).
- The project needs to take place over a long period, a minimum of eight weeks.

Furstenberg et al. (2001, 75) summarize their goals as follows: "Results from the Cultura experiment suggest that there is a significant structural difference between French and American semantic networks pertaining to the cultural items our students explored. Explicating these differences is one way to develop cultural literacy. This form of cultural literacy is not so much acquiring a checklist of 'knowledge,' as developing awareness of the relation between selfhood and otherness. Not only the target culture comes under study but fundamental elements that structure the source culture are revealed as well."

O'Dowd (2005, 47–51) takes issue with the stipulation that all the ACMC must be carried out in L1. In carrying out a Cultura exchange between Spanish and American students, he and the other American instructors compromised so that all students wrote about certain topics exclusively in English, about others only in Spanish, and about still others using the respective L1 according to the Cultura guidelines. This adjustment was necessitated by the Spaniards' lack of online access at their university and/or living environments and their need to practice English before their final exams.

Ironically, the role of the teacher is not lessened by the Cultura project; the dynamics call for more of an expert guide than the typical showman found in the teacher-centered classroom. The teacher is critical in giving students stimulating supporting materials, focusing on particular linguistic expressions, and generally knowing how to channel their students' reactions into constructive analytical patterns rather than emotional meltdowns or hasty generalizations that only serve to reinforce cultural stereotypes. On the micro level, the teacher draws attention to contradictions, irony, humor, and sarcasm in search of charged linguistic expressions that are the product of deeply ingrained values. This process does not necessarily lead either teachers or students to closure but rather to a persistent interrogatory approach to L2 culture. The teacher should insist that students provide evidence for their observations by quoting pertinent language or examples gleaned from the questionnaire, films, articles, or supplementary materials.

O'Dowd (2006, 139) found the opposition between teacher-centered and student-centered NBLT to be too simplistic; more specifically, he rejected the portrait of the NBLT teacher as a "guide on the side" (O'Dowd 2003, 138). The cultural differences often present L2 students with an insurmountable barrier that only the teacher can remove using direct intervention: "Teachers need to lead classroom discussions, but they also need to explicitly develop learners' knowledge and skills and cultural awareness by providing factual information, by modeling the analysis of texts from the partner class, by helping learners to create their own correspondence and also by encouraging them to focus on the meanings which the target culture attributes to behavior as opposed to simply focusing on the behaviour itself. These, I would argue, are all teacher-centred or teacher-led activities which have a justifiable presence in the network-based foreign language classroom."

Clearly L2 students, in addition to their respective linguistic limitations, are not naturally aware of how to carry out intercultural exchanges. Accordingly, no matter how the debate is framed, the findings in this study have highlighted the need for a proactive approach to telecollaboration and the necessity for teachers to play a constant role in organizing and adapting their guidelines and activities according to the circumstances with which they and their partner-teacher are confronted. Very often it will be this flexibility and willingness to react creatively to problems that will mean the difference between success and failure in online collaborations.

CMC and Best Practice

The interactionist framework and the sociocultural approach may not be as much at odds as one might think. It is not coincidental that most telecollaboration projects and ICC activities involve intermediate or advanced L2 students. First-year students would be hard-pressed to successfully carry out deep intercultural reflections, such as that described above, using L2 as the basis of communication in either a classroom or a CMC context.

When one thinks about face-to-face interaction or CMC, it is hoped that students are negotiating meaning, noticing gaps, working collaboratively, and directing the discourse in ways that satisfy their own particular learning concerns of the moment. As students gain more L2 competence, the opportunities to reflect on and absorb new cultural values must expand accordingly. Intermediate and advanced students cannot remain stunted in a never-ending transactional universe; they also need to tackle the ever demanding and constantly shifting challenge of developing real ICC on their road to bilingualism.

The classroom reality, at all levels, is often very different, especially in the many FL classrooms that continue to endorse teacher-centered rather than more student-centered approaches. At the beginning levels, the asymmetric power relationship between the teacher, the all-knowing expert, and the L2 beginner can pose a significant deterrent to fostering the necessary interactions that prime the SLA pump, over and beyond the usual affective barriers engendered by worry over public embarrassment. Still, many FL professionals hold dear the idea that the classroom locus, the mere physical presence of all participants being in the same time and place, affords students an inherent advantage for language learning, no matter what pedagogy is employed (for further discussion, see chapter 6 on distance language learning). Beliefs need no proof in order to be widely held and defended; most language professionals continue to be skeptical about the efficacy of students' interacting online precisely for this reason. More to the point would be to recognize that each SLA theory—interactionist and sociocultural—and each instructional format has respective strengths and weaknesses.

In this chapter I have illustrated, especially through an analysis of bimodal chatting, that CMC can play a crucial role in stimulating linguistic interactions in a fashion that produces similar benefits to those generated by face-to-face collaborations. I deliberately present an instructor–learner CMC exchange from the first year to illustrate the feasibility of adding a CMC component and to highlight the instructor's role in this environment. The transcripts reveal that negotiations of meaning are commonplace. Students have ample opportunities to focus their attention on gaps in their interlanguage, direct the flow of their own learning on an equal footing with that of the teacher, and carry out intensive practice of these new structures both in writing and in speech with the real expectation of adding them to their growing L2 grammar. Obviously, at the intermediate and advanced levels, much more can be accomplished and classroom activities can be complemented by telecollaborations as well.

The benefits of these CMC practices accrue during the early stages of L2 study even with students of low verbal abilities. Payne and Whitney (2002) have shown that written chat has a positive influence on the development of oral proficiency (also see Abrams 2003). Bimodal CMC of the sort examined above appears to provide another form of glue that helps maintain interest in the subject matter outside class. These benefits do not automatically or deterministically derive from the tools themselves but rather from how CMC is used in the service of promoting meaningful interactions and real intercultural reflections.

Either written and/or voice chat is not without its communicative problems. Breakdowns are frequent, but they also provide golden opportunities for students and teacher alike to focus attention on the emerging L2 system as well as new ways of conceiving of one's bilingual identity. This heightens rather than diminishes the teacher's role in raising awareness and task setting (O'Rourke and Schwienhorst 2003). Just as the classroom's supposed a priori edge of the here and now can be thoroughly neutralized, or even undermined, by poorly designed activities, successful CMC just does not happen because the tool is there—it must be carefully planned. Again, the teacher's initiative is crucial to the success of CMC activities.

Both students and instructors need training in how to profit from bimodal CMC; it is not an activity that comes naturally to most teachers or students. In fact, the bimodal aspects and the persistent problems of time lag can be quite confusing, if not disconcerting, for the first few sessions. The incessant chants of "Can you hear me now?" or the frequent written responses of "Are you still there?" clearly attest to some of CMC's inherent difficulties. To say the least, it is not intuitively obvious to even the seasoned language instructor how such a tool must be employed in the service of L2 language learning. How teachers can put all the different aspects of new technologies together as a whole so as to create a successful learning experience is the topic of the next chapter.

Discussion Questions and Activities

1. What does Kramsch (1993) mean when she says that the goal of L2 students should be to find their own third place?
2. Describe three situations where asynchronous CMC (e.g., e-mail, e-bulletin boards/forums, blogs, wikis) would be preferred over synchronous CMC.
3. Go online to the Cultura website (http://cultura.mit.edu), study the materials, and write a two-paragraph summary of the project. Would this framework work for the language you teach? Give reasons why and why not, and make specific reference to proficiency levels: first year, second year, third year.

4. Conduct a survey of five students or five colleagues to determine what kinds of CMC tools they use and how frequently. Fill in the chart below using the following Likert values:

0 = not at all 3 = several times a week
1 = once a week 4 = relatively frequently during the week
2 = more than once a week 5 = every day

Persons interviewed	e-mail	Forums	Blogs/ wikis	IM or Facebook	Phone texting	Chat with sound/ video
1						
2						
3						
4						

How have these usage patterns changed in the last five years?

5. Design a jigsaw task for your students to accomplish working in pairs. Each partner should have only part of the knowledge necessary to complete the task to help ensure that the participants work together. Share the task with your colleagues and try it out. What types of FonF or negotiations of meaning do you expect to occur when your students try to accomplish this task?

Notes

1. For an excellent overview of CMC tools, see Lafford and Lafford (2005). For a review of synchronous CMC research, see Sauro (2011).
2. See www.slf.ruhr-uni-bochum.de/index.html.
3. E.g., see www.blogger.com/start; www.duber.com/oncall/; http://uniblogs.la.psu.edu.
4. See www.bjfogg.com.
5. An additional complication derives from the fact that the personal "*a*" allows for a highly flexible word order, although different pragmatic interpretation can be motivated: "A mi esposo le gusta la carne"; "Le gusta la carne a mi esposo."
6. See http://themecraft.net/www/freinet.org.
7. See http://cultura.mit.edu/.

CHAPTER 5

Theory into Practice
Putting It All Together

Common Threads

With the publication of *Brave New Schools*, Cummins and Sayers (1995) challenged the language-teaching profession to radically rethink, if not transform, the FL curriculum using global learning networks along the lines of Freinet's (1994) classic dialogic approach. Throughout this book on technology and language teaching, I have either explicitly or implicitly advocated these and other similar steps, albeit from a slightly less sweeping framework, by emphasizing the following pedagogical threads that should guide the integration of technology into the FL curriculum:

1. Multiple technological entry points (i.e., Web pages and exercises, CALL applications, CD-ROMs/DVDs, and CMC; and then later, in chapters 6–8, hybrid courses, DL courses, social networking, games).
2. Theory-driven applications of new technologies, not just for the sake of the use of any specific digital tool.
3. Student-centered classrooms.
4. Interactivity, agency, and students as coproducers of technologically enhanced materials.
5. Pursuit of a third place in the quest for bilingualism and the development of intercultural communicative competence.

In the following subsections I review each of these themes separately before moving on to more advanced topics in chapters 6 through 8, such as DL, social networking, and games for language learning.

Multiple Technological Entry Points

In chapter 1 (see myth 1), I stressed that the term *technology* must be seen as an overarching concept that refers to an array of electronic tools that can be harnessed to assist humans in carrying out certain activities without implying any particular hierarchical ranking. That means that there exists no single best technological tool, just as there is no single pedagogical approach that everyone should follow. Consequently, it should not be said that teachers who employ chat programs or social networking, for example, are inherently superior to those CALL practitioners who only use Web pages or those who only use e-mail to promote interactions among the members of their own classes. Each technique has its own appropriate time and place. Some teachers may feel comfortable using a relatively simple set of technological tools, such as what is called for by the Cultura project, whereas others will plunge headfirst into using all possibilities, with or without any sense of what they are doing; personalities and teaching styles will differ widely. Nevertheless, a successful deployment of technology in service of the FL curriculum will also involve thinking through the entire process and planning carefully.

It is worth reminding ourselves that today's FL curriculum encompasses not only the time spent in class (ten hours at the very most and, more likely, five or less per week) but also the effort spent outside the classroom working in groups, with or without contact with the target speech community at large, as well as all those moments of the night and day spent alone, quietly studying the L2. Again, one tool does not fit all times and places; rather, all available tools have a proper place given a felicitous set of learning conditions created by the teacher, supported by the learning environment, and accepted by the learners.

Although I have mostly argued in chapter 3 for using a type of CALL that goes beyond the drill-and-kill model, the time alone spent studying a language through drills might be well motivated with an appropriately designed CALL application, as Hubbard and Bradin Siskin (2004) and Heift (2010) have suggested. Steady improvements in feedback routines afforded by advances in iCALL (see chapter 3) will surely continue to heighten a new sense of worth for tutorial CALL.

From another viewpoint, no one should think that the mere use of technology by itself would create educational change in the FL classroom and improve the curriculum (see chapter 1, myth 2). In other words, technology is not a self-determining agent (Selber 2004, 8); only social forces—teachers and students working together—can create curriculum change and innovation. Nevertheless, tools of all kinds facilitate and encourage the performance of particular activities over others—what the CALL field terms *affordances*. Technology can rarely be said to be entirely free of ideological content or to be completely *transparent*, as computer engineers would like to describe highly effective computer tools and interfaces. Sociocultural researchers, however, quite rightly, reject altogether the notion that tools are transparent; they focus on the social structures and the cultures of use or practice that technological tools help reinforce (Thorne 2003; van Dijk 2005).

Ironically, computer engineers can only discover which tools are relatively easy to use or *transparent* by letting users use them and then observing the results. Consequently, both positions—technology conceived of only as a tool versus technology as a cultural artifact that reflects the discursive, cultural, economic, and geographical systems of power—share the basic notion that one cannot separate the tool from how it is used or embedded in social interactions and institutions. How technology is used should always be the focus and the testing ground for the brave new digital classroom.

Not What but How Technology Is Used

The consequences of realizing that tools are not self-determining agents means that *how* any given technological tool is used far outweighs the importance of which tool is selected to carry out a particular activity. Following Chapelle's (2001) earlier example, I have stressed the use of technology in service of a vision of SLA tied to negotiations of meaning, according to the Interactionist Hypothesis (Long and Robinson 1998). Although the Interactionist Hypothesis may not be the definitive word concerning SLA theoretical discussions, it surely represents one of the most cogent frameworks for research and praxis that the field enjoys at present (Doughty and Long 2003b).

By adopting this general framework, I do not mean to suggest that tutorial CALL has no place in the FL curriculum or that developers should not strive to make tutorial CALL exercises as meaningful as possible, a worthy goal even if the format does not immediately lend itself to practice that stimulates negotiations of meaning. Nor should the negotiation-of-meaning approach lead us to a reductionistic classroom practice that prevents students from entering into profound reflections about the sociocultural issues that are intimately entwined with L2 learning. For instance, many SLA researchers (Kramsch 2002, 2005; Byrnes 2006) have recently cautioned the field about falling into a servile application of a transactional methodology of language learning where language negotiations simply reinforce the dominant corporate model of social interaction. They advise the profession not to teach only to the needs of negotiating business, tourist transactions, contracts, and economic exchanges—goals that are too limiting for any meaningful L2 learning environment. Byrnes (2006, 242) warns us of the dangers originating from the present communicative classroom, where transactional exchanges tend "to perpetuate self-referential notions of the other language and culture." In other words, students learning in this most basic transactional framework end up thinking that other cultures simply carry on their lives in exactly the same way by merely using a different language—a conclusion that ignores all the relevant sociocultural dimensions of the L2 culture and the profound differences with the students' L1 culture.

Accordingly, teachers must put the same kind of thought into using technology in the service of the curriculum that they regularly do in selecting specific L2 readings or preparing in-class discussions and other such classroom activities. Using new technologies will not make up for a lack of planning or foresight but rather will tend to intensify existing classroom methodological deficiencies. Moreover, teachers need to plot out how the introduction of a given technological tool and its accompanying tasks will empower students to take control of their own learning process and, consequently, stimulate a more student-centered classroom.

A Student-Centered Classroom

The idea of a student-centered classroom remains an elusive if not threatening goal for most language teachers, and for good reason. Most teachers were trained in a tradition that puts them at center stage, as the sole providers of authentic, comprehensible input. Krashen's model (see chapter 1) might also be said to reinforce this sense of the teacher-centered classroom because the burden of providing students with comprehensible input rests on the teacher. Abandoning this time-honored role seems strange and unnatural. More important, the student-centered classroom predictably blurs the traditional roles of authority and expertise (Warschauer, Turbee, and Roberts 1996)—and, for most teachers, that is a disturbing feeling without some previous experience or guidelines on how to handle it.

Integrating technology properly into the curriculum can accelerate the focus on the student-centered classroom. Wikis, blogs, social networking (see chapter 7), and asynchronous and synchronous chat tend to foster a more egalitarian sense of authorship. As the students look at it, why should any single person's contribution to a wiki, even the teacher's, be more important than anyone else's? In the case of webquests (http://webquest.org), L2 students might not always reach the same informed conclusions about the L2 culture that the teacher had in mind. This is dangerous ground for most teachers: Are not teachers supposed to tell the students what is important about the target culture in their role as the resident expert? Relinquishing the compulsion to control the flow of information comes hard for most teachers, but, in the case of using technology, many of today's new tools may actually provide affordances to do just that.

Teachers should redirect their energies away from notions of control toward learning objectives that ensure that the tasks and tools will motivate students to become active participants who engage in reflections about both their own culture and the target one. However, sending L2 students to a chat forum (synchronous or asynchronous) to engage NSs from abroad without a clear lesson plan or preparations will most likely lead to communication breakdowns that reinforce stereotypes and frustrate everyone involved (see Ware and Kramsch 2005). In reaction to these breakdowns, some teachers are prone to intone the familiar mantra, "Well, technology failed me again today." But more often than not, the teacher failed to plan properly; using technology never obviates the need for lesson planning and careful technical preparation, especially if the goal is to involve students as willing and active participants in the process.

Interactivity, Agency, and the Student as Producer

Selber (2004, 24–26)—whose principal interests lie in teaching English composition, but whose observations are equally valid for L2 language study—argued that students need to develop three types of computer literacy: (1) functional, using the computer as a tool; (2) critical, viewing computer functions as cultural artifacts that imply social dynamics, conventions, and cultures of practice that need to be analyzed; and (3) rhetorical, reflecting and then producing new computer-mediated (hyper)texts or materials. This model closely parallels Kern and Warschauer's (2000) view of CALL development (see chapter 3) as having moved away from structural and communicative to more integrative concerns. Clearly teachers and students alike must have a firm grounding in how the tools work (i.e., functional literacy), but a successful incorporation of technology into the language curriculum demands that students reflect on what they are doing (i.e., critical literacy) and then put it into practice (i.e., rhetorical literacy). Students must be guided into probing and analyzing, from both an L1 and an L2 perspective, the cultural values and historical contexts that are embedded in language, computer use, the internet, chat exchanges, blog entries, Web pages, and multimedia. In short, sociocultural research maintains that all things human are embedded in a social context.

As part of the path to reaching critical literacy, Selber (2004, 95–103) suggested that teachers should provide their students with a set of analytical or problem-solving strategies, known in classical rhetoric as *heuristics*, that can aid students in formulating possible responses to a website activity, a chat exchange, a blog entry, an authentic hypertext with images, or any new set of cultural values or expressions.

Interestingly enough, new technologies have engendered innovative forms of expression that challenge traditional notions of authorship and standard genres. For instance, chat exchanges are blurring the distinctions between oral and written genres. Students, then, are charged with not just negotiating meaning in L2 but also with trying to make sense of their world with the inclusion of new L2 elements and forms of expression.

Selber's (2004, 138) next step toward realizing a rhetorical literacy is much bolder: He asks students to produce their own hypertexts so as to become multimedia authors in their own right, "designers of information environments that span time as well as space." Blogs, wikis, and shared Google Docs come readily to mind. Selber expects a rhetorically literate student to be able to engage with others (or with other materials) in acts of deliberation, reflection, persuasion, and social actions. As discussed in chapter 2, Laurillard (2002, 23) also considers the goal of teaching to be fundamentally a rhetorical one: "seeking to persuade students to change the way they experience the world through an understanding of the insights of others." Teachers should strive to guide their students during this process of change so that they can successfully find their own third place as an evolving bilingual.

The Third Place: Intercultural Communicative Competence

In chapter 4 I discussed how Kramsch (1993, 2000) and Byram (1997) have championed the idea that students must find their own voice as incipient bilinguals, what Kramsch (1993) has called finding a *third place* that combines both their L1 and L2 experiences and knowledge, but is not identical to either. In essence, Laurillard (2002, 21–22) is referring to this same basic idea when she talks about the mediating role of language, especially with reference to academic as opposed to direct experiential learning. Consider figure 5.1.

The ideal learning pathway from many teachers' point of view would have students experience and interpret L2 culture directly through the L2 language without interference from the L1, harkening back to an old behaviorist tenet, "speak only in the target language in class!" In fact, this is exceedingly unhelpful for beginning, intermediate, or even some advanced students and does not appear to be a reasonable path for integrating past experiences with new ones (as those who work in bilingual education programs can readily verify—see Cook 2001; Levine 2011). The L1 language and especially the L1 culture unavoidably constitute the student's principal

Figure 5.1 The Individual's L2 Learning as Mediated by L1 Language and Culture

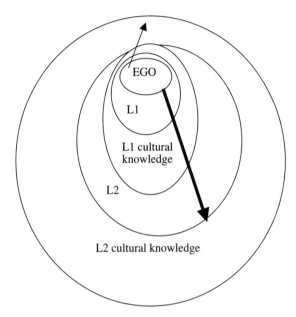

warp and woof for interpreting, conjecturing about, evaluating, and judging all new experiences—even more so with respect to gaining academic knowledge about the L2, its NSs, and L2 culture. In figure 5.1 this process is represented by the heavy arrow that proceeds from the individual (i.e., EGO) through the L1, through the L1 world knowledge, through the L2, and finally to L2 cultural knowledge. As time goes by, students will consolidate their knowledge of L2 and become more proficient, enjoying a more direct pathway to the L2 culture (the lighter arrow). Support for this interpretation of bilingualism comes from the Revised Hierarchal Model (Kroll and Stewart 1994). Yet in the process of constantly defining and redefining a third place, no one is entirely free from the effects of previous experiences, especially those that are as deeply engrained as L1 language and culture.

If teachers and/or students ignore this mediation dynamic in constructing the L2 learning environment, the goal of reaching a more profound understanding of ICC becomes all the more difficult or unpleasant. Not surprisingly, the process of arriving at that third place will probably end up having the most life-altering consequences for students who attempt to learn another language and not merely another culture—they are intimately bound together. Nevertheless, long after finishing formal language study, our students will most probably only remember their intensely personal insights gained about L2 culture, while quite naturally allowing the details of the pluperfect subjunctive forms to lapse into oblivion. This is as it should be, if language teachers stop for a moment to contemplate the nature and value of academic learning.

Striving for a third place, then, is not only a goal for a more internationally oriented curriculum but also a principal objective for those students who will never travel abroad, which is 97 percent of our students (Davidson 2007). Because of the changing US demographics, increased diversity at home has heightened the importance of promoting learning languages as part of the core curriculum from a need to embrace multiculturalism in the United States, quite apart from increasing one's attractiveness to the corporate world that is seeking to hire multilingual employees to work abroad. Cummins and Sayers (1995, 109) argued for an FL classroom that would rely on collaborative critical inquiry, which will, in turn, "promote pride in students' cultural identities and respect for other cultural realities." Technology can facilitate the process of this collaborative critical inquiry if teachers are aware of these goals.

The Cultura Project Revisited

I return, again, to the goals of the Cultura project (see chapter 4) as an embodimentt of this sense of a rhetorical praxis, as well as a realization of Cummins and Sayers's (1995) plea for incorporating global networks into the learning environment. It is not that the technology used in Cultura has become so transparent or sophisticated, but rather that the tools are used in conjunction with lesson plans that make students from both countries work toward a new sense of intercultural competence. Notice that I did not say that students will "achieve true understanding" or "will come to like or appreciate the target culture." That may or may not happen. Each student must find his or her own third place, a process that surely will involve tension and conflict. But only this type of dialogic approach stands any chance of imparting meaningful intercultural competence as part of the L2 process.

By design, the technology used in the Cultura project is limited to online survey materials, Web postings on a bulletin board, and asynchronous e-mail listserv communication. The creators (Furstenberg et al. 2001) eschew synchronous chat on purpose so as to force the participants to spend time reflecting on and analyzing what they are going to say before they write it. This strategy lowers the emotional stakes, eliminates direct confrontations, and stimulates a willingness to carefully listen to the opinions of the other and, then, enter into reflections. There is nothing dogmatic or magical about these choices; another teacher could adapt the Cultura curriculum so that synchronous chat would make perfect sense, given local circumstances.

The Cultura curriculum further stipulates that each L2 population—whether French L1 speakers or English L1 speakers in the case reported by Furstenberg and colleagues (2001)—expresses their theories and opinions in their respective native languages. In theory, no single group holds a linguistic advantage over another. These L1 thoughts become fodder (i.e., authentic texts) for linguistic analysis in each of the respective L2 classrooms that are conducted in the L2.

The Cultura project is much less about technology and much more about curricular design. The tools provide the right learning environment to allow the teachers and students to accomplish the stated goals, following Hubbard's (2006) advice to take into account both the student fit and teacher fit (see chapter 3). It should be remembered as well that the Cultura curriculum is used starting with the intermediate level. I could imagine that efforts to apply this approach with beginners would be too frustrating, if not actually counterproductive. Obviously, a realistic consideration of linguistic level of competence is also part of finding the right fit.

Toward a Rhetorically Based Digital Classroom

In the last section I reviewed the common threads that underlie the preceding chapters and general ideas about using technology in the FL curriculum. In this section I outline a specific pedagogy for a rhetorically based digital classroom, with particular attention to Laurillard's work (2002).

With respect to higher education, Laurillard (2002, 21–22) carefully distinguishes between first-order or direct experiential learning—such as what happens in the course of acquiring L1 from birth—and second-order or academic learning, which is necessarily mediated in SLA development by the L1, by the L1 culture, and, in the present case, by the use of the computer. Accordingly, academic knowledge relies on symbolic representations, a fact that has drawn considerable attention with respect to mathematical education but has been taken relatively for granted by practitioners in the language field. Laurillard explains that academic knowledge comes about through exposition, argument, interpretation, and reflection—a process very close to Selber's (2004) notion of rhetorical literacy, Cummins and Sayers's (1995) process of collaborative critical inquiry, or Kramsch's (1993) quest for a third place. Consequently, the act and/or art of teaching consists of helping students go beyond their first-order experiences to change the way they experience the world. That is why it can be said that teachers are engaged in a practice of rhetoric, the art of influencing the thought and conduct of an audience.

Laurillard (2002, 20) captured this epistemological difference by contrasting the terms *percept*, a result of direct experiential learning (i.e., perceptions), with *precept*, a product of artificial or formal learning environments. The real challenge that teachers face every day in the classroom is how to impart decontextualized knowledge, precepts about L2 language and culture, given that most students will not experience the L2 in a direct way by living in the target society but rather only in an academic setting. Her solution was to propose using an iterative conversational framework that first reveals and then takes into account what teachers and students alike bring to the learning environment (e.g., their respective theories, ideas, conceptions, and observations; Laurillard 2002, 87). In processing the variation that exists between them, teachers must also imagine themselves as the learner, which will determine the focus of further dialogue and classroom activities (p. 71). As a consequence of this iterative process, more than one way of teaching a topic or subject always exists. Teachers may start out following certain rhetorical heuristics, as mentioned above, but the formulation of specific lesson plans must be based on this dialogic process, which in turn depends on the variation of student responses (Marton and Booth 1997, 179).

Herein lies one of the reasons why teachers might resist creating a student-centered learning environment and/or introducing technological assistance: The lesson plans need to be constantly reviewed and adapted based on the students' reception of them. Teaching in this fashion—with or without technology—becomes a discovery process, not a deductive exercise in hypothesis testing. Laurillard (2002, 69, 86–87) calls this discovery process a *phenomenographic* teaching strategy because it asks teachers to qualitatively assess and then incorporate the variation in students' conceptions into the learning environment, according to the following basic pathway:

- Present the learner with new ways of seeing.
- Focus on a few critical issues and show how they relate.
- Integrate substantive and syntactic structures.
- Make the learner's conception explicit to them.
- Highlight the inconsistencies within and the consequences of the learner's conceptions.
- Create situations where learners center attention on relevant aspects.

At all points in the process, teachers must gauge student reaction. Of course, it would be easier to ignore all of this and just give a lecture or play the role of the principal provider of comprehensible input. A pedagogy based on the inspirational lecture or class performance, however, is inherently flawed, as Laurillard explains (2002, 93): "Academics will always defend the value of the *inspirational* lecture, as though this could clinch the argument. But how many inspirational lectures could you reasonably give in a week? How many could a student reasonably absorb? Inspirational lectures are likely to be occasional events. Academics [in their role] as *students* typically think little of the method. It is commonplace to observe that the only valuable parts of an academic conference are the informal sessions."

As part of the conversational framework, Laurillard uses the following twelve-step evaluation checklist to review the affordances that an assortment of educational media may provide: lectures, print, television, video, DVD, hypermedia, enhanced hypermedia, Web resources, interactive television, simulations, virtual environments, tutorial programs, games, digital document discussion environments, audio conferencing, videoconferencing, microworlds, collaborative microworlds, and modeling (i.e., creating new software):

1. Teacher can describe conception.
2. Student can describe conception.
3. Teacher can redescribe in light of student's conception or action.
4. Student can redescribe in light of teacher's conception or action.
5. Teacher can adapt task goal in light of student's description or action.
6. Teacher can set task goal.
7. Student can act to achieve task goal.
8. Teacher can set up world to give intrinsic feedback on actions.
9. Student can modify action in light of feedback given.
10. Student can adapt actions in light of teacher's description or student's redescription.
11. Student can reflect on interaction so as to modify redescription.
12. Teacher can reflect on student's action to modify redescription.

Notice that the conversational framework heightens, rather than lessens, the active intervention of teachers, although not necessarily in the role of doing all the talking. Educational media, depending on their respective affordances, contribute to at least some of the twelve steps of the conversational framework. Print, TV, video, and DVDs provide students with narratives; DVDs and Web resources offer students an interactive space; CMC tools assist communications; simulations and iCALL make available an adaptive environment; and, finally, modeling allows students to become productive agents in their own right. An intelligent language curriculum uses a variety of educational media in ways that enable and activate as many steps of the iterative conversational pedagogy as possible.

Teaching Pigs How to Fly: Defining the Limits of Technology

On the one hand, it should be abundantly clear by now that not all technology satisfies all the goals of the ideal classroom pedagogy, digitally enhanced or otherwise. But no matter; the parts can and do add up to a whole, if carefully thought out in advance. On the other hand, using technology in place of what people do best is tantamount to trying to make pigs fly. And what people do best is carry on dialogues. Using technology to help people carry out conversational exchanges (ACMC or SCMC), then, is a good fit. Because academic knowledge is a "consensual description of experience" (Laurillard 2002, 177), the role of teachers who use technology in the curriculum becomes more important than ever, but perhaps not as the principal protagonist, as is the case in the more traditional teacher-centered classroom.

Accordingly, discussion and dialogue remain the linchpin, the glue of the language learning process that will continue to be labor intensive despite any and all exemplary uses of technological tools and the persistent administrative pressure to increase productivity (i.e., maintain high student/instructor ratios) through the use of new technologies. Technology, however, does not supplant the teacher (chapter 1, myth 4)—quite the opposite—but its use does impose the requirement that teachers learn how to find the best fit in a way that precludes doing business as usual. The tool by itself cannot be carrying on a dialogue, but teachers can learn a new, more student-centered, more computer rhetorically literate way of presenting the curriculum where new technologies can help feed the dialogic process. How can teachers learn to do this?

Fortunately, teachers now have recourse to many online language journals dedicated to providing guidance and the latest research about using technology in the service of the language curriculum.[1] These resources exist to stimulate and guide teachers to incorporate technology into the curriculum; but again, teachers must want to do it.

Likewise, the CALL field now exhibits a marked desire to discuss issues of teacher training in the use of technology in the service of the L2 curriculum, as evidenced by the recent spate of publications—for example, Beatty (2003); Colpaert (2006); Donaldson and Haggstrom (2006); Egbert (2005); Egbert, Paulus, and Nakamichi (2002); Felix (2003); Hubbard and Levy (2006b); Kassen and colleagues (2007); Lai and Zhao (2005); Lomicka and Cooke-Plagwitz (2004); and Hauck and Stickler (2006).

Kassen and colleagues (2007, ix) point out that concerns dealing with teacher training and technology fall into five broad categories: national frameworks (e.g., standards, European Common Framework of Reference for Languages, No Child Left Behind), specific contexts (e.g., retraining faculty to teach in e-learning environments, graduate student training), e-communities or communities of practice, toolboxes, and critical reflections.[2] Hubbard and Levy (2006a, 11) define four possible roles for teachers with respect to CALL: practitioner, developer, researcher, and trainer. Although teachers are minimally asked to perform in the classroom as practitioners, they should aspire to assume other roles as well. Hubbard (2004) also counsels teachers to experience CALL themselves so that they can better understand the students' challenges and frustrations.

Egbert, Paulus, and Nakamichi (2002, 110) observe that language teachers frequently incorporate into the curriculum only those technologies that they use outside the school environment in their own personal lives, despite whatever preservice and in-service training course they have received on CALL. The tendency is to use new technologies to fit current practice rather than transforming practice through the application of a new technology (Egbert, Paulus, and Nakamichi 2002, 111). Lam's (2000) study shows that teachers' decisions regarding technology depend crucially on whether the teacher was *personally* convinced of the benefits of using technology for L2 instruction. Given the rapid pace of change in the CALL field (see chapter 1, myth 3), teachers will have to accept that much of their training and retraining will have to come from self-directed learning (Robb 2006). By any measure, then, the key factor for enacting the brave new digital classroom still remains each teacher's will to change toward a more student-centered approach that incorporates CALL.

Ironically, constant change is exactly what we are asking our students to do when they step into the language classroom: transform themselves by learning an L2 and finding a new third place vis-à-vis both the L1 and L2. If our best and most experienced language teachers are afraid to harness the power of new technologies or only do so with halfhearted and uninformed attempts (i.e., the "technology failed me again today" syndrome), their students cannot be expected to rise to the challenge of becoming bilingual, which will radically alter their knowledge systems.

Without a doubt, technology will continue to seep into all facets of US society, including the educational sector (Crystal 2001a). The new language classroom will most likely be digitally enhanced, along with the entire educational curriculum at all levels. Continuing education and e-learning will gain more and more prominence as well. Teachers will still be needed to help students make sense of an increasingly multilingual and multicultural world within a progressively more digital learning environment. In this context, training new professionals and retraining seasoned educators in order to enter the brave new digital classroom is the responsibility of the field as a whole, but it begins with each teacher's desire to participate in the process of changing how they and their students view the world.

The next three chapters examine the new language learning environments of DL, social networking, and language games. However, the key to taking advantage of these new learning environments continues to be linked to the extent to which teachers are willing to enact a more rhetorically based pedagogy, as outlined in the present chapter. Admission into the brave new digital classroom is just as much about a change in educational approach as it is about the introduction of new technologies.

Discussion Questions and Activities

1. Explain to a colleague or student what "multiple entry points for using technology" means in terms of teaching or learning an FL.
2. Under what conditions does using a CALL exercise of the drill-and-kill type make sense?
3. What do researchers mean when they say that culture is mediated by language? What repercussions does this statement have for L2 teaching and learning?
4. Conduct a survey of your colleagues as well as your students: How many of them have reached (1) functional computer literacy, (2) critical computer literacy, or (3) rhetorical computer literacy? What implications do the survey results have for designing your curriculum? What impact would your survey results have on preservice or in-service training?
5. Review Laurillard's twelve-step checklist for creating a conversational framework for using technology, then examine a single use of technology in your curriculum (e.g., a webquest, a CALL exercise, a CD-ROM activity, a wiki assignment, a CMC task). How many of

these steps are implied by your use of technology? Share your results with your colleagues.

6. What are the similarities and differences between creating a classroom activity that is enhanced with technology and one that is not?

Notes

1. E.g., *CALICO Journal* (www.calico.org/); Computer Assisted Language Learning (CALL) (www.tandf.co.uk/journals/titles/09588221.asp/); *Heritage Language Journal* (http://hlj.ucdavis.edu/); and *Language, Learning & Technology* (http://llt .msu.edu/); On-CALL: *Australasian Journal of Educational Technology* (www.ascilite .org.au/); ReCALL (www.eurocall-languages.org/recall/index.html); and South Asia Language Pedagogy and Technology (http://salpat.uchicago.edu/).

2. Also for teachers, e.g., MERLOT, www.merlot.org.

CHAPTER 6

Distance Learning for Languages

The Roots of Distance Learning

Online learning is gradually gaining a more prominent role in the mainstream curriculum, including the language learning field. L2 researchers are becoming increasingly interested in measuring its role in L2 language development (Thorne 2006). The following subsections are intended to help the professional evaluate when online language learning is appropriate for their curriculum, as well as determine if online learning presents the right fit for their students.

Background

"Do you use technology in your foreign language classroom?" Few language teachers would dare to answer "no" to this leading question for fear of being classified as outdated or out of touch with best practices. Not surprising, most teachers routinely employ Web pages to distribute syllabi assignments, often through their institution's learning management system, where they post cultural materials, place lecture notes created in PowerPoint, and organize webquests (see chapter 2). Many instructors also make good use of the bank of Google apps or other Web 2.0 tools already reviewed in chapter 3. But at the point that the faculty is polled about accepting credit for language courses delivered in a hybrid or entirely distance learning format on an equal footing with classroom instruction, the smiles begin to fade and the positive attitudes toward technology tend to evaporate.

Many FL teachers still harbor deep-seated doubts as to whether a hybrid course, much less a completely online language learning experience, could ever provide L2 learners with an accepted way to gain linguistic proficiency in a second language, especially when speaking is a priority. In some cases, language instructors might secretly worry that these new distance learning (DL) classes will displace them or, at the very least, force them to change radically their time-honored, teacher-centered practices into an educational environment that is more student centered.

Despite these fears, national education trends increasingly include online classes as a delivery format for all disciplines; online education is rapidly becoming part of the accepted curricula. Allen and Seaman (2006, 2007, 2010; and see table 6.1) reported that approximately 3.2 million higher education students in the fall of 2005 were taking at least one course online—a 40 percent increase from the previous year. By the fall of 2006 there were 3.5 million DL students, or a little less than one in five students overall, a 10 percent increase from 2005. By the fall of 2008, 4.6 million students participated in some way with an online curriculum—that means that one in four college-age students were involved in some type of online learning experience. In other words, online learning is growing at a rate of 9.7 percent versus the 1.5 percent growth experienced in enrollment for the rest of higher education. Most of this expansion occurred in two-year associate institutions, which constitute approximately one-half of all online enrollments, as well as in the larger, public universities with enrollments of fifteen thousand or more.

The principal advantages reported for online learning centered on increased access, especially for nontraditional students, which allowed them to complete their degrees. In terms of quality, the majority of chief academic officers at these institutions felt that the online courses were equivalent or even superior to their face-to-face counterparts. Faculty acceptance, however, lagged behind due to the low perceived acceptance in the marketplace and the rigorous self-discipline and independence demanded of students by the online learning format—conditions that often discourage faculty from pursuing online implementations and students from completing an online course. No doubt, some faculty are scared away from teaching online when faced with the challenges of learning new online teaching methods and new technological tools.

DL for languages is a complicated enterprise. On the one hand, there are only a handful of DL language courses being offered for credit in our

Table 6.1 Postsecondary Total and Online Enrollments for the Fall of 2002 through the Fall of 2008

Fall Term	Total Enrollment	Annual Growth Rate Total Enrollment (%)	Students Taking at Least One Online Course	Annual Growth Rate Online Enrollment (%)	Online Enrollment as a Percentage of Total Enrollment
2002	16,611,710	N.A.	1,602,970	N.A.	9.6
2003	16,911,481	1.8	1,971,3976	23.0	11.7
2004	17,272,043	2.1	2,329,783	18.2	13.5
2005	17,487,481	1.2	3,180,050	36.5	18.2
2006	17,758,872	1.6	3,488,381	9.7	19.6
2007	17,975,830	1.2	3,938,111	12.0	21.9
2008	18,199,920	1.2	4,606,353	16.9	25.3

Note: N.A. = not available.

Source: Adapted from Allen and Seaman (2010).

universities and even fewer evaluation studies available that could be used to establish a strong track record with which to assess their impact and argue for or against offering students this alternative (Goertler and Winke 2008; also see below). On the other hand, no language professional, not even the most technologically enamored instructor or CALL researcher, would dispute the notion that in order to reach advanced or superior proficiency levels (Interagency Language Roundtable Scale, or ILR, level 3 or higher), L2 students need to interact face to face with native speakers, preferably in a country where the language is spoken. How else could L2 students develop the appropriate level of pragmatic and sociolinguistic competence that is a requisite part of advanced/superior L2 competence?

Using a student record database maintained by the American Council of Teachers of Russian that spans more than thirty years, Davidson (2004, 2007) has analyzed the gains in listening, reading, and spoken competency of approximately 3,500 L2 students of Russian who have gone abroad. His results document without any doubt that the gains toward advanced proficiency are due to study abroad—especially when carried out in full-year study programs as opposed to just one semester or quarter.[1] Unfortunately, of the 45 percent of entering US freshmen who profess the intent to study abroad, fewer than 3 percent actually undertake it (Davidson 2007). This explains why both administrators and the FL profession obviously need to bring more pressure to bear on the university curriculum to include study abroad as a requirement for graduation.[2]

In this light, perhaps, intercultural CMC projects such as those described in chapter 4 might be used to advantage as a way of whetting beginning-level students' appetite for study abroad by providing direct contact through telecollaboration or text/sound chatting with speakers of the target culture (also see chapter 7). What role, then, do DL courses have to play in the general FL curriculum? There is probably not a single ideal answer. Critics of learning language at a distance routinely tend to couch the debate in terms of all or nothing—all DL courses versus no DL courses— whereas the real issue is how to obtain a smooth articulation of DL offerings into the overall FL curriculum in ways that accommodate the needs of an institution's learners without compromising quality. In other words, DL language courses should be conceived as part of a diversified path (including opportunities for study abroad) that FL departments routinely employ to meet different needs of their students.

A discussion of DL issues could focus on any level, especially when higher levels of literacy come into the picture, but the debate most frequently deals with only the first two years by asking the following question: Can a hybrid or a completely virtual format engender linguistic progress comparable to that fostered within a traditional L2 classroom environment that meets five days a week, especially with respect to oral proficiency? This is the heart of the matter for those who doubt the efficacy of the DL learning format: the development of oral proficiency. In other words, do DL classes have a role to play in the FL curriculum, perhaps as one way to begin the journey down the long road to advanced proficiency—a feat, as discussed in chapter 1, that requires a minimum of 700 to 22,000 hours of instruction depending on the complexity of the L2? The answer is particularly important in the case of the less commonly taught languages (LCTLs), where access to beginning instruction is especially limited due to teacher shortages, low enrollments, and the concomitant financial constraints.

Even with respect to a language like Arabic—an LCTL in high demand partly because of world affairs—the lack of trained classroom teachers puts in jeopardy the chances of meeting national priorities for Arabic language readiness, especially if delivery is limited to the traditional classroom format (Al-Batal 2007). Wiley (2007) has argued for harnessing the power of the diverse language communities or heritage speakers residing in the United States in order to meet the national language priorities in the short run. But in the long run, the US educational system also needs to produce more nonheritage Americans who are able to speak Arabic, Farsi, Punjabi, and other LCTLs; in other words, the United States needs to produce more bilinguals from the population of nonheritage learners as well as take advantage of the rich bilingualism that already exists among the increasingly international communities in this country.

In the remainder of this chapter, the different types of DL formats are discussed, along with the existing evaluation studies regarding their respective effectiveness. This discussion serves as background for a general discussion of how DL language courses can fit into the FL curriculum and what an instructor needs to know in order to provide a seamless articulation between a department's DL and non-DL courses.

What Is Distance Learning?

The term *distance learning* has been loosely applied to many different types of learning environments, including blended, hybrid, teleconferencing, or virtual (for a recent overview of DL education, see Hauck and Stickler 2006; Goertler and Winke 2008; also see Holmberg, Shelley, and White 2005; White 2006). Teaching languages through teleconferencing (i.e., two-way interactive closed-circuit TV) has the longest track record in the field, although this medium does not relieve either students or instructors of the burden of showing up at some specific time and place (i.e., the campus TV studio or satellite campus studio), not unlike the demands imposed by the classroom. Teleconferencing allows a teacher to reach students who might otherwise have no access to instruction. For example, the US Arabic

Distance Learning Network based at Montana State University (www.ara bicstudies.edu/index.shtm) provides an excellent illustration built on this type of teleconference model currently serving approximately fifteen small colleges that would not normally have access to Arabic language instruction. For the students this is a felicitous outcome, given that their administrators have no immediate plans to add Arabic to the curriculum at these respective institutions.

Without a doubt the live TV/video environment is exciting but not without its limitations with respect to issues of interactivity. Laurillard (2002, 103) considers this format to be heavily oriented toward a teacher-driven pedagogy, despite the purely technical capacity for students to participate. Only with great difficulty do students work together using this format in a more autonomous and constructivist manner (Goodfellow et al. 1996). Normally, teleconferences are organized around the teacher's delivery of information, much as a lecture with limited group drill activity and interactivity. Nevertheless Fleming, Hiple, and Du (2002, 18–29) described successful efforts at the University of Hawaii to incorporate meaningful group and pair activities into their teleconference format.

O'Dowd (2006, 189) classified videoconferencing into three types: teacher to class, student to student, and class to class. All three types of videoconferencing potentially suffer from sound delays, gaps in fluidity in handovers that make the medium critically different from face-to-face interactions, the tendency toward passive viewing, and other logistical problems (O'Dowd 2006, 191–93). Practical difficulties can become formidable obstacles to carrying out successful videoconference projects when implemented among institutions that do not share the same calendar (i.e., semesters vs. quarters) or do not have adequate mechanisms for sharing credit and financial resources.

Ironically, teleconferencing language courses are more readily accepted by faculty curricular committees as being equivalent to the classroom experience with little extra justification—despite whatever difficulties might exist in duplicating the same learning experience found in a communicative classroom, the so-called gold standard for best practice in the United States (Magnan 2007). This might be due to the visual image/presence of the teacher and the more recognizable teacher-driven paradigm. In other words, the presence of the teacher via a teleconference video image projected in real time leads the profession to validate the learning experience on a par with what happens in traditional language classrooms. In the rest of this chapter, the other types of DL formats are examined in detail because they allow for a more autonomous learning environment than what is afforded by the tele-conference format. Many refer to this type of DL as "anywhere anytime," a concept that includes asynchronous as well as synchronous online learning.

Hybrid or *blended* courses combine in-class instruction for part of the week together with independent work the rest of the time that is supported by a combination of dedicated CALL programs, internet activities, and/or online chatting. Hybrid courses have become popular with administrators and faculty alike because both can identify with the direct control main-tained by the instructors, even if the classroom meetings have been reduced (usually two or three times a week). Administrators, in particular, recog-nize the financial potential for stretching an institution's expensive human resources (i.e., teaching assistants and lecturers) to the maximum using the hybrid format (Scida and Saury 2006; Arvan and Musumeci 2000). One implementation of hybrid courses allows language departments to increase the number of language sections with the same number of instructors with-out totally abandoning the face-to-face component that appears to be emblematic as a guarantee of quality (Young 2002). Nevertheless, many hybrid course teachers tend to view the computer components of this for-mat as only suitable for drill and kill, or mechanical grammar practice, so as to free up the classroom meetings for more communicative activities. Scida and Saury (2006, 520) exemplify this attitude concerning the hybrid cur-riculum: "Our goals for the use of technology were very simple: going back to the 1980s, literature on use of computers in language instruction and other fields have noted the one thing that the computer can do comparable to what a human being can do is *rote exercises or drills*" (emphasis added).

This view of technology, as Scida and Saury clearly stated, was tied to a pedagogy spawned in the 1980s, with roots in behaviorism, well before the explosion of internet 2.0 use, CMC, and social networking. Hybrid or blended classrooms are not necessarily constrained by this vision of technology, as illustrated by Bañados's (2006) DL implementation, a blended approach to English as an L2 for Chilean students that included

(1) dedicated CALL programs, (2) online monitoring, (3) face-to-face teacher-led classes in English as a foreign language, and (4) conversation classes with native speakers of English both face-to-face and online. In Bañados's framework (2006, 539) both teachers and students were challenged by new roles: Teachers acted more like guides and collaborators while students assume a more autonomous participatory status. Likewise, Allen and Seaman (2010) have characterized the hybrid learning format as representing the best of both worlds in the sense that it provides the learner with all the conveniences of online learning while still maintaining the vital face-to-face (F2F) link found in the classroom experience.

With completely virtual online language courses, the teachers and students interact exclusively online with no face-to-face meetings, which may account for some of the negative reactions to DL typically voiced by language faculty, in contrast to the tolerance shown toward the teleconferencing format and the marginal acceptance of hybrid courses. But entirely online courses come in all shapes and sizes and encompass different combinations of asynchronous and/or synchronous modes. More often than not, virtual language courses take advantage of the authoring features provided by standardized course management systems (see chapter 3), such as WebCT, Blackboard, Sakai, or Moodle (Brandl 2005)—for instance, archived lessons, Web links, multimedia libraries, drop boxes, announcements, internal mail or message systems, bulletin boards or discussion forums, wikis, chat tools (synchronous textual exchange with voice or video exchanges, too), whiteboards, quiz templates, and customized gradebooks.

Within these three main delivery formats, substantial portions of a course can involve CMC of either an asynchronous (deferred–time communication such as IM and/or a synchronous nature (i.e., real-time communication). The CMC tools themselves vary, offering students the ability to exchange just text, text and audio, text and video, or text, video, and whiteboards/screen sharing (see Lafford and Lafford 2005; and any Robert Godwin-Jones column on emerging technologies published in *Language, Learning & Technology*). Understandably, applied linguists have devoted much attention to examining how CMC exchanges take place from an interactionist, social-cultural, or discourse perspective. Some researchers have endeavored to determine whether CMC is at least as effective as classroom face-to-face exchanges in promoting oral proficiency development (Blake 2011).

Simplifying a great deal of previous research in this area, CMC exchanges all seem to provide additional language practice, whether or not they can be classified as exactly equivalent experiences to F2F interactions. In Malcolm Gladwell's context of meeting the prerequisite 10,000 hours to become an expert at some endeavor (2008), then, it is irrelevant to ask whether CMC can replace F2F exchanges: More is always better, and students need more and more in order to reach just functional proficiency (600+ hours), not to mention a more advanced state of bilingualism. But chat sessions undoubtedly add greatly to language development, as can be seen from the following student comments collected two years after they enrolled in an entirely online first-year Arabic course (Blake and S'hiri 2012). In this course, students were asked to chat with both classmates and instructors using Wimba Voiceboards that provided text and audio exchanges:

I enjoyed the chat sessions and I feel I learned a lot from them. They were probably the more intensive part of the class and they helped me keep the rhythm throughout the semester.

One key to a successful class, and indeed a successful education, is the student-to-student interaction that takes place [in the chat sessions]. For that, I'd like to say a special thanks to those of you who took time to correspond with me, even a little.

I loved the fact that part of our grade was to constantly communicate with the professor, TA, and classmates (though late at night when I still had a ton of homework to do, I didn't feel the same way!!) :-> I am thankful for it and for the struggle.

Student X and I met, on average, four times a week [online via *Wimba*] and went through the assignments together. I found this very helpful, because not only did it force me to put aside a few hours each day to study Arabic, it also gave me the opportunity to practice speaking Arabic with a peer (those online chats can be terrifying), work through questions we had, and have the real-life interaction of the standard real-life class.

The popularity of CMC exchanges like those reported above can be confirmed by the explosive popularity of social computing (i.e., Facebook, LiveMoca, Twitter, and texting in general) and is the subject of the next chapter. Social networks offers the profession another avenue to engage language students outside the classroom, especially with respect to tandem learning (i.e., pairs of students learning each other's native language) with the goal of further developing intercultural competence. Although tandem learning has enjoyed much success (Schwienhorst 2008), these online collaborations have sometimes led to some unpleasant breakdowns in communication, as has been reported in the literature (Ware and Kramsch 2005; Belz 2002), and should not be undertaken without considering the obstacles to intercultural understanding, especially when the dialogue is mediated through technology. As with most every activity carried out inside or outside the classroom, careful selection and planning of the task itself helps to guarantee a felicitous exchange and mitigates the possibilities of the type of breakdowns chronicled in the literature. Clearly, student autonomy constitutes one of the strengths of these different DL formats with the implicit understanding that students are prepared for this challenge.

In addition to CMC tools described here, a plethora of other internet 2.0 tools provides helpful ways of delivering engaging language materials and activities: interactive Web pages, blogs, wikis, clouds, apps, bots, and tutorial CALL databases that can respond to frequent errors with finely tweaked feedback messages (Heift 2010). How instructors mix and match these components in implementing an online course is entirely up to their respective discretion and creativity. This helps explain why comparing one hybrid course to another is such a difficult research proposition—in other words, comparing technologically supported courses is as hard as comparing one F2F teacher with another. Methods, tasks, personalities, and individual student factors vary wildly, which makes comparisons difficult, as is discussed below.

Student Demand for DL Classes

Why would anyone want to take a language course without face-to-face instruction five days each week? This is an excellent question, which implies that the DL format might not be an appropriate learning environment for everyone. In actual fact, DL tends to be self-selecting. A completely virtual course appeals, in particular, to people who work full time and, therefore, need special access to instruction, as well as to those who prefer to work independently. The popularity of a hybrid course also responds to these factors but in a somewhat more disjunctive relationship: those who want fewer in-class hours (and some think this means less work too!) or those who like to work independently. Many students belatedly find out that hybrid or totally online formats require much more self-motivation and self-discipline than they are willing to give. These factors might explain the usually high dropout rate for the DL learning environment for all disciplines (Carr 2000). Ironically, students with strong motivation to learn LCTLs such as Arabic, Farsi, Filipino, or Punjabi, to name only a few, may find to their dismay that there are no classroom language offerings available locally, making the DL format the only way to get started in these cases. Slowly the FL profession is beginning to respond to this demand for more LCTL instruction.

Evaluation of Online Language Learning

As stated above, few empirical research studies have examined the overall effectiveness of online language learning or compared the progress of students participating in such courses with that of those enrolled in traditional classes. Likewise, little is known about students' perceptions of their online learning experiences.

One common assumption among educators is that all face-to-face (F2F) classes are inherently better than any online classes, without any regard to size (lecture vs. discussion format) or the instructor's classroom talents or lack, thereof. Sadly, it is simply not the case that a poor instructor lecturing to 300 students will necessarily create a superior learning experience as compared with other formats, including online options. As we all know, good teachers are wonderful and bad teachers are not and may even do damage to a student's progress. Obviously, there are many cases of teaching that lie in between these extremes and depend on a host of idiosyncratic factors.

Bad teachers using technology will still most probably deliver bad teaching and a discouraging educational experience for the students. Merely being physically present in the same classroom should not constitute the gold standard for either teaching or learning—it works both ways. Achieving a sound curricular design should always be the responsibility of the faculty and the overriding concern, whether or not the delivery method partially involves technology as in hybrid courses or provides an entirely online experience. Nevertheless, many language professionals persist in worrying about the onslaught of online courses despite the fact that language instructors must clearly be involved at all stages of design and implementation of such a curriculum (for a good exemplar of faculty involvement and the process of online curricular planning and instruction, see Coleman et al. 2010, and their report on the Open University).

Many instructors fear—and, sometimes, quite rightly—that administrators will attempt to use these new technologies to reduce the faculty payroll and make class delivery less expensive by increasing class size. First of all, the cost-benefit analyses that have addressed this question have shown that using technology only marginally saves money without necessarily improving student performance in any significant way (Maher et al. 2005; but for a rosier estimation of savings for online delivery, see Herman and Banister 2007).

Second, only asynchronous formats have any chance of drastically scaling up the number of enrolled students, but online language courses should ideally involve an SCMC component to stimulate oral proficiency as already discussed above, which would make them as time-intensive, if not more so, than F2F classes. Third, and closely related, choosing not to include CMC opportunities turns the online class into little more than an electronic workbook, which is not what our profession should have in mind when contemplating online language education.

Once again, the proper use of technology can increase student access through anytime anywhere learning and the sharing of faculty among different institutions, which is something that the FL profession is just beginning to explore. For the students, some prefer to work in a hybrid manner because it fits their learning styles, others enjoy the flexibility offered by working online, while still others do not thrive very well in these new digital learning environments if they lack a strong sense of conscientiousness or learner autonomy (see Arispe and Blake 2012).

But with respect to granting college credit for online language courses, many faculty members demand to see the research on the teaching effectiveness for online courses as a prerequisite for taking any action to legitimize this format and recognize that an *equivalent educational experience* is being provided. This is a thoroughly slippery notion based on the premise, once again, that all courses delivered in the classroom already share equivalent educational value. The truth is that language courses, whether delivered in situ or online, enjoy certain affordances while suffering from other specific limitations. To a great degree, the differences among same-level language courses owe more to the individual instructor talents and limitations and the quality of the learning materials they use, rather than the format itself. This is not to imply that the course format will not also shape the nature of the learning experience in significant ways. Although the exercise of equating courses delivered by different instructors via different formats remains an elusive goal, making sure that students can move seamlessly back and forth between in-class and online learning experiences should be and is, moreover, an absolute faculty responsibility for a well-articulated language curriculum with online options. Since second language development is a slow process, as previously discussed, each learning experience along the way should be, above all else, stimulating, motivating, and well articulated. Clearly, there exists more than one pathway to reach the goal of becoming bilingual—no matter how much some in our profession value the in-class format over any other avenues of language study (i.e., independent study, hybrid classes, online courses, or study abroad).

Returning now to the specific issue of comparative studies, the present-day language assessment tools are often inadequate to tease out significant differences in linguistic proficiency during the first year (see the discussion given by Blake et al. 2008, 123–24; Blake 2009). This is hardly surprising when one considers the limited first-year vocabulary (less than 1,000 words) and limited time on task entailed by the first-year curriculum, which is, minimally, only about 150 contact hours. This is just the nature of what can be achieved during the first year of L2 language study, not a criticism of any student, teacher, or curriculum; the brain is still overwhelmed with processing issues that mitigate against the short-term memory (i.e., the explicit cognition system) holding items long enough in memory so as to convert them into permanent knowledge (i.e., the implicit cognition system). Thankfully, a new plateau seems to be achieved when students reach the 200-hour contact mark, which is intuitively captured by the ACTFL beginner rubrics of novice low, novice mid, and novice high and the ILR scale's less gentle classification system of 0 or 0+. In other words, students need about 200 hours of instruction or contact with the L2 in order to bump up from the first-year plateau to the next level of intermediate low. Accordingly, measuring progress during those first 200± hours remains a dicey proposition, at least with the present assessment tools, clouding our ability to track student progress in the first year. Not surprisingly, more often than not researchers have discovered no significant difference between in-class and online student outcomes. With these caveats in mind, let us examine previous research on hybrid and totally online language learning.

To date, most studies of online language learning for beginners have evaluated hybrid courses that combine regular class meetings with computer-mediated instruction. The results indicate that online activities can be substituted for some of the class time normally required in language courses without adversely affecting students' progress. As a whole, they also suggest that students who learn a language online may develop literacy skills that are superior to those of students enrolled in traditional courses (Warschauer 1996).

Two groups of researchers—Adair-Hauck, Willingham-McLain, and Earnest-Youngs (1999) and Green and Earnest-Youngs (2001)—compared the achievement test scores of students enrolled in standard elementary French and German classes, respectively, that met four days per week (control group) with the scores of other learners who attended class three days a week and who participated in technologically enhanced learning activities in lieu of a fourth hour of in-class contact (treatment group). Adair-Hauck, Willingham-McLain, and Earnest-Youngs (1999) found that students participating in the treatment group did as well as those in the control group on tests of listening, speaking, and cultural knowledge. In addition, these students performed significantly better than the control group on measures of reading and writing ability. The authors speculate that online students were more motivated to write, but they offer no explanation with respect to the reading results. In contrast, Green and Earnest-Youngs (2001) found no significant difference between the scores of the treatment and control groups on the same type of tests used in the study adapted for the Web by Adair-Hauck and colleagues. Why these two studies report different findings is not immediately clear.

Chenoweth and Murday (2003) examined the outcomes of an elementary French course, *Elementary French Online*, developed at Carnegie Mellon University in 2000 and delivered mostly online, along with an hour-long, face-to-face class meeting once per week as well as weekly twenty-minute individual or small-group meetings with a native speaker tutor. Chenoweth, Jones, and Tucker (2006) provide an update on the project that includes a Spanish counterpart, Spanish Online Learning, to the French hybrid course that has now been thoroughly revamped and upgraded into free open source courseware available at https://oli.web.cmu.edu/openlearning/forstudents /freecourses/french.

The progress of French and Spanish L2 students in the online group was compared with that of others who attended a traditional class four hours per week on tests of oral production, listening comprehension, reading comprehension, grammar knowledge, and written production. The results showed that the scores for the treatment and control groups were not significantly different for oral production and only slightly different for the writing samples, with essays by students in the online group being judged superior to those of the control group on a variety of measures including grammatical accuracy and syntactic complexity (Chenoweth, Jones, and Tucker 2006, 158–59). All students were weakest in the use of transitions and general essay organization. Likewise, other measures for listening comprehension, grammar knowledge, and reading comprehension registered minimal statistical differences. The first study also found that the online students spent approximately one hour per week less studying than did those in the traditional class, suggesting that the online course was more efficient because students achieved results similar to those attained by learners in the conventional class with less time expenditure. But the second study that included the Spanish course showed that students spent an equal amount of time regardless of learning format (e.g., 8.5 hours per week).

Nieves (1996) reported on the performance of students enrolled in Éxito (Federal Language Training Laboratory 1990), an introductory Spanish course in a format very similar to that of the online French program in the study by Chenoweth and Murday (2003). The Éxito program was the basis for a survival Spanish course developed for government employees. It was originally a ten-day course with each day devoted to learning to survive in Spanish with regard to some aspect of daily life such as ordering meals, getting driving directions, and so on. Nieves expanded it into a semester-long course in which students worked with the materials primarily on their own and attended a one-hour face-to-face class meeting per week. Besides the video newscast, the other multimedia components were audiocassettes and graphics. There were no Web-based activities, as the study was done in 1994 when the Web was not yet widely employed in language teaching. Nieves used her own set of outcome listening measures to show that students who participated in the multimedia-based course outperformed those enrolled in traditional courses on measures of aural and oral communication skills but scored slightly lower on a test of writing ability.

Finally, another group of researchers (Scida and Saury 2006; Epps 2004; Walczynski 2002; Echávez-Solano 2003) followed the progress of students using Mallard, a drill/quiz exercise and tracking program designed and supported by the University of Illinois (Champaign-Urbana). In general, these four studies show no significant differences among the experimental (Mallard) group and the control group, with Scida and Saury's (2006) study registering slightly higher final grades for the group using Mallard. These researchers attributed much of the student success with the Mallard program to students' ability to continue working on the exercises until reaching 100 percent accuracy. In essence, the availability of the tutorial CALL program allowed students to dedicate more time to making more automatic their control of the basic language structures.

Blake and colleagues (2008) compared the placement results for in-class, hybrid, and completely online Spanish learners. They found no clear separation among student scores from course 1–3 no matter what format of instruction was used as measured by Versant for Spanish by Pearson, an assessment instrument designed to determine oral proficiency automatically graded with the aid of voice recognition software and a parsing algorithm (Bernstein et al. 2004).[3] Versant depends heavily on a well-known psycholinguistic technique of sentence repetition: Students cannot repeat what does not reside in their long-term memories or interlanguage grammar. For the 258 in-class students, the Versant scores separated the students into three statistically observable groups: beginners consisting of students from quarters 1–4 (in other words, the first 200 hours of instruction!), intermediates from quarters 5–7, and heritage speakers.

Two other studies (Cahill and Catanzaro 1997; Soo and Ngeow 1998) have evaluated language courses taught entirely online using empirical data. In both cases online learners were found to outperform students in conventional courses on the grammar output measures. Cahill and Catanzaro (1997) reported on an introductory online Spanish class that might be considered somewhat low tech, as it did not have a multimedia component. The *Dos Mundos* textbook (Terrell et al. 2002), along with the accompanying audiocassettes and lab manual, were used as the core course materials. Online activities included synchronous chat sessions, open-ended Web assignments, practice tests, and a substantial number of pen-pal writing assignments. Responses to two essay questions were used to compare the progress of students participating in the experimental group to that of students enrolled in conventional Spanish classes. Based on ratings of global quality and percentage error scores, the writing samples of students in the online course were judged to be significantly better than those in the traditional classes. Although not discussed by the authors, it seems clear that more writing was demanded of the online students, thereby making it hard to ascertain whether this effect was due solely to the online teaching format.

Soo and Ngeow (1998) compared the performance of 77 students enrolled in conventional English classes with 111 students who studied English exclusively through a multimedia CALL program. A comparison of pre- and posttest TOEFL scores showed that students in the online group not only made significantly greater improvement than those in conventional classes but also did it in a shorter period of time, as the experimental course was five weeks shorter due to technical difficulties.

As is the case for the hybrid courses reviewed above, the results from these two studies suggest that online language learning can be effective, at least as a means of improving writing, reading, and listening comprehension abilities. But these studies did not explain why the online environment produced these results, and more research is needed to substantiate these initial observations. Cahill and Catanzaro's (1997) results must be viewed with caution, as it could easily be argued that the reason distance students wrote better final essays was simply a function of the large amount of writing practice.

Finally, the burden of isolating the experimental treatment so as to focus on the medium alone (DL vs. classroom instruction), to the exclusion of all other factors, remains a daunting, if not insurmountable, challenge. Much of the research done in comparing student outcomes between traditional classroom delivery and the DL environment in all disciplines has given rise to no significant differences (Russell 2001). Again, one of the difficulties in this line of research is isolating the format variable from all the other factors that contribute to L2 learning outcomes—for example, learner characteristics, instructional method, and media attributes.

One might even say that this type of research, medium comparison studies, is inherently flawed as it is not grounded in examining the premises and/or predictions of any particular theory of learning (Pedersen 1987; Horn 1992; Burston 2006). After all, students learning a second language in whatever format have to do a great deal of language practice, which tends to level the performance outcomes for everyone. Nevertheless, both administrators and the profession at large continue to demand these types of comparative studies to bolster either claims of adequacy or, conversely, inadequacy.

Students' Perceptions of the Online Learning Experience

A handful of studies have asked students to describe and rate the quality of their experience in online language classes (Adair-Hauck, Willingham-McLain, and Earnest-Youngs 1999; Chenoweth and Murday 2003; Green and Earnest-Youngs 2001; Blake and S'hiri 2012).

Adair-Hauck, Willingham-McLain, and Earnest-Youngs (1999) used a self-report questionnaire to compare the attitudes and opinions of students in their hybrid French course with those of students taking a conventional class. They found that a higher percentage of students in the hybrid class reported meeting their personal language-learning goals over the course of the semester than did those in the traditional class. A number of students in the technology-enhanced class also indicated that the flexibility of the multimedia materials contributed to their progress in the class, noting the advantage of being able to spend more time on activities they found particularly difficult; in short, there was more student-centered learning. This is not to say that student-driven materials cannot be incorporated into the regular classroom but rather that students often perceive that the classroom is teacher driven as opposed to the student-driven nature of the online format.

Responses to a self-report questionnaire administered to online and offline students by Green and Earnest-Youngs (2001) and the results of course evaluations collected by Chenoweth and Murday (2003) shed a less positive light on the online language learning experience. Students in the hybrid and conventional courses studied by Green and Earnest-Youngs (2001) reported equal levels of satisfaction with the progress they had achieved. However, students who completed Web-based activities in place of a fourth hour of class time found some Web pages too difficult and some of the activities not sufficiently well organized. The mostly online French course evaluated by Chenoweth and Murday (2003) received a lower overall rating on student evaluations than did a conventional class taken by learners in the control group. The authors note that the low course ratings may be due to factors other than its technological component, because students' complaints dealt with organization and grading.

Murray (1999) also reported on students' assessment of their experiences learning language with CALL materials. He interviewed Canadian university students who used an interactive videodisc program to study French for one semester and obtained responses that were very similar to those found by Adair-Hauck, Willingham-McLain, and Earnest-Youngs (1999). For example, students in Murray's study commented that they liked the ability to work at their own pace and focus their efforts on activities that were particularly difficult for them, indicating once again the benefit of student-directed learning. In addition, a number of students stated that they found that working independently with the videodisc materials caused them less anxiety than participating in a conventional language class.

Notwithstanding the limited amount of research available at this time, students' reactions to the experience of learning language online seem to be mostly positive. Students appreciate the flexibility afforded by CALL materials and their potential for self-directed learning. Murray's (1999) results also indicate that working with CALL may make language learning less stressful for some students.

The FL profession, however, is now more concerned with oral proficiency than with discrete grammar tests or even attitudes, undoubtedly as a result of the dominant role accorded to the ACTFL's Oral Proficiency Interviews, the primary means for assessment at present, although this test is not without its critics, who fault this evaluation procedure for its limited conception of what knowing another language and culture is supposed to mean (see Kramsch 1986).

Final Remarks on Online Language Evaluation Studies

To summarize, the result of no significant difference between the in-class students and the online students was the most frequent finding from these comparative studies for first-year language study. Occasionally, the online students performed slightly better, but never worse. Obviously, the number of uncontrolled and uncontrollable variables—namely, the talents of different instructors, different types of students, different technological tools, different tasks, different delivery modes, different time frames—abounds and will continue to confound this line of research. But because we are all in L2 education for the long haul (10,000 hours or bust!), our profession should concentrate more on making the curricular design the very best it can be with or without technology and providing students with well-articulated options to different learning formats whenever possible.

Implementing Online Language Instruction

The Sloan Consortium (Moore 2004) has suggested the following guidelines with respect to offering online language instruction:[4]

- Orient students on how to learn online and help them adjust to their new role as more self-directed and independent learners.
- Write clear learning objectives at both the macro (i.e., syllabus) and micro (i.e., day-by-day) levels of curricular planning.

- Ensure that the quality of the online course is comparable to that of traditional classroom materials.
- Provide ready help in both technical and content issues and respond within twenty-four hours (or sooner, if possible).
- Minimize technical difficulties for obtaining the necessary plug-ins and software.
- Feature interaction—with instructors, classmates, and the interface— at all possible moments.
- Include student feedback in shaping the instructional goals for specific activities (see Laurillard's *conversational framework*, as discussed in chapter 5).
- Recycle instruction, materials, topics, concepts, and practice through the course.
- Allow students to practice before oral exams to ensure positive outcomes.
- Demonstrate to students in palpable ways the progress being made throughout the course.

Remember that with completely virtual courses there is no *there* there: Students are not physically present at any time. Even teleconferencing offers a live image of students, which is reassuring in human terms. As a consequence of this, online learning must compensate with increased opportunities for interactions using the CMC tools already reviewed in chapter 4. The interface design should also give the sense of interactivity whenever possible (see Reeves and Nass 1996; Fogg 2003).

Online Language Learning for Now and the Future

The FL profession should not lose sight of the fact that attaining advanced proficiency (ILR level 3) is a most arduous task that requires five or more years of college instruction and critically depends on the nature of the language involved. Languages such as Arabic, Korean, Japanese, and Chinese that have been classified as group IV languages in terms of their learning difficulties (McGinnis 1994) require more hours of instruction than do the Romance languages to reach the same proficiency level, especially given the complexities of their respective writing systems. Yet advanced proficiency is precisely where the nation should want to go, especially in this post–September 11 era, given the urgent need to develop a national language capacity in some of the more strategic LCTLs (Blake and Kramsch 2007). In order to get there, no method of language instruction should be privileged or discarded, although a well-articulated and prolonged study-abroad component along the way might well be a hard-and-fast requirement, as Davidson's (2004, 2007) research has shown.

The current interest in the online formats, then, must be situated within this context: (1) L2 students need access, (2) students need to work at it for a long time, and (3) students need to study abroad. A DL course is only one piece in this equation but an important avenue to afford students access to introductory instruction of LCTLs when local classroom options are lacking. The increasing number of DL studies should offer the FL profession the comforting knowledge that adding a DL component as a curricular option is a responsible and reasonable format of language instruction, with similar benefits of oral proficiency as those produced in traditional classrooms.

The profession should concern itself with providing legitimate options and increasing all avenues of access to language instruction, especially where LCTL instruction is concerned. The DL format can respond effectively to the challenges of best practices in language delivery (Keeton 2004, 86–87), namely, the need to tailor the curriculum to individual student readiness and potential, to make learning goals and paths clear, to link inquiries to genuine problems to enhance motivation, and to provide prompt constructive feedback.

The real challenge, however, lies in implementing online language instruction within a sound pedagogical framework, a truly conversational framework, as Laurillard (2002, 23) has named it, that seeks "to persuade students to change the way they experience the world through an understanding of the insights of others," blending experiential and formal knowledge. This formidable task is academic in nature and most properly should reside under the purview of those in the FL profession. I have endeavored throughout this book to argue that while technology requires knowledge of new tools (which are constantly changing; see myth 3 in chapter 1: *Today's technology is all I need to know*), it is the language instructors themselves, not the technology, that stand in the way of adopting new paradigms and pedagogies. The FL teachers, not the medium, will ultimately determine whether e-learning will make a positive contribution to the L2 student's long march to advanced proficiency. Whether in the context of the classroom or distance learning, each teacher has to learn to give sway to teacher centeredness in favor of a more student-centered and student-autonomous paradigm.

In the process of making the change to this new learning paradigm, both teachers and students must learn to cultivate what Selber (2004) has called a rhetorical computer literacy. This new rhetoric must proceed from what has been the FL profession's solid base: communicative language teaching, but more in the sense that Hymes (1974) originally meant it—a socially constructed notion that changes the student into a bilingual and bicultural individual as defined uniquely by the individual's own context and experiences (Magnan 2007). This is what Kramsch (1993, 236) means when she refers to students' constantly needing to resituate themselves and their cultural identity in a third place, somewhere between two monolingual idealizations, one defined by the students' mother tongue and the other by the problematic concept of the native speaker. What that new pedagogy consists of and how to get there with the assistance of technology is the topic of the final chapter.

Overall, the CALL research supports the idea that hybrid and online language courses constitute a responsible option for the FL curriculum, especially for those students who are strongly self-motivated or conscientious. Hybrid courses with an online self-study component empower individual language study and provide the needed practice to support the learning path of low-verbal students, in particular. By the same token, a synchronous chat component will help maintain course quality and oral proficiency, although mitigating the ability to scale up the class size in the online format.

Whether or not hybrid courses represent *the best of both worlds*, as Allen and Seaman (2010) have suggested, is not really a necessary claim. Hybrid language courses are a good fit for conscientious, high-verbal, and even low-verbal learners—and that covers a significant proportion of our student population (see Arispe and Blake 2012). Now, the language profession must endeavor to create and implement online materials that adequately provide a curriculum that includes pedagogically sound chatting tasks as well as tutorial CALL and, along the way, train a new generation of graduate students how to teach in this environment, even when most of the faculty has never done so.

On a more cautionary note, I have said little about what contribution online language learning can make toward the attainment of advanced proficiency, a level where subtle but crucial pragmatic and cultural knowledge comes into play. What affordances, if any, can online courses offer in lieu of having access to the benefits offered by study abroad (Davidson 2007)? The processes involved in learning online are just beginning to be examined with a focus other than the proverbial comparative question, "Which is better?" Many interesting challenges await us in the CALL field as practitioners carefully integrate technology into the FL curriculum.

Discussion Questions and Activities

1. Discuss whether you would or would not accept credit from another institution that taught your particular language in an online format and explain why. Would you accept first-year credit? Second-year credit?

2. Defend why you would prefer to teach either a hybrid course or a totally online language course.

3. List five of the requirements needed to succeed in a DL course from both the student's and the instructor's points of view.

4. Imagine that you are teaching a language class online to first-year students. Assume that these students are computer savvy (which is, of course, a big assumption). Design a step-by-step lesson plan for teaching them the present tense. Which technological tools (Web pages, apps, CALL exercises, blogs, wikis, and synchronous video/voice chat) would you use, and for what purpose?

5. Imagine that you are teaching a second-year language class in the classroom. You have students who took the first-year course online and others who were in a classroom. List the strengths and weaknesses that each of these types of students would have. What adjustments would you have to make in order to mesh these two populations together smoothly?

6. Evaluate and discuss the merits of using voice or video chat to support online learning.

7. Defend or refute the following statement: "Online learning language classes are appropriate for all language students." What issues does this statement ignore?

Notes

1. For earlier work on this topic, also see Brecht, Davidson, and Ginsberg (1995).
2. See the Lincoln Commission Report at www.nafsa.org/publicpolicy/default.aspx.
3. See www.versanttest.com/news/versant.jsp.
4. See www.sloan-c.org/effective/.

CHAPTER 7

Social Networking and L2 Learning

Social Networking as a Way of Life

The distinction between using CMC tools to carry out L2 learning tasks (see chapter 4) and social networking may not be immediately obvious, but it remains important nonetheless. Although CMC Web 2.0 tools abound, allowing users to communicate synchronously or asynchronously with their peers and teachers, social networking is an entirely more encompassing and personal activity and, consequently, is more resistant to teacher control and integration into the FL curriculum. Nevertheless, the usage statistics for social networking should command our attention: Teenagers spend nine hours a week engaged in social networking—on an average, over an hour each day. Facebook, by far the preferred social networking choice not only for teenagers but for people of all ages, enjoys upward of 650 million users, 250 million of whom are most probably accessing Facebook right now through their mobile devices (http://how manyarethere.net/how-many-facebook-users-are-there/). Seventy percent of Facebook members live outside the United States, making this forum an ideal site to meet speakers from a wide range of the world's languages all over the globe. With respect to adults in the developed countries, the statistics show that they tend to spend one-third of their leisure time on two major social networking sites and regularly meet sixteen people *virtually* on the internet (Truly Global Industry 2008). Stutzman (2006) pointed out that 90 percent of university undergraduate students are Facebook users, along with 22 percent of graduate students.

Social networking sites (SNS) also form part of the new set of Web 2.0 tools that allow users to focus more on the content knowledge than on the details of Web development and design. First-generation Web activities require contributors to obtain a certain level of computer literacy, creating a barrier for many who want to publish online, share ideas, and collaborate on projects. Web 2.0 tools link information with people as well as people to people without requiring advanced computer skills; the same is true for SNSs dedicated to L2 learning (Reinhardt and Zander 2011).

Livemocha, an SNS specifically focused on language learning, is reportedly patronized by 11 million users from 190 countries; Mixi in Japan has more than 27 million users (Hamachiya 2010); Busuu boasts of 2 million users; Shared Talk (Rosetta Stone) asserts that its membership originates from users in more than 150 countries; Transparent Language has released its Byki social networking site in 30 languages; iTalki hosts a social network in more than 100 languages; ACTFL's Hello-Hello purportedly serves 12,000 educators engaging in tandem learning; and Dickinson College provides the Mixxer, a tandem exchange with patronage from around 40,000 users worldwide.

SNSs not only provide information and tutorials, they also become a part of the participants' social life. Typically, a language SNS offers its members free courses, chat rooms, practice and feedback with vocabulary and grammar, additional paid features and extra tutorials, and a place to meet and socialize with people online in a chosen L2 language.

These language-oriented SNSs offer language tutorial materials as well as opportunities to learn through social interaction by facilitating the process of finding language exchange partners. Once users submit their oral and written exercises, they may also receive feedback from peers and follow this up with free exchanges in the target language community. Classroom teachers may seek to use these SNSs to extend their communicative language teaching outside class time. Despite the phenomenal growth of SNSs, SLA researchers are currently unsure of the nature and the extent to which these websites contribute to improving language skills.

According to Lin and Warschauer's (2011) extensive 2009 survey of adult LiveMocha users from around the world, four languages accounted for 84 percent of the languages spoken on this site: Portuguese (27.4 percent), English (22.3 percent), Spanish (20.6 percent), and Chinese (13.6 percent). English was the target language most in demand and involved 59 percent of the survey respondents. Their motivations for L2 learning could be characterized as either *integrative* (i.e., to establish new friendships and contacts in a given L2 community) or *instrumental* (i.e., to get ahead in their career path).

According to the 2009 survey, using LiveMocha increased the participants' self-confidence and motivation, which in turn increased their motivation to spend additional time learning a language and return repeatedly to the SNS. Unlike the traditional bottom-up learning, participants on the LiveMocha site quickly grabbed ready-to-use sentences and had more than sufficient opportunities to practice with NSs. The chat function was a key component for success in using the site. Chatting online, as analyzed in chapter 4, helps to lower anxiety levels as compared with talking face to face (Warschauer 1996, 1999; Young 2002). With written chat exchange, participants enjoyed more time to review their output before sending it on to NSs; this asynchronous delay helps them avoid embarrassments and slows down the overall pace of the discourse. For the NS partners, there undoubtedly exists a certain amount of satisfaction helping other people learn a given speaker's mother tongue.

Autonomous Learning

Crucially important for success in using SNSs such as LiveMocha is the notion of autonomous learning (AL), an educational approach that asks learners to take responsibility for their own learning process (Arispe 2012; Benson 2006; Blin 2004; Little 2004, 2007; Murphy 2008; Porto 2007; Reinders and White 2011). Those who engage in AL are encouraged to reflect constantly on their learning processes with an eye to choosing the most felicitous course of study for their L2 development.

Holec (1979) pioneered the AL concept and posited five steps for its success: (1) The learner must first understand clearly the learning objectives; (2) then, the learner must define the contents and progression that will guide the path toward the learning objective; (3) next, the learner selects appropriate methods, techniques, and tools that will allow the objectives to be achieved; (4) meanwhile, the teacher should encourage the learner to monitor the entire acquisition procedure; and (5) the learner should finally evaluate what has been accomplished. A teacher or NS partner should ideally be actively involved at each stage along the way, helping all learners take responsibility for their L2 learning development.

Little (2004) posits a shorter list of three necessary characteristics for AL to take place, which overlaps some with Holec's list: (1) *learner empowerment*, whereby learners assume control of their learning and build on (and are limited by) what they already know; (2) *learner reflection*, whereby learners analyze what they have learned at both the macro (i.e., overall knowledge) and the micro (i.e., specific language structures) levels as well; and (3) *appropriate target language use*, whereby the teacher and/or NSs scaffold the utterances and the discourse in such a way that learners are able to use the target language for genuine communicative purposes from the very beginning.

Clearly, the notion of autonomous learning draws theoretical support from both the explicit and implicit approaches to L2 learning. Each learner constructs L2 knowledge through an interaction between what is already known (i.e., the implicit knowledge system) as well as from an examination of new ideas, information, and linguistic experiences (i.e., the explicit knowledge system). The recognition of an interface between the two knowledge systems led Little (2004) to suggest that autonomous learners are also limited by what they already know, their present level of proficiency as derived from past experience, as they strive to move forward in their language development.

In other words, AL succeeds when the learner strategically builds upon previous implicit learning in order to reach a higher level of language development. AL principles seek to help learners mediate between what they already know and what they are trying to learn by explicitly building upon previous knowledge and elaborating it. One might assume that the AL framework is applicable only to independent and self-learning environments. Schwienhorst (2008, 19), however, also values the dynamic relationship that can exist with peer-to-peer AL and affirms the importance of the major tenets of social interactionism, following Vygotsky's (1986) classic ideas of the advantages afforded by the zone of proximal development—or, in more commonsense terms, the notion that two heads are better than one.

Accordingly, learners become autonomous in a socially interactive environment by exploring the target language through communication, collaboration, and experimentation. The AL social community values the role of experimentation and collaboration among peers, teachers, and NSs.

A typical example of AL embedded in a social community might be a collaborative writing assignment. The first step centers on getting the group to agree on the first words. That text provides a basis for what might come next, more words, and gradually the text becomes large enough for the participants to begin to evaluate the overall product as good or bad or as capable of being improved. During this collaborative phase, the AL learners must read and reread the text aloud, which helps pronunciation and the internalization of language forms. Little by little, the participants scaffold their way to the completion of the assignment with plenty of speaking practice that reinforces reading and writing.

Tandem Learning

Very much connected with the AL approach discussed above is a time-honored tradition of promoting tandem language learning—namely, two individuals with different L1s teach each other an L2, what is known on the Web as *e-tandems* or tandem language learning as carried out through a social networking site rather than face to face. This practice of matching up two people to learn each other's language dates back to international efforts to establish pen pals. In fact, many online tandem organizations still use the acronym PAL in advertising Partners in Acquiring Languages.

O'Dowd (2007) and Bower and Kawaguchi (2011) have stressed that student preparation for e-tandem projects is critical to its success. Tandem partners do not naturally know how to facilitate language learning. As might be expected, then, students give better feedback when they receive clear e-tandem instructions and develop learning strategies as both learners and instructors. Corrective feedback—such as recasts, clarifications, comprehension checks, repetitions, and explicit corrections—tends to be low among tandem participants (Bower and Kawaguchi 2011), unless it is encouraged by instructors or the tasks themselves. E-tandem exchanges readily contribute to an increased level of intercultural knowledge and help to expand the participants' vocabulary. More training is needed if the e-tandem feedback is to address the correction of incorrect or awkward linguistic forms, grammar, and pragmatic competence.

Tandem language learning and e-tandems crucially depend on the participants embracing two guiding principles: reciprocity and autonomous learning. The concept of AL has already been discussed above, but reciprocity bears closer examination. Reciprocity means that learners must devote the same amount of time to both languages, so that the contribution and benefits are similar for both individuals. This exchange can occur within a pure e-tandem, as in what happen in SNSs such as LiveMocha, a controlled e-tandem embedded into an L2 class or, finally, a semicontrolled e-tandem that is organized by an educational institution as an extracurricular event. Controlled tandems and telecollaborations are usually not conceived as part of the core offerings in L2 education (O'Dowd 2010). But any successful tandem or e-tandem project will need substantial administrative support, which means full inclusion into the core curriculum, and careful screening to ensure pairings at approximately the same level. Understandably, this process demands much extra work and effort on the part of the instructor, along with an institution that values the type of learning that occurs in tandem education.

L2 Classroom Applications with Facebook

Despite scant research findings concerning the impact of SNSs on L2 development, language teachers have already begun to experiment with this popular electronic social forum as a way of motivating their students to increase practice of their speaking of the L2. In his L2 teacher's blog (November 11, 2010; http://iltl.wordpress.com), Hamilton-Hart described in detail a procedure for introducing Facebook into the language curriculum. But a set of security issues must be faced immediately because classroom students, especially those children from the secondary level, need to work in a protected learning environment. Hamilton-Hart solved this hurdle by having students first use any digital drawing program to create a picture/avatar of some imagined L2 persona, complete with a made-up name, birthdate, birthplace in the L2 country, profession, personality, hobbies, likes, and dislikes. All information about this persona must be reported in both oral and written form in the L2 to the teacher and/or classmates. By asking the students to make this person from five to thirty years older than themselves, their imagination can run wild and the power of play takes hold of the class (see chapter 8 for an in-depth analysis of the importance of play).

Next, the students have to do a run-around of the usual Facebook e-mail accounts—Facebook does not like a single individual to have dual accounts—by creating an alternate e-mail account through Gmail or Yahoo with the invented name, saved digital image, and a character description of the L2 persona. Now the students can return to Facebook and register this alternate e-mail account on Facebook and create a Facebook page with the information about their respective L2 personae accompanied by their respective digital image or L2 avatar. Everyone in the class will add each other's imaginary Facebook page to their own, and then the class can begin to get to know all the other L2 personae and invented biographies—the teacher could even give a prize for the most imaginative persona. In addition, all the students can set the interface instructions for Facebook to the language under study.

After introductions and basic personality inquiries, the class is ready to accomplish a list of more ambitious tasks in the L2. Either individually or in groups, the students can first describe an imaginary trip to the L2 country's capital. The students can search the Web for appropriate videos, photos, and graphics that help familiarize everyone with that city, its people, and its culture.

Likewise, students can search for a good lunch or dinner restaurant and then provide a description of the menu, prices, decor, food quality, service, and clientele for this locale. Later, they can write up their opinions of the restaurant as if it were a culinary review. The menu can be illustrated with pictures or sound bites of what this restaurant offers to its clientele.

Next, students can describe a random encounter with someone from the L2 culture based on any video found on YouTube of a person talking in the L2. The students will need to imagine that they interviewed this person directly in order to produce the video. They can even make up reasons or motivations for why this person in the video did or said certain things. The whole class can engage in a discussion as to whether this person is representative of the target culture in general or whether the views expressed are unique to this particular individual.

The same procedure can be applied to find a cultural event: Students identify a video of a museum, park, or monument where a group of students can visit virtually and, subsequently, describe their reactions. Perhaps the event can be nocturnal, such as a visit to a club, film, theater, cabaret, or concert.

This fictitious Facebook account and the activities briefly described above immerse students in the L2 environment by using this very popular social network. The Facebook interface allows students to create visually appealing pages in short order with little programming knowledge. The fact that the tasks themselves do not involve preselected Web addresses but rather instructions for what to look for eliminates the worry over nonoperative Web pages (i.e., link rot).

The account also opens the door for taking full advantage of the group functions available through Facebook. The group functions that Facebook and most other SNSs offer their users can be leveraged by any L2 teacher to create a sustainable community of practice (Blattner and Fiori 2009). Any user can create a group open to any other users or restricted to a preselected audience. Facebook, if anything else, is rooted in community building, social networking, and interpersonal relationships, but the Group application can be utilized in language classes in a variety of socially constructive and psychologically satisfying ways. Once a Facebook member is part of a Group, a variety of options are possible for sharing views, ideas, and topics, and engaging in virtual cyberdiscussions. Again, these tools keep them socially connected via e-mail notifications of Group postings of any type (e.g., wall postings, audio and video files, event invitations). In addition, any Group member can contact other classmates in a variety of ways through the Group application, or in a more conventional manner by using the Message application, by writing directly on their classmates' wall, or by sending a confidential e-mail.

Furthermore, outside the confines of the L2 class, students can use Facebook to join other groups where the participants exclusively use the L2 for their interactions. In these electronic forums, students will no doubt suffer some of the consequences of pragmatic and social stumbles—experiences that will further teach them about the L2 and its culture. If all goes well, L2 students will first enter such groups through peripheral participation, where they can first observe and learn the norms for acceptable patterns of behavior and linguistic practices of the community, including dialectal and social variation. Experiencing this type of language variation is extremely important for intermediate and advanced students who are trying to move their linguistic knowledge forward and gain control of the more colloquial forms and complicated L2 speech acts.

As a final point, it needs to be noted that increased motivation and improved performance in language classes have long been associated with the feeling of classroom community (Rovai 2002). Using Facebook can clearly enhance a student's sense of belonging. Recent investigations have pointed out that Facebook can have a positive effect on the student-to-student and student-to-teacher relationship (Mazer, Murphy, and Simmonds 2007). Students enjoy learning something more personal about their teachers as well because it decreases the asymmetric power relationship normally maintained in the standard classroom hierarchy by putting everyone on more of an equal footing. This, in turn, promotes a feeling of comfort and trust, which are important conditions for building an effective community of practice. In any event, SNSs are here to stay and only increasing in membership; teachers should learn to take full advantage of their positive aspects for promoting L2 learning.

Discussion Questions and Activities

1. Draw a digital image of a fictitious L2 persona and create a profile for this character, just as the students would have to do as described above in Hamilton-Hart's blog. Now that you have done this, what advice would you give your students when they do the same? Search Hamilton-Hart's blog for other good ideas for using Facebook in the classroom.

2. Explore any Web log written by a language teacher commenting on how Facebook can be used in class or as part of the curriculum. What aspects of this implementation would transfer to your class? What strikes you as not being feasible given any restrictions imposed at your institution or the special circumstances of your classroom? Is there any way to work around these restrictions?

3. Name the five principles of autonomous learning. Which ones are most important to you and your students? Why?

4. Sign up for a language social networking site such as LiveMocha and describe all the positive and negative aspects that you experienced joining this learning community.

5. Why does tandem learning work or not work? Debate the issue with a classmate; one person should take the affirmative position, and the other one should take the negative position.

6. Design an AL task and specify both the topic and the role of the instructor. In other words, what aspects of the task will be left in the hands of the learners? How can you, the teacher, assist them to realize their own goals?

7. Write down a list of five guidelines to give your students who are about to engage in an e-tandem project.

CHAPTER 8

Homo Ludens
Games for Language Learning

Why *Homo Ludens* Is Important for L2 Learning

CALL researchers and curriculum developers have recently begun to turn to the gaming environment and the notion of play as a viable way to stimulate learning an L2 (e.g., Arnseth 2006; Gee 2007; Green, Sha, and Liu 2011; Peterson 2006, 2010, 2011; Piirainen-Marsh and Tainio 2009; Reinhardt 2011; Reinders and Wattana 2011; Sørensen and Meyer 2007; Sykes, Reinhardt, and Thorne 2010; Thorne, Black, and Sykes 2009; Zheng et al. 2009). Games have the potential to combine the best of what has been developed over recent years in tutorial CALL programs with the powerful affordances of social computing (Thorne 2008). Accordingly, students can work individually but also share their results by working in teams using chat programs to facilitate textual and/or audio exchanges. Usually, the visual representation of a student's game persona is mediated through the use of an avatar (Peterson 2010), which increases the sense of play. Games are most always task oriented and often imply group collaboration. For instance, in the World of Warcraft environment (whether in English, French, Spanish, or another language), online players navigate through a fantasy world of beasts and warriors in pursuit of different quests or battle goals. In Second Life, people dress in whimsical costumes in order to pursue their own social or academic agendas. In the Forgotten World (Green, Sha and Liu 2011), English-as-a-second-language (ESL) learners participate in an online comic-strip drama that develops their English linguistic skills while helping to solve the adventure story at hand.

These gaming environments, as well as many others, all tap into a deep-seated imperative to play that may constitute part of our basic nature as *homo ludens*, "man/woman the player," as was first suggested by Huizinga (1955) in 1938. In what way is play of importance to learning in general? A report titled "Harnessing the Power of Videogames for Learning" from the 2006 Summit on Educational Games by the Federation of American Scientists found that students only remember 10 percent of what they read; 20 percent of what they hear; 30 percent if they see visuals, too; 50 percent, if they watch someone model something while explaining it; and 90 percent, if they engage in the job themselves, even if only as a simulation or game. In her brilliant book *Rethinking University Teaching*, Diana Laurillard (2002), former provost at the Open University, also singled out simulations (i.e., games, but real, serious games) as the most interactive of all technologies used in support of learning.

Likewise, returning to an earlier theme expressed in chapter 1 concerning the numbers of hours that students must devote to L2 learning (e.g., seat-time in class, individual study, immersion, study abroad), the power of *homo ludens* appears very attractive as a way to increase student engagement with the L2, especially if these language games can be well integrated into the curriculum (Cook 2000; Crystal 2001b). Although many educators dislike the notion of using *entertainment* to promote learning, I argue in this chapter that games also embody sound pedagogical practices that should normally be at the heart of the communicative and student-centered classroom. Undoubtedly, this chapter will leave many questions unanswered, along with a number of frowning, skeptical faces. That is to be expected, because not every language game is appropriate for the foreign-language curriculum just because it appears to be fun or encourages playful behavior. Likewise, the potential of language games is just beginning to be imagined, much less fully developed, and even less of it has been tested for results (for a good review, see Thorne, Black, and Sykes 2009). Nevertheless, the fact that $125 million was spent on the first day of release of *Halo 2* on November 9, 2004, should give us reason alone to be interested in games for the purposes of language learning (Squire 2006). Total online gaming constitutes a multi-billion-dollar industry rivaling that of movie theaters. Lenhart, Jones, and Macgill (2008) report that 81 percent of Americans age eighteen to twenty-nine years play digital games on a multitude of platforms (e.g., gaming consoles, computers, and mobile devices). Clearly, games have irrevocably captured the attention of our best customers, our students and, to an even greater extent, that of the younger students coming up from the ranks.

The Nature of Games

Language teachers have harnessed the power of games for the FL classroom for years, usually with great success (Boucquey et al. 2007). Classroom-based games motivate students to engage in L2 practice with exercises involving dice, cards, and other props that stimulate thinking and provoke pleasure and/or productive competition. For a sample list, see http://ms.loganhocking.k12.oh.us/~madame/teacher/presentations/Games.html. Online games can have similarly pedagogical effects, while they also appeal to students in a more up-to-date environment, the online gaming world.

Understandably, not all online games are the same: There are single-player games, cooperative or two-player games, and massively multiplayer online role-playing games, or MMOs (also MMOGs) for short. Each has its own rhythms, affordances, and dynamics. Multiple-player games often provide online chat during play, through either textual and/or audio exchanges. Thorne, Black, and Sykes (2009) use their own tripartite classification: (1) "social virtualities," such as Second Life and Active Worlds (Peterson 2006, 2010); (2) "commercial MMOs," such as World of Warcraft (Soares 2010; Thorne 2003); and (3) made-for-education synthetic immersive environments, such as Croquelandia (for Spanish, see Sykes 2011; Sykes, Oskoz, and Thorne 2008) or Zon for Chinese. These different gaming platforms are all part of the virtual environment and gaming spaces that can be harnessed in the service of online L2 learning.

What do games in general do that might assist students in learning (Gee 2007; Prensky 2000; Squire and Jenkins 2004; Steinkuehler 2004, 2006) and, in particular, in L2 learning? First and foremost, games allow people to play—an obvious fact, with language games being no exception. But games are not entirely free or unstructured play; they are *designed experiences*, as Squire (2006) describes them, with defined goals and rules that one must follow. Learners submit to these goals and rules as part of the price they pay in order to continue playing (Klopfer, Osterweil, and Salen 2009).

With emergent games, however, the random interaction of rules creates playful behavior that is unpredictable and hard to systematize into patterns that would be useful for explicit language practice (Juul 2005).

Play itself is rather like an act of faith that invests the game with special meaning. Players accept the rules of the designed experience, just as people accept the protocols of the live stage or a masquerade ball, thereby allowing the game to have verisimilitude, along with variety. Verisimilitude constitutes the very essence of play—the game has to seem real, feel real, or at least allow participants to pretend that it is based in reality just enough to suspend disbelief and achieve full involvement in storyline or quest (Calleja 2007). The cognitive or psychological benefits of play are certainly real, whereas the potential risks are minimized or even nonexistent in the play environment. This is the mechanism that draws us into play—it represents a preparation for real life without having to undergo any painful or psychologically crippling experiences during the process of the learning. The benefits for the L2 learner, who is engaged in a very psychologically stressful activity (i.e., SLA), should be clear: Play allows the learner to experiment, make errors, retry, and practice without any penalties.

Role playing is another way to think about play and verisimilitude; games allow students to explore new identities in a unique state of relative pseudonymity in a persistent or ever-present game world. This quality parallels what language instructors are trying to get their students to do when they learn an L2: Expand their identity into a new bilingual or multilingual self, something akin to what Kramsch (2009) has described with references to the multilingual subject by finding a *third place* that is neither equivalent to the identity in the first language nor that of the NS from the L2 world.

The environment of Second Life (SL) constitutes a good example of a learning environment where playacting can take place, although SL play may not fit the strict definition of a game because it has an open structure without rules. All this playacting, however, has an effect on language as well. Yee and Bailenson (2007) have called this the *Proteus effect*: An individual's verbal behavior is affected by his or her digital self-presentation through the avatar. In other words, the ways in which students play crucially affect how they learn and how they speak.

Second, and closely related to the idea of role playing, games foster agency, allowing players to do something such as carrying out a task or constructing meaning. Games make the users feel they are being competent and independent problem solvers. Games encourage a participatory culture with different rates and learning paths in response to the gamers' interests and abilities. Within these designed experiences, the participants enjoy the freedom to fail with low risks, to experiment, to fashion identities, to exert varying degrees of effort, and to interpret. Gee (2007) concluded that games let players be producers, not just consumers, by promoting agency, control, and ownership. Game players have to think like scientists as well, because they must hypothesize, probe the micro world, get a reaction, reflect on the results, and then probe it again in order to get better results.

This last phase of the process really is a clear nod to the role of practice. Purushotma, Thorne, and Wheatley (2008) insist that game's design must dedicate at least as much thought about failure states as to success states—a trait that shares much in common with the stated goals of iCALL programs (see chapter 3). In other words, repetitive practice, with instructive and customized feedback, must be an integral part of game design and the participant's learning cycle. Again, this sounds very similar to what students need to go through when learning an L2 in any educational environment—face-to-face or online—and very much in line with the Interactionist SLA theory described in chapter 1.

Prensky (2001) summarizes the basic characteristics of a game as follows:

- Games are a form of *fun*. That gives us *enjoyment and pleasure*.
- Games are a form of *play*. That gives us *intense and passionate involvement*.
- Games have *rules*. That gives us *structure*.
- Games have *goals*. That gives us *motivation*.
- Games are *interactive*. That gives us *doing*.
- Games have *outcomes and feedback*. That gives us *learning*.
- Games are *adaptive*. That gives us *flow*.
- Games have *win states*. That gives us *ego gratification*.

- Games have *conflict/competition/challenge/opposition*. That gives us *adrenaline*.
- Games have *problem solving*. That sparks our *creativity*.
- Games have *interaction*. That gives us *social groups*.
- Games have *representation and story*. That gives us *emotion*.

Gee (2007), in his fascinating book *What Video Games Have to Teach Us about Learning and Literacy*, offers a more theoretically phrased set of thirty-six learning principles that are followed in using or designing games, but he insists that these principles should be built into or rather inherently exist in any good learning environment. Here I have selected fourteen of the most salient pedagogical properties of good games listed by Gee, which can also serve as guiding principles for CALL design; note that they share much in common with Prensky's list given above:

- Critical Learning Principle: Active, not passive, learning.
- Psychosocial Moratorium Principle: Learners can take risks in a space where real-world consequences are lowered.
- Identity Principle: Games allow learners to meditate on (and mediate between) new and old identities.
- Amplification of Input Principle: For a little input, get a lot of output.
- Achievement Principle: For all levels there are intrinsic rewards, customization, and growing mastery.
- Practice Principle: Learners get lots of practice that is not boring; lots of time on task.
- Regime of Competence Principle: Similar to Krashen's $i + 1$ (see chapter 1); players operate at the edge of their competencies, but they are challenged with tasks that are doable.
- Multiple Routes Principle: Explore alternative styles.
- Situated Meaning Principle: Meaning is not decontextualized.
- Multimodal Principle: Meaning and knowledge are built up through multimodal channels, not just words.
- Explicit Information On-Demand and Just-in-Time Principle: Explicit instruction can be very helpful if it comes at the right moment; think about the feedback from iCALL programs.

- Discovery Principle: Overt telling is kept to a well-thought-out min-imum, allowing ample opportunity for the learner to experiment and make discoveries.
- Insider Principle: The learner is an insider, teacher, and producer from the beginning and throughout the gaming experience.
- Material Intelligence Principle: Thinking, problem solving, and knowledge are "stored" in smart tools, smart technologies, mate-rial objects, and the environment. This frees learners to engage their minds with other things and then combine the results of their own thinking with the knowledge stored in these tools.

Gee's last principle, the *material intelligence principle*, provides a tie-in to tutorial CALL and iCALL. Gee is suggesting here that tutorial CALL and social CALL should come together in the gaming environment, merg-ing into a single seamless learning space that can be harnessed for language learning purposes. In a report from the National Science Foundation (2008, 28, 41), researchers described the role of games in what they call a new cyberlearning environment (also see Salen 2007). Although recent inter-est in CALL research has been dominated by topics in social computing, recent advances in iCALL research (e.g., Heift 2010; Amaral and Meurers 2009; Nagata 2010) should make us rethink the value of tutorial CALL and its balance vis-à-vis social CALL in future language cyberlearning environ-ments. In the gaming environment, both activities are called upon and lev-eraged in pursuit of play.

Understandably, all language instructors want their students to chat bimodally (text and audio) with each other online, but also to use smart tools and apps, such German Tutor and Tagarela or Scott Payne's LangBot, at the same time, so that they can search for and experiment with new words and phrases as they negotiate meaning with their peers and accom-plish tasks of interest to them. Accordingly, in addition to working in groups, students should be spending hours and hours of individual lan-guage study by playing games that promote learning linguistic and cul-tural knowledge in a more independent fashion. If the games are built correctly, according to the key principles and characteristics mentioned above, they will motivate students to continue playing, which keeps them coming back for more language study and more time on task—the ultimate the key to L2 learning.

Clearly, Gee and Prensky's principles describe a pedagogy applicable to all learning, not just L2 learning and not just online learning. Perhaps the use of language games can help more traditional teachers begin to see how students will thrive in a classroom that also provides structured play, identity experimentation, repeated but meaningful practice, low stakes or risks, and hypothesis testing. Failures become opportunities to explore more fully not only the correct answer but what principles underlie the right answer.

And finally, the game metaphor can help students build new communities of practice where the *beta vets*, the more experienced players, assist with the development of the inexperienced players, or *noobs* (Steinkuehler 2004, 2006; Soares 2010). Passing from the ranks of the *noobs* into that of the *beta vets* motivates today's youth in ways far superior to explaining the cultural benefits of learning a new L2.

Language Games, Language Play: Research and Caveats

Despite the rosy picture painted here with respect to language games, some words of caution are in order. To date, there have been few experimental studies that examine how L2 learners fare within a virtual learning environment. Soares (2010) and Thorne (2008) have begun the exploration of World of Warcraft as a learning platform for Spanish and Russian, respectively. The data are intriguing but limited, and much of the practiced language in the World of Warcraft environment remains highly routine, formulaic, and full of gamer slang.

Peterson (2010) reported on seven studies dealing with a German-language MOO, an English-language SIMCOPTER, an ESL-based SIMCITY, a Japanese-based application programmed in Active Worlds, an ESL example realized in World of Warcraft, and an Arabic language multimedia tutorial/simulation called Tactical Iraqi. Peterson described these gaming experiences in positive terms, especially because they helped learners increase their target language production, improve negotiations of meaning, and enhance good learner reception, but a common assessment framework was missing or not possible to implement.

Ranalli (2008) used SIMCITY to teach vocabulary and included a rigorous set of assessment measures, but only nine students participated. The use of Croquelandia as a learning medium has already been discussed above (see Thorne, Black, and Sykes 2009; Sykes and Cohen 2009), but Cohen and Sykes (2010) reported only marginal progress in developing strategic competence in L2 pragmatics for students working in this medium.

Similarly, with respect to the chatting that often accompanies gaming, Thorne and colleagues (2009, p. 809) correctly pointed out that social computing within a game environment does not "significantly extend the findings from previous negotiation-oriented studies that have focused on purely text-based synchronous CMC chat spaces." It is just another environment open to explore the type of CMC research questions reviewed in chapter 4.

Curriculum development for language learning games is proceeding ahead on many fronts, but without a framework that has been vetted by the FL profession. With their online publication of *The Forgotten World* and the Xenos platform, the LearningGamesNetwork (www.learninggamesnetwork.org) has effectively employed online ESL games in China (Green, Sha, and Liu 2011), with an eye to expanding this environment to other languages in the near future. Languagelab.com has an extensive ESL presence in Second Life and had previously launched Ciudad Bonita as a locus for teaching Spanish. Likewise, there are other locations in SL where speaking in languages other than English can take place spontaneously (e.g., for Spanish, visit Plaza Barcelona, SL coordinates: 169, 68, 23). Any instructor can adapt existing commercial games such as World of Warcraft, Travian.com, the Sims 2, Grim Fandango, Curse of MonkeyIsland, or Runescape for classroom use, but adapting them to support specific L2 language tasks will require considerable extra work.

Without any doubt, using games for learning languages opens up an exciting new area for future research, but its curricular development faces serious caveats. The literature often refers to environments such as Second Life and the Sims 2 as *digital dollhouses*, where people just dress up and act out without much significant learning taking place. Likewise, the school-age population is increasingly intolerant of unsophisticated graphics, which increases the possibility that incursions into the gaming curriculum will become an expensive proposition. Pedagogically well-designed games should be able to exist in black and white or color, with more or less pixel details but, ultimately, the students themselves will have to determine what is acceptable.

Finally, programming games, whether for a stand-alone or online platform, such as for an adventure in Croquelandia or SL, remains a thoroughly time-consuming and, consequently, expensive endeavor even for a programmer, relegating the development process to well-financed commercial ventures that have little stake in the educational curriculum or to highly collaborative research groups, which are hard to keep funded and cohesive.

Clearly, more research is called for with respect to using games for online learning, but games have captured the attention of today's students, as has been well documented in the forward-looking recommendations contained in the federal report *Transforming American Education* from the US Department of Education (2010). One might ask where the language-teaching profession could go if the power of gaming were combined with the affordances offered by mobile devices. Christopher Holden and Julie Sykes (2011), two professors at the University of New Mexico, have begun to work out this scenario for intermediate Spanish by loaning their students iPhones or iPads that they use to play an interactive, place-located murder mystery, Mentira "Lie." This interactive story/game exhibits many of the classic advantages of games, as can be seen in the following analysis.

Mentira: A Mobile, Place-Based, Augmented Reality Game

Mentira is a mobile-enhanced, place-based, augmented reality game for intermediate Spanish built and run on the ARIS augmented reality for interactive storytelling open source platform maintained by the Department of Curriculum and Instruction at the University of Wisconsin, Madison (http://arisgames.org). ARIS allows the game creators to program an online interactive storyline/quest that utilizes locally embedded clues that can be accessed using the Global Positioning System and via the Quick Response Codes available to iPhones and iPads. In this fashion, game players experience a hybrid world of virtual interactive characters, items, and media placed in physical space, in this case, a Spanish-speaking neighborhood in

Albuquerque. Some of the plot's characters are game-generated nonplaying characters, but others are real people and places from a predominantly Hispanic neighborhood, Los Griegos.

The Mentira project began in 2009 and continues at present with new versions updated yearly to include innovations and suggestions from the student players. Intermediate Spanish students must choose an identity from among four Hispanic families. The murderer is a member of one of those families. Players are required to follow the murder investigation online and then, eventually, to visit the Los Griegos neighborhood in order to collect additional clues and, ultimately, solve the mystery by determining the responsible party and, with luck, absolving their own chosen family's name in the process. The first three weeks are spent getting oriented with the facts and shifting through clues surrounding the murder by reading about the four families and interacting with the ARIS program via the iPhone/iPad. The last two weeks involve group trips to the Los Griegos neighborhood to collect more specific information as guided by their mobile devices and the ARIS program prompts. The final dissection of clues to solve the mystery is carried out as an in-class assignment, not as part of the narrative of the game.

Mentira plays out much like a historical novel, where fact and fiction are interwoven so as to require the students to participate linguistically in meaningful ways with simulated nonplaying characters, other players, and local citizens. In this fashion, these university L2 students must explore both virtual and physical places, practice written Spanish, produce oral language in their final game report, and collaborate in Spanish with their classmates in a variety of learning contexts, especially the environment of real Spanish-speakers from the Albuquerque community. Ultimately, the pathway for solving the murder mystery is student driven and is the result of a series of interactions and decisions carried out in response to proddings generated by the game.

A game such as Mentira provides L2 learners with a place where they can exercise their own agency, try out new bilingual identities, practice language with relatively low stakes, create a storyline path that no one else has experienced, and experience direct knowledge of Spanish speakers and hispanic culture as embodied in the local communities. This type of game and the use of the students' favorite device, the mobile phone, expands learning far beyond the walls of the classroom and successfully captures the students' interest and augments their investment of time in L2 learning tasks. If Gee or Prensky's checklists were applied to this implementation of game learning, most of the characteristics would apply. The Albuquerque community can leverage benefits from a Spanish-speaking neighborhood such as Los Griegos. Although that aspect might not be easily replicated in other locales near universities and schools, other options via the internet might be substituted. Nevertheless, the principles that make this game so attractive will continue to obtain in other adaptations. The actual production of a game such as Mentira could even be the focus of a class project that would involve game planning, scriptwriting and serious L2 learning. Undoubtedly, the next years will see many new advances in infusing the L2 classroom with some of these game principles.

Brave New Digital World Revisited: Games and the L2 classroom

The previous discussion of games for language learning should have made it abundantly clear that adapting games for the L2 classroom and curriculum is not a straightforward proposition, despite the tremendous promise that gaming holds for stimulating and capturing student attention. Nevertheless, Gee (2007) has convincingly argued that game principles should be imbued readily into any learning environment, the L2 classroom being no exception, whether or not the learning tasks are specifically delivered via a game. Many of these benefits derive from more general notions of play and its importance to human pyschology. The role of play in learning fits very well with the trend toward fostering a more student-centered, student-driven classroom.

However, the collaborative effort needed to produce language games—for example, computer programmers, scriptwriters, artists, and educational designers—will also inhibit the language profession's ability to readily introduce games into the curriculum. The commercial MMOs presently available are very dominated by war metaphors and may not be appropriate for or of interest to all educational audiences. Undoubtedly, development platforms such as ARIS will become more numerous and user friendly in the future, which will mitigate against the current costs and large time investment that damper the efforts of instructors wishing to innovate their own language games.

The dynamics of games—and the mechanisms of play, in general—should be studied as part of teacher training and professional development. When these learning principles can be melded with the affordances of mobile devices and other new technologies, language teaching becomes more relevant to students, both the present generation and the ones coming up. But the language profession should examine and adapt what will work for both teachers and students. Again, what we know today about technology is not enough (myth 3, see chapter 1) to move the language profession's agenda forward.

Arnseth (2006) has pinpointed the real challenge of implementing games into the language curriculum: Are students *learning to play* or *playing to learn*? Clearly, the approach of *learning to play* is process oriented and takes advantage of the full motivational powers afforded by the games, whereas explicit language learning merely disguised as a game, while still useful, may not be very motivating in the long run. The latter approach sees language as a product, a skill, or content that must be learned as the end result of the game. This subtle but critical difference in meaning belies a more general methodological conflict: language learning as process versus language learning as product. Pedagogues, curriculum designers, and classroom practitioners alike will have to struggle with this distinction in order to find the right balance.

Discussion Questions and Activities

1. From either Gee's or Prensky's lists of game characteristics, select four qualities that you try to foster among your students in your in-class learning environment and describe how you do this.
2. Write a fifty-word paragraph to the parents of your students that justifies the use of L2 games.
3. Agree or disagree with the "Proteus effect" (Yee and Bailenson 2007), which argues that your avatar's appearance changes the way you speak.

Then explain your reasons. What benefits do avatars have for gaming? Why would the Proteus effect be potentially helpful for L2 learning?

4. Use the internet to find one online game played in the FL you teach. Describe how you would integrate this game into your curriculum or, if it does not meet your approval, analyze why you would not use it with your curriculum.

5. Sketch out your ideas for the ideal L2 game. What tasks would students accomplish? What "material intelligence" would be available to them while playing the game? How would the student's progress be incorporated into the classroom?

6. Which approach do you favor with respect to language games: learning to play or playing to learn? Justify your answer.

GLOSSARY

ACMC (asynchronous CMC). Asynchronous computer-mediated communication programs in deferred time allow students to exchange text messages and, sometimes, sound recordings in the format of an electronic bulletin board organized around threads or topics.

affective filter. A term first proposed by Stephen Krashen to refer to the psychological inhibitions that students erect when learning a foreign language.

affordances. This term refers to the advantages and disadvantages that every technological tool provides its users. Some tools predispose users to doing things in a particular way, which could be both positive and negative.

apperception. This is a process whereby someone learns new information by relating it to the previous knowledge base. In terms of learning language, linguists talk about students' needing to realize the gap between where they are now and where they need to go.

ASR (automatic speech recognition). The process of using computers and their programs to render speech signals into words represented through digital data.

authoring tool. A program that allows nonprogrammers to produce sophisticated software quickly and without extensive knowledge of the programming language that makes it possible. Authoring tools usually have certain preset programming routines or templates that are easy to produce but are relatively inflexible in terms of their design.

autonomous learning. Autonomous learning is a school of education that sees learners as individuals who can and should be responsible for their own learning climate.

blended or hybrid format. A blended or hybrid language class mixes a reduced number of classroom sessions with individual work done outside of class and assisted by technology.

browser. A program that interprets HTML code to create a graphics user interface that is visually oriented.

CALI. Computer-assisted language instruction is similar to CALL and refers to stand-alone programs that aid language learning.

CALL. Computer-assisted language learning refers to any software program that aids students in learning another language.

CBI. Content-based instruction for language learning asks students to focus on the subject content first and approaches learning the linguistic features as a by-product of content work.

CD-ROM. Compact disc read-only memory refers to a medium that holds digital information, games, programs, and music.

CGI scripts. Common gateway interface is a programming protocol used with servers to pass information or requests collected by the server to external applications or other individual users.

chat. This is a form of CMC communication that most often refers to synchronous online communication.

chatterbot program. The chatterbot program provides users with a conversational agent that simulates having artificial intelligence. Most chatterbot programs match key words to a stock set of responses in order to feign interactivity.

CMC (computer-mediated communication). Any program that allows users to exchange language—through text or audio. For instance, e-mail, blogs, wikis, forums, instant messaging, and chat.

CMS/LMS. Course management systems or learning management systems are a suite of authoring tools that allow teachers and students to organize their online e-learning materials, complete with content posting, grade books, and communication tools.

comprehensible input. This term was made popular by Stephen Krashen and refers to linguistic input that is just slightly more difficult than the learner is used to but still comprehensible (i.e., <i + 1>).

DVD. The digital video disc provides large amounts of optical storage of information. DVDs are the same physical dimension as CD-ROMs but with six times the amount of storage capacity.

F2F. Face-to-face learning environment—in other words, the classroom.

FonF (focus on form). Focus on form should be contrasted with focus on forms, where the former allows students to discover form differences through meaningful practice, whereas the latter imparts information (i.e., lectures) about the linguistic form differences without contextualized practice.

forums, discussion boards, or electronic bulletin boards. These terms refer to online message boards where posts are displayed chronologically or in threaded discussions.

FTP. File transfer protocol, which is used to transfer files from local areas (a single computer) to a server, where files can be made publicly available through the internet.

GUI. A graphical user interface turns machine code into a visual metaphor that can be modified and manipulated.

hosting. Programs that are accessible on the internet must be publicly published on a server connected to the World Wide Web. Someone or some institution must offer hosting on a server for their users where they can store their programs.

HTML. Hypertext markup language is the programming language that browsers can interpret in order to create Web pages with a graphics interface.

HTTP. Hypertext transfer protocol is the programming convention used for publishing pages on the internet.

ICALL. Intelligent computer-assisted language learning refers to programs that exhibit a modicum of artificial intelligence, the ability to respond to users' needs and demands.

ICC (intercultural communicative competence). As a counterpoint to Noam Chomsky's notion of linguistic competence, ICC refers to knowledge of another people's culture as mediated through language.

ILR rating scale. The Interagency Language Roundtable scale is a set of descriptions of abilities to communicate in a language. It was originally developed by the US Foreign Service Institute, the predecessor of the National Foreign Affairs Training Center. Thus, it is also often called Foreign Service Levels. It consists of descriptions of five levels of language proficiency.

interactionist theory. For language, interactionist theory consists of the process of social interactions with actions, reactions, and mutual adaptation between two or more individuals as a means of L2 learning.

interlanguage. When people learn a second language, the developing internal grammar, albeit incomplete, is referred to as their interlanguage.

internet. A worldwide, publicly accessible network of interconnected computers that transmit data by packet switching using the standard internet protocol. It includes millions of smaller domestic, academic, business, and government networks.

JavaScript. This programming language can be used in conjunction with HTML code to enhance a Web page's interactivity.

LAD. Language acquisition device; the innate capacity to construct a grammar.

link rot. When the address of a Web page is no longer operative.

MOO. A MUD (multiuser domain) Object Oriented is a type of domain that allows users to connect to each other via the computer and share a virtual reality.

PERL (practical extraction and reporting language). A dynamic programming language that is used to create highly interactive programs and Web pages.

Proteus effect. An individual's verbal behavior is affected by his or her digital self-presentation online by means of an avatar.

SCMC (synchronous CMC). This refers to chat in real time that includes the exchange of text, audio, and/or video.

Second Life (SL). A virtual world where users can socialize, customize an avatar, connect, and create using free voice and text.

SLA. Second language acquisition: The study of how learners acquire a second (or third or fourth, etc.) language.

social networking site (SNS). Web-based services that allow individuals to construct a public profile within a bounded system and then share thoughts with a list of other users with whom they share a connection.

synthetic immersive environments. Virtual environment and gaming spaces that can be harnessed in service of online L2 learning.

tandem language learning. This term refers to the pairing up of two speakers of different languages so that each one can teach the other his or her native language.

task-based language teaching (TBLT). A teaching approach that offers students material with they have to actively engage in the processing of problem solving in order to achieve a goal or complete a task.

telnet. The telecommunication network is a protocol used to allow users to communicate with each over the internet. It was originally developed for the UNIX operating system.

Unicode. A standardized protocol that permits computers to represent the text of any language in a consistent way. Only Unicode-compliant programs allow users to type in non-Roman alphabets used in such languages as Chinese, Arabic, or Korean.

URL. The uniform resource locator is the address for a Web page that follows the HTTP protocol.

VoIP. A program that implements voice over internet protocol or internet telephony allows users to speak to one another via computer as if they were using a telephone.

webquest. An educational research activity where students use the Web to investigate and analyze assigned topics.

World of Warcraft. An online game where players from around the world assume the roles of heroic fantasy characters and explore a virtual world full of mystery, magic, and endless adventure.

World Wide Web. A system of interlinked hypertext documents available through the internet.

WYSIWYG. What you see is what you get refers to a system that makes the content editing appear identical to the final visual product.

zone of proximal development (ZPD). The difference between what a learner can do without help and what he or she can do with help.

REFERENCES

Abrams, Z. I. 2003. The effects of synchronous and asynchronous CMC on oral performance. *Modern Language Journal* 87 (2): 157–67.

———. 2006. From theory to practice: Intracultural CMC in the L2 classroom. In *Calling on CALL: From theory and research to new directions in foreign language teaching*, edited by L. Ducate and N. Arnold. CALICO Monograph Series 5. San Marcos, TX: CALICO.

ACTFL (American Council on the Teaching of Foreign Languages). 1996. Standards for foreign language learning: Executive summary. www.actfl.org/i4a/pages/index.cfm?pageid=3324.

Adair-Hauck, B., L. Willingham-McLain, and B. Earnest-Youngs. 1999. Evaluating the integration of technology and second language learning. *CALICO Journal* 17 (2): 269–306.

Al-Batal, M. 2007. Arabic and national language educational policy. *Modern Language Journal* 91 (2): 268–71.

Allen, I. E., and J. Seaman. 2006. *Making the grade: Online education in the United States, 2006.* Needham, MA: Sloan Consortium. www.sloan-c.org/publications/survey/index.asp.

———. 2007. Online nation: Five years of growth in online learning. Needham, MA: Sloan Consortium. www.sloan-c.org/publications/survey/pdf/online-nation/pdf.

———. 2010. Learning on demand: Online education in the United States, 2009. Babson Survey Research Group. www.sloan-c.org/publications/survey/index.

Amaral, L., and D. Meurers. 2009. Little things with big effects: On the identification and interpretation of tokens for error diagnosis in ICALL. *CALICO Journal* 26: 580–91.

Arispe, K. 2012. Why vocabulary still matters: L2 lexical development and learner autonomy as mediated through an ICALL tool, *Langbot.* Doctoral diss., Spanish and Portuguese, University of California, Davis.

Arispe, K., and R. J. Blake. 2012. Individual factors and successful learning in a hybrid course. *System Journal* 40 (3): 449–65.

Arnold, N., and L. Ducate. 2006. CALL: Where are we and where do we go from here? In *Calling on CALL: From theory and research to new directions in foreign language teaching,* edited by N. Arnold and L. Ducate. CALICO Monograph Series 5. San Marcos, TX: CALICO.

Arnseth, H. C. 2006. Learning to play or playing to learn: A critical account of the models of communication informing educational research on computer gameplay. *Game Studies* 6 (1). http://gamestudies.org/0601/articles/arnseth.

Arocena, F. 2006. *Webmaestro.* www.axis.org/ usuarios/farocena/.

Arvan, L., and D. Musumeci. 2000. Instructor attitudes within the SCALE efficiency projects. *Journal of Asynchronous Learning Networks* 4 (3): 193–210.

Bañados, E. 2006. A blended-learning pedagogical model for teaching and learning EFL successfully through an online interactive multimedia environment. *CALICO Journal* 23 (3): 533–50.

Barson, J. 1991. The virtual classroom is born: What now? In *Foreign language acquisition research and the classroom,* edited by B. F. Freed. Lexington, MA: Heath.

Bauer, B., L. deBenedette, G. Furstenberg, S. Levet, and S. Waryn. 2006. The Cultura project. In *Internet-mediated intercultural foreign language education,* edited by J. A. Belz and S. L. Thore. Boston: Thomson Heinle.

Beatty, K. 2003. *Teaching and researching computer-assisted language learning.* London: Longman.

Belz, J. A. 2002. Social dimensions of telecollaborative foreign language study. *Language Learning & Technology* 6 (1): 60–81. http://llt.msu.edu/vol6num 1/belz/.

———. 2003. Linguistic perspectives on the development of intercultural competence in telecollaboration. *Language Learning & Technology* 7 (2): 68–117. http://llt.msu.edu/vol7num2/belz.

Belz, J. A., and S. L. Thorne, eds. 2006. *Internet-mediated intercultural foreign language education*. Boston: Thomson Heinle.

Benson, P. 2006. *Learner autonomy 8: Insider perspectives on autonomy in language teaching and learning*. Dublin: Authentik.

Bernstein, J., I. Barbier, E. Rosenfeld, and J. De Jong. 2004. Development and validation of an automatic spoken Spanish test. In *InSTIL/ICALL 2004 symposium on computer-assisted learning, NLP and speech technologies in advanced language learning systems, Venice, June 17–19, 2004, ISCA Archive*. www.isca-speech.org/archive/icall2004.

Bertin, J.-C. 2001. CALL material structure and learner competence. In *ICT and language learning: A European perspective*, edited by A. Chambers and G. Davies. Lisse: Sets and Zeitlinger.

Bialystok, E., and K. Hakuta. 1994. *In other words*. New York: Basic Books.

Bickerton, D., T. Stenton, and M. Temmerman. 2001. In *ICT and language learning: A European perspective*, ed. A. Chambers and G. Davies. Lisse: Sets and Zeitlinger.

Blake, R. 2000. Computer-mediated communication: A window on L2 Spanish interlanguage. *Language Learning & Technology* 4 (1): 120–36.

———. 2005a. Bimodal chatting: The glue of a distance language learning course. *CALICO Journal* 22 (3): 497–511.

———. 2005b. Review of Wimba: Voice management system 4.0. Ed. Jack Burston. *Digital Language Lab Solutions, IALLT*, 54–66.

———. 2006. Two heads are better than one: C[omputer] M[ediated] C[ommunication] for the L2 Curriculum. In *Changing language education through CALL*, edited by R. P. Donaldson and M. A. Haggstrom. Abingdon: Routledge, 229–48.

———. 2008. New trends in using technology in the language curriculum. *2007 Annual Review of Applied Linguistics* 27 (March): 76–97.

———. 2009. From Web pages to distance learning: Technology in the foreign-language curriculum. In *Teaching literature in language online*, edited by Ian Lancashire. New York: MLA Press 23–37.

———. 2011. Current Trends in Online Language Learning. *Annual Review of Applied Linguistics* 31: 19–35.

Blake, R., J. Blasco, and C. Hernández. 2001. *Tesoros CD-ROM: A multimedia-based course*. Boecillo, Valladolid, and New York: Boecillo Editorial Multimedia and McGraw-Hill.

Blake, R., and A. Delforge. 2005. Language learning at a distance: Spanish without walls. In *Selected papers from the 2004 NFLRC symposium: Distance education, distributed learning and language instruction (NetWork#44)* [HTML document], edited by I. Thompson and D. Hiple. Honolulu: National Foreign Language Resource Center, University of Hawaii. http://nflrc .hawaii.edu/NetWorks/NW44.

Blake, R., M. V. González Pagani, A. Ramos, and M. Marks. 2003. *Al corriente: Curso intermedio de español*. New York: McGraw-Hill.

Blake, R., and C. Kramsch. 2007. Introduction to perspective volume. *Modern Language Journal* 91 (2): 247–49.

Blake, R., and S. S'hiri. 2012. Online Arabic language learning: What happens after? *L2 Journal* (Berkeley Language Center) 4 (2): 230–46.

Blake, R., N. Wilson, C. Pardo Ballester, and M. Cetto. 2008. Measuring oral proficiency in distance, face-to-face, and blended classrooms. *Language Learning and Technology* 12 (3): 114–27.

Blake, R., and E. Zyzik. 2003. Who's helping whom? Learner/heritage speakers' networked discussions in Spanish. *Applied Linguistics* 24 (4): 519–44.

Blattner, G., and Fiori, M. 2009. Facebook in the language classroom: Promises and possibilities. *International Journal of Instructional Technology and Distance Learning* 6 (1). www.itdl.org/journal /jan_09/article02.htm.

Bley-Vroman, R. 1990. The logical problem of foreign language learning. *Linguistic Analysis* 20 (1–2): 3–49.

Blin, F. 2004. CALL and the development of learner autonomy: Towards an activity-theoretical perspective. *ReCALL: The Journal of EUROCALL* 16 (2): 377–95.

Blyth, C. S. 1999. *Untangling the Web: Nonce's guide to language and culture on the internet*. New York: Nounce Publishing Consultants.

Boucquey, T., K. Flores, J. Kramer, L. McPherson, M. Pettit, H. Silverstein, and E. Tjuanakis. 2007. 100 games and activities for the introductory foreign language classroom. Larchmont, NY: Eye On Education.

Bower, J., and S. Kawaguchi. 2011. Negotiation of meaning and corrective feedback in Japanese/English eTandem. *Language Learning & Technology* 15 (1): 41–71.

Brandl, K. 2002. Integrating internet-based reading materials into the foreign language curriculum: From teacher- to student-centered approaches. *Language Learning & Technology* 6 (3): 87–107. http://llt.msu.edu/vol6num3/brandl/default.html.

———. 2005. Are you ready to MOODLE? *Language Learning and Technology* 9 (2): 16–23. http://llt.msu.edu/vol9num2/review1/default .html.

Brecht, R., D. Davidson, and R. Ginsberg. 1995. Predictors of foreign language gain during study abroad. In *Second language acquisition in a study abroad context*, edited by Barbara F. Freed. Amsterdam: John Benjamin.

Brinton, D., M. A. Snow, and M. Wesche. 1989. *Content-based second language instruction*. Boston: Heinle & Heinle.

Brown, H. D. 2001. *Teaching by principles: An interactive approach to language pedagogy*. White Plains, NY: Addison Wesley Longman.

Bruner, J. 1996. *The culture of education*. Cambridge, MA: Harvard University Press.

Burston, J. 1998. Antidote 98. *CALICO Journal* 16 (2): 197–212.

———. 2003. Software selection: A primer on sources and evaluation. *CALICO Journal* 21 (1): 29–40.

———. 2006. Working towards effective assessment of CALL. In *Changing language education through CALL*, edited by R. P. Donaldson and M. A. Haggstrom. London: Routledge.

Byram, M. 1997. *Teaching and assessing intercultural communicative competence*. Clevedon, UK: Multilingual Matters.

Byram, M., B. Gribkova, and H. Starkey. 2002. *Developing the intercultural dimension in language teaching: A practical introduction for teachers*. Strasborg: Council of Europe.

Byrnes, H. 2000. Languages across the curriculum: Interdepartmental curriculum construction. In *Languages across the curriculum: Interdisciplinary structures and internationalized education*, edited by M.-R. Kecht and K. von Hammerstein. Columbus: National East Asian Languages Resource Center, Ohio State University.

———. 2006. Perspectives. *Modern Language Journal* 90 (2): 244–46.

Cahill, D., and D. Catanzaro. 1997. Teaching first-year Spanish on-line. *CALICO Journal* 14 (2): 97–114.

Calleja, G. 2007. Digital game involvement: A conceptual model. *Games and Culture* 2 (3): 236–60.

Carnegie Mellon University. 2000. *Elementary French online*. http://ml.hss.cmu.edu/languageonline/overview/overview.html.

Carr, S. 2000. As distance education comes of age, the challenge is keeping up with the students. *Chronicle of Higher Education*, February 11, A3. Available at www.chronicle.com.

Chapelle, C. 2001. *Computer applications in second language acquisition: Foundations for teaching, testing, and research*. Cambridge: Cambridge University Press.

———. 2005. CALICO at center stage: Our emerging rights and responsibilities. *CALICO Journal* 23 (1): 5–15.

Chen, Chin-chi. 2006. How webquests send technology to the background. In *Teacher education in CALL*, edited by P. Hubbard and M. Levy. Language Learning & Language Teaching Series 14. Philadelphia: John Benjamin.

Chenoweth, N. A., C. M. Jones, and G. R. Tucker. 2006. Language online: Principles of design and methods of assessment. In *Changing language education through CALL*, edited by R. P. Donaldson and M. A. Haggstrom. Abingdon: Routledge.

Chenoweth, N. A., and K. Murday. 2003. Measuring student learning in an online French course. *CALICO Journal* 20 (2): 284–314.

Chomsky, N. 1986. *Knowledge of language: Its nature, origin, and use*. New York: Praeger.

Chun, D. 1994. Using computer networking to facilitate the acquisition of interactive competence. *System* 22 (1): 17–31.

———. 1998. Using computer-assisted class discussion to facilitate the acquisition of interactive competence. In *Language learning online: Theory and practice in the ESL and L2 computer classroom*, edited by J. Swaffar, S. Romano, P. Markley, and K. Arens. Austin: Labyrinth.

———. 2006. CALL technologies for L2 reading. In *Calling on CALL: From theory and research to new directions in foreign language teaching*, edited by L. Ducate and N. Arnold. CALICO Monograph Series 5. San Marcos, TX: CALICO.

Chun, D. M., and J. L. Plass. 1997. Research on text comprehension in multimedia environment. *Language Learning & Technology* 1 (1): 60–81.

Clifford, R. 1987. The status of computer-assisted language learning. *CALICO Journal* 4 (4): 9–16.

Cobb, T. 2007. Computing the vocabulary demands of L2 reading. *Language Learning & Technology* 11:38–63.

Cohen, A., and J. Sykes. 2006. *Dancing with words: Strategies for learning pragmatics in Spanish*. www.carla.umn.edu/speechacts/sp _pragmatics/home.html.

———. 2010. Language learner strategies and their effect on speech act performance. *Applied Linguistics Forum, 30.* www.tesol.org//s_tesol/article.asp?vid=142&DID=13196&sid=1&cid=695&iid=13190&nid=2857.

Coleman, J. A., R. Hampel, M. Hauck, and U. Stickler. 2010. Collaboration and interaction: The keys to distance and computer-supported language learning. In *Critical and Intercultural Theory and Language Pedagogy*, edited by G. Levine, A. Phipps, and C. Blythe. Florence, KY: Cengage Learning.

Colpaert, J. 2006. Pedagogy-driven design for online language teaching and learning. *CALICO Journal* 23 (3): 477–97.

Cook, G. 2000. *Language play, language learning*. Oxford: Oxford University Press.

Cook, V. J. 2001. Using the first language in the classroom. *Canadian Modern Language Review* 57 (3): 402–23.

Crandall, J., and G. R. Tucker. 1990. Content-based instruction in second and foreign languages. In *Foreign language education: Issues and strategies*, edited by A. Padilla, H., Fairchild, and C. Valadez. Newbury Park, CA: Sage.

Crump, B., and A. McIlroy. 2003. The digital divide: Why the "don't–want–tos" won't compute: Lessons from a New Zealand ICT project. *First Monday* 8 (12). http://firstmonday.org/issues/issue8_12/crump/ index.html.

Crystal, D. 2001a. *Language and the internet.* Cambridge: Cambridge University Press.

———. 2001b. *Language play.* Chicago: University of Chicago Press.

Cummins, J. 1998. E-Lective language learning: Design of a computer-assisted text-based ESL/EFL learning system. *TESOL Journal* 7 (3): 18–21.

Cummins, J., and D. Sayers. 1995. *Brave new schools: Challenging cultural literacy through global learning networks.* New York: St. Martin's Press.

Cziko, G. A., and S. Park. 2003. Internet audio communications for second language learning: A comparative view of six programs. *Language Learning & Technology* 7 (1): 15–27. http://llt.msu.edu/vol7num1/review1/default.html.

Davidson, D. 2004. Capabilities and outputs of the US education system: Proficiency outputs. In *The Proceedings of the National Language Conference.* www.nlconference.org/docs/NLC_Commentary_Davidson.doc.

———. 2007. Study abroad and outcomes measurements: The case of Russian. *Modern Language Journal* 91 (2): 276–80.

Davies, G., ed. 2006. *Information and communications technology for language teachers (ICT4LT).* Thames Valley University, Slough. Available at www.ict4lt.org.

Davies, M. 2006. *A frequency dictionary of Spanish: Core vocabulary for learners.* New York: Routledge.

Debski, R. 1997. Support of creativity and collaboration in the language classroom: A new role for technology. In *Language learning through social computing: ALAA's occasional papers*, edited by R. Debski, J. Gassin, and M. Smith. Melbourne: Applied Linguistics Association of Australia.

DeKeyser, R. M. 2000. The robustness of critical period effects in second language acquisition. *Studies in Second Language Acquisition* 22 (4): 499–533.

Delcloque, P. 2001. Disseminate or not? Should we pursue a new direction—Looking for the *third way* in CALL development? In *ICT and language learning: A European perspective*, edited by A. Chambers and G. Davies. Lisse: Sets and Zeitlinger.

Dodge, B. 2002. *Webquest taskonomy: A taxonomy of tasks.* http://webquest.sdsu.edu/taskonomy.html.

Donaldson, R. P., and M. A. Haggstrom. 2006. *Changing language education through CALL.* Abington: Routledge.

Doughty, C. 1998. Acquiring competence in a second language: Form and function. In *Learning foreign and second languages*, edited by Heidi Byrnes, 128–56. New York: Modern Language Association.

Doughty, C. J., and M. H. Long, eds. 2003a. *The handbook of second language acquisition.* London: Blackwell.

———. 2003b. Optimal psycholinguistic environments for distance foreign language learning. *Language Learning & Technology* 7 (3): 50–80. http://llt.msu.edu/vol7num3/doughty.

Dubreil, S. 2006. Getting perspective on culture through CALL. In *Calling on CALL: From theory and research to new directions in foreign language teaching*, edited by L. Ducate and N. Arnold. CALICO Monograph Series 5. San Marcos, TX: CALICO.

Ducate, L., and L. Lomicka. 2005. Exploring the blogosphere: Use of Web logs in the foreign language classroom. *Foreign Language Annals* 38 (3): 408–19.

Echávez-Solano, N. 2003. A comparison of student outcomes and attitudes in technology-enhanced vs. traditional second-semester Spanish language courses. PhD diss., University of Minnesota, Minneapolis.

Egbert, J. 2005. *CALL essentials: Principles and practice in CALL classrooms*. Alexandria, VA: TESOL.

Egbert, J., T. Paulus, and Y. Nakamichi. 2002. The impact of CALL instruction on classroom computer use: A foundation for rethinking technology in teacher education. *Language Learning & Technology* 6 (3): 106–26. http://llt.msu.edu/vol6num3/egbert /default.html.

Ehsani, F., and E. Knodt. 1998. Speech technology in computer-aided language learning: Strengths and limitations of a new CALL paradigm. *Language Learning & Technology* 2 (1): 54–73. http://llt .msu.edu/vol2num1/article3/.

Ellis, N. C. 2002. Frequency effects in language processing: A review with implications for theories of implicit and explicit language acquisition. *Studies in Second Language Acquisition* 24 (2): 143–88.

Ellis, R. 1994. *A study of second language acquisition*. Oxford: Oxford University Press.

———. 1997. *Second language acquisition*. Oxford: Oxford University Press.

———. 2003. *Task-based language teaching and learning*. Oxford: Oxford University Press.

Epps, M. 2004. CALL: How does it make you feel? Master's thesis, University of Virginia, Charlottesville.

Eskenazi, M. 1999. Using automatic speech processing for foreign language pronunciation tutoring: Some issues and a prototype. *Language Learning & Technology* 2 (2): 62–76. http://llt.msu.edu /vol2num2/article3/.

Eskenazi, M., and J. Brown. 2006. Teaching the creation of software that uses speech recognition. In *Teacher education in CALL*, edited by P. Hubbard and M. Levy. Language Learning & Language Teaching Series 14. Philadelphia: John Benjamin.

Federal Language Training Laboratory. 1990. *Éxito: High technology teaching basic Spanish*. Washington, DC: Federal Language Training Laboratory.

Felix, U. 2003. Teaching language online: Deconstructing the myths. *Australasian Journal of Educational Technology* 19 (1): 118–38.

Fidelman, C. 1995–96. A language professional's guide to the World Wide Web. *CALICO Journal* 13 (2–3): 113–40.

Fleming, S., D. Hiple, and Y. Du. 2002. Foreign language distance education: The University of Hawai'i experience. In *New technologies and language learning: Cases in the less commonly taught languages*, edited by C. A. Spreen. Technical Report 25. Honolulu: Second Language Teaching & Curriculum Center.

Fogg, B. J. 2003. *Persuasive technology: Using computers to change what we think and do*. Amsterdam: Morgan Kaufmann.

Freinet, C. 1994. *Les oeuvres pédagogiques*. Paris: Edition Seuil.

Fryer, L., and R. Carpenter. 2006. Emerging technologies: Bots as language learning tools. *Language Learning & Technology* 10 (3): 8–14.

Fukkink, R. G., J. Hulstijn, and A. Simis. 2005. Does training of second-language word recognition skills affect reading comprehension? An experimental study. *Modern Language Journal* 89 (1): 54–75.

Furstenberg, G., S. Levet, K. English, and K. Maillet. 2001. Giving a virtual voice to the silent language of culture: The Cultura project. *Language Learning & Technology* 5 (1): 55–102. http://llt.msu.edu/vol5num1/furstenberg/default.html.

Gale, L. E. 1989. *Macario, Montevidisco, and interactive Dígame*: Developing interactive video for language instruction. In *Modern technology in foreign language education: Applications and projects*, edited by W. F. Smith. Lincolnwood, IL: National Textbook.

Garrett, N., and P. Liddell. 2004. The new language centers: New mandates, new horizons. In *New perspectives on CALL for second language classrooms*, edited by S. Fotos and C. Browne. Mahwah, NJ: Lawrence Erlbaum Associates.

Garrett, Nina. 1986. The problem with grammar: What kind can the language learner use? *Modern Language Journal* 70 (2): 133–48.

———. 1988. Computers in foreign language education: Teaching, learning, and language-acquisition research. *ADFL Bulletin* 19 (3): 6–12. www.mla.org/adfl/bulletin/V19N3/193006.htm.

———. 1991. Technology in the service of language learning: Trends and issues. *Modern Language Journal* 75 (1): 74–101.

Gass, S. M. 1997. *Input, interaction, and the second language learner.* Mahwah, NJ: Lawrence Erlbaum Associates.

Gass, S. M., A. Mackey, and T. Pica. 1998. The role of input and interaction in second language acquisition: Introduction to the special issue. *Modern Language Journal* 82 (3): 299–307.

Gass, S. M., and L. Selinker. 2001. Second language acquisition: An introductory course, 2nd ed. Hillsdale, NJ: Lawrence Erlbaum Associates.

Gass, S. M., and E. Varonis. 1994. Input, interaction and second language production. *Studies in Second Language Acquisition* 16 (3): 283–302.

Gee, J. P. 2007. *What video games have to teach us about learning and literacy.* New York: Palgrave Macmillan. Orig. pub. 2003.

Genesee, F. 1994. *Integrating language and content: Lessons from immersion.* Educational Practice Report 11. National Center for Research on Cultural Diversity and Second Language Learning. www.ncbe.gwu.edu/miscpubs/ncrcdsll/epr11.htm.

Gladwell, M. 2008. *Outliers.* New York, NY: Little, Brown and Company.

Global Reach. 2004. http://global-reach.biz/globstats/index.php3.

Godwin-Jones, B. 1998. Dynamic Web page creation. *Language Learning & Technology* 1 (2): 9–15. http://llt.msu.edu/vol1num2/emerging/default.html.

———. 2002. Multilingual computing. *Language Learning & Technology* 6 (2): 6–11. http://llt.msu.edu/vol6num2/emerging/default.html.

———. 2003a. Emerging technologies: Blogs and wikis—environments for on-line collaboration. *Language Learning & Technology* 7 (2): 12–16. http://llt.msu.edu/vol7num2/emerging/.

———. 2003b. Emerging technologies: Tools for distance education—toward convergence and integration. *Language Learning & Technology* 7 (3): 18–22. http://llt.msu.edu/vol7num3/emerging/.

———. 2004. Language in action: From webquests to virtual realities. *Language Learning & Technology* 8 (3): 9–14. http://llt.msu.edu/vol8num3/emerging/default.html.

Goertler, S., and P. Winke, eds. 2008. *Opening doors through distance language education: Principles, perspectives, and practices.* San Marcos, TX: CALICO.

Gonglewski, M. 1999. Linking the internet to the National Standards for Foreign Language Learning. *Foreign Language Annals* 32 (3): 348–62.

Goodfellow, R., I. Jeffreys, T. Miles, and T. Shirra. 1996. Face-to-face learning at a distance? A study of a videoconferencing try-out. *ReCALL* 8 (2): 5–16.

Grabe, W. 2004. Research on teaching reading. *Annual Review of Applied Linguistics* 24 (March): 44–69.

Green, A., and B. Earnest-Youngs. 2001. Using the Web in elementary French and German courses: Quantitative and qualitative study results. *CALICO Journal* 19 (1): 89–123.

Green, P. J., M. Sha, and L. Liu. 2011. *The US–China E-Language Project: A Study of a Gaming Approach to English Language Learning for Middle School Students.* Research Triangle Park, NC: RTI International. www.eric.ed.gov/ERICWebPortal/contentdelivery /servlet/ERICServlet?accno=ED521516.

Grefenstette, J. N. 2000. Estimation of English and non-English language use on the WWW. In *Proceedings of RIAO [Recherche d'Information Assistée par Ordinateur]#213, 2000: Content-based multimedia information access.* Paris: Recherche d'Information Assistée par Ordinateur.

Gregg, K. 1984. Krashen's monitor and Occam's razor. *Applied Linguistics* 5 (2): 79–100.

Hamachiya. S. 2010. Mixiカウンター :: ぼくはまちちゃん！. http://s .hamachiya.com/mc/.

Hamilton-Hart, J. 2010. Using Facebook for language learning. In *Innovation in language teaching and learning: A blog for language teachers and learners.* http://iltl.wordpress.com/2010/11/11 /using-facebook-for-language-learning/.

Hanson-Smith, E. 2006. Communities of practice for pre- and in-service teacher education. In *Teacher education in CALL*, edited by P. Hubbard and M. Levy. Language Learning & Language Teaching Series 14. Philadelphia: John Benjamin.

Hatch, E. 1978. Acquisition of syntax in a second language. In *Understanding second and foreign language learning: Issues and approaches*, edited by J. Richards. Rowley, MA: Newbury House.

Hauck, M., and U. Stickler. 2006. What does it take to teach online? *CALICO Journal* 23 (3): 463–75.

Heift, T. 2001. Intelligent language tutoring systems for grammar practice. *Zeitschrift für Interkulturellen Fremdsprachenunterricht* [online], 6 (2): 15. www.spz.tu-darmstadt.de/projekt_ejournal/jg-06-2 /beitrag/heift2.htm.

———. 2002. Learner control and error correction in ICALL: Browsers, peekers and adamants. *CALICO Journal* 19 (3): 295–313.

———. 2004. Corrective feedback and learner uptake in CALL. *ReCALL* 16 (2): 416–31.

———. 2010. Prompting in CALL: A longitudinal study of learner uptake. *Modern Language Journal* 94: 198–216.

Heift, T., and M. Schulze. 2007. *Parsers and pedagogues: Errors and intelligence in computer assisted language learning.* London: Routledge.

Herman, T., and Banister, S. 2007. Face-to-face versus online coursework: A comparison of costs and learning outcomes. *Contemporary Issues in Technology and Teacher Education* 7 (4). www.citejournal .org/vol7/iss4/currentpractice/article1.cfm.

Holden, C., and J. M. Sykes. 2011. Leveraging mobile games for place-based language learning. *International Journal of Game-Based Learning* 1 (2): 1–18.

Holec, H. 1979. *Autonomy and Foreign Language Learning.* Oxford: Pergamon Press.

Holliday, L. 1995. NS syntactic modifications in NS-NSS negotiation as input data for second language acquisition of syntax. PhD diss., University of Pennsylvania, Philadelphia.

Holmberg, B., M. Shelley, and C. White. 2005. *Distance education and languages: Evolution and change.* Clevedon, UK: Multilingual Matters.

Horn, R. 1992. How to get little or no effect and make no significant difference. *Performance and instruction* 31 (January): 29–32. http://66.249.93.104/search?q=cache:dpTmrkyUrogJ:www.stan ford.edu/~rhorn/a/topic/edu/artclHowtoGetLttleorNoEffct .pdf+no+significant+differences&hl=en&gl=es&ct=clnk&cd=6& client=firefox-a.

Hubbard, P. 1996. Elements of CALL methodology: Development, evaluation, and implementation. In *The power of CALL*, edited by M. Pennington. Bolsover, TX: Athelstan.

———. 2004. Learner training for effective use of CALL. In *New perspectives on CALL for the second language classroom*, edited by S. Fotos and C. Browne. Mahwah, NJ: Lawrence Erlbaum Associates.

———. 2006. Evaluating CALL software. In *Calling on CALL: From theory and research to new directions in foreign language teaching*, edited by L. Ducate and N. Arnold. San Marcos, TX: CALICO.

Hubbard, P., and C. Bradin Siskin. 2004. Another look at tutorial CALL. *ReCALL* 16 (2): 448–61.

Hubbard, P., and M. Levy. 2006a. The scope of CALL education. In *Teacher education in CALL*, edited by P. Hubbard and M. Levy. Philadelphia: John Benjamin.

———, eds. 2006b. *Teacher education in CALL*. Language Learning & Language Teaching Series 14. Philadelphia: John Benjamin.

Huizinga, J. 1955. *Homo ludens: A study of the play element in culture*. Boston: Beacon Press. Orig. pub. 1938.

Hymes, D. 1974. *Foundations in sociolinguistics: An ethnographic approach*. Philadelphia: University of Pennsylvania Press.

Internet World Stats. 2006. www.internetworldstats.com/stats7.htm.

Jeon-Ellis, G., R. Debski, and J. Wigglesworth. 2005. Oral interaction around computers in the project-oriented CALL classroom. *Language Learning and Technology* 9 (3): 121–45. http://llt.msu.edu/vol9num3/jeon/default.html.

Jones, C. M. 1999. Introduction to special issue on language courseware design. *CALICO Journal* 17 (1): 5–7.

Juozulynas, V. 1994. Errors in the compositions of second-year German students: An empirical study for parser-based iCALL. *CALICO Journal* 12 (1): 5–17.

Juul, J. 2005. *Half-real: Video games between real rules and fictional worlds*. Cambridge, MA: MIT Press.

Karp, A. 2002. Modification of glosses and its effect on incidental L2 vocabulary learning in Spanish. PhD diss., University of California, Davis.

Kassen, M. A., R. Z. Lavine, K. Murphy-Judy, and M. Peters. 2007. *Preparing and developing technology-proficient L2 teachers.* CALICO Monograph Series 6. San Marcos, TX: CALICO.

Keeton, M. T. 2004. Best online instructional practices: Report of phase I of an ongoing study. *Journal of Asynchronous Learning Networks* 8 (2): 75–100.

Kern, R. 1995. Restructuring classroom interaction with networked computers: Effects on quantity and quality of language production. *Modern Language Journal* 79 (4): 457–76.

Kern, R., P. Ware, and M. Warschauer. 2004. Crossing frontiers: New directions in online pedagogy and research. *Annual Review of Applied Linguistics* 24 (March): 243–60.

Kern, R. G., and M. Warschauer. 2000. Theory and practice of network-based language teaching. In *Network-based language teaching: Concepts and practice,* edited by M. Warschauer and R. Kern. Cambridge: Cambridge University Press.

Klopfer, E., S. Osterweil, and K. Salen. 2009. Moving learning games forward: Obstacles, opportunities and openness—an educational arcade paper. http://education.mit.edu/papersMovingLearning GamesForward_EdArcade.pdf.

Knight, S. 1994. Dictionary use while reading: The effects on comprehension and vocabulary acquisition for students of different verbal abilities. *Modern Language Journal* 78 (3): 285–99.

Kramsch, C. 1986. Proficiency versus achievement: Reflections on the proficiency movement. *ADFL Bulletin* 18:22–24. http://web2 .adfl.org/adfl/bulletin/v18n1/181022.htm.

———. 1993. *Context and culture in language teaching.* Oxford: Oxford University Press.

———. 2000. Social discursive construction of self in L2 learning. In *Sociocultural theory and second language learning,* edited by J. Lantolf. Oxford: Oxford University Press.

———. 2002. In search of the intercultural. *Journal of Sociolinguistics* 6 (2): 275–85.

———. 2005. Post 9/11: Foreign languages between knowledge and power. *Applied Linguistics* 26 (4): 545–67.

———. 2009. *The multilingual subject: What foreign language learners say about their experience and why it matters.* Oxford: Oxford University Press.

Kramsch, C., and R. Anderson. 1999. Teaching text and context through multimedia. *Language Learning & Technology* 2 (2): 31–42. http://llt.msu.edu/vol2num2/article1/index.html.

Kramsch, C., F. A'Ness, and W. S. E. Lam. 2000. Authenticity and authorship in the computer-mediated acquisition of L2 literacy. *Language Learning & Technology* 4 (2): 78–104. http://llt.msu .edu/vol4num2/kramsch /default.html.

Krashen, S. 1982. *Principles and practice in second language acquisition.* London: Pergamon.

———. 1985. *The input hypothesis: Issues and implications.* London: Longman.

———. 2004. *The power of reading.* Westport, CT: Libraries Unlimited.

Krashen, S., and T. Terrell. 1983. *The natural approach: Language acquisition in the classroom.* Oxford: Pergamon Press.

Kroll, J. F., and E. Stewart. 1994. Category interference in translation and picture naming: Evidence for asymmetric connections between bilingual memory representations. *Journal of Memory and Language* 33: 149–174.

Lafford, B. 2004. Review of *Tell me more. Language learning & technology* 8 (3): 21–34. http://llt.msu.edu/vol8num3/review1.

Lafford, P., and B. Lafford. 2005. CMC technologies for teaching foreign languages: What's on the horizon? *CALICO Journal* 22 (3): 679–710.

Lafford, B., P. Lafford, and J. Sykes. 2007. *Entre dicho y hecho* . . : An assessment of the application of research from second language acquisition and related fields to the creation of Spanish CALL materials for lexical acquisition. *CALICO Journal* 24 (3): 497–529.

Lai, C., and Y. Zhao. 2005. Introduction: The essence of second language education and technology integration. In *Research in technology and second language learning: Developments and directions*, edited by Y. Zhao. Greenwich, CT: Information Age.

Lai, P., and J. Biggs. 1994. Who benefits from mastery learning? *Contemporary Educational Psychology* 19 (1): 13–23.

Lam, Y. 2000. Technophilia v. technophobia: A preliminary look at why second language teachers do or do not use technology in their classrooms. *Canadian Modern Language Review* 56 (3): 389–420.

Lange, D. L., C. A. Klee, R. M. Paige, and Y. A. Yershova, eds. 2000. *Culture as the core: Interdisciplinary perspectives on culture learning in the language curriculum*. Minneapolis: Center for Advanced Research on Language Acquisition.

Lantolf, J., ed. 2000. *Sociocultural theory and second language learning*. Oxford: Oxford University Press.

Lantolf, J., and W. Frawley. 1988. Proficiency: Understanding the construct. *Studies in Second Language Acquisition* 10 (2): 181–95.

Larsen-Freeman, D., and M. Long. 1991. *An introduction to second language acquisition research*. New York: Longman.

Laurillard, D. 2002. *Rethinking university teaching*, 2nd ed. London: Routledge.

Leaver, B. L., and J. R. Willis. 2004. *Task-based instruction in foreign language education: Practices and program*. Washington, DC: Georgetown University Press.

Lee, L. 2004. Learners' perspectives on networked collaborative interaction with native speakers of Spanish in the US. *Language, Learning & Technology* 8 (1): 83–100. http://llt.msu.edu /vol8num1/lee.

LeLoup, J. W., and R. Ponterio. 2003. Interactive and multimedia techniques in online language lessons: A sampler. *Language Learning & Technology* 7 (3): 4–17.

———. 2004. FLTEACH: On-line professional development preservice and inservice foreign language teachers. In *The Heinle professional series in language instruction, Vol. 1, Teaching with technology*, edited by L. Lomicka and J. Cooke-Plagwitz. Boston: Heinle.

———. 2005. On the Net: Vocabulary support for Independent online reading. *Language Learning & Technology* 9 (2): 3–7. http://llt .msu.edu/vol9num2/net/default.html.

Lenhart, A., S. Jones, and A. Macgill. 2008. *Adults and video games*. Pew Internet and American Life Project. Washington, DC: Pew

Research Center. www.pewinternet.org/Reports/2008/Adults-and-Video-Games/1-Data-Memo.aspx.

Lenhart, A., M. Madden, and P. Hitlin. 2005. Teens and technology: Youth are leading the transition to a fully wired and mobile nation. *Pew International & American Life Project.* www.pewinter net.org/PPF/r/162/report_display.asp.

Levelt, W. 1989. *Speaking: From intention to articulation.* Cambridge, MA: MIT Press.

Levet, S., and S. Waryn, S. 2006. Using the Web to develop students' in-depth understanding of foreign cultural attitudes and values. In *Changing language education through CAL*, edited by R. P. Donaldson and M. A. Haggstrom. Abingdon: Routledge.

Levine, G. 2011. *Code choice in the language classroom.* Tonawanda, NY: Multilingual Matters.

Levine, G., and S. Morse. 2004. Integrating diverse digital media in a global simulation German course. In *The Heinle professional series in language instruction, Vol. 1, Teaching with technology*, edited by L. Lomicka and J. Cooke-Plagwitz. Boston: Heinle.

Levy, M. 1997. *Computer-assisted language learning: Context and conceptualisation.* Oxford, UK: Clarendon.

———. 2006. Effective use of CALL technologies: Finding the right balance. In *Changing language education through CALL*, edited by R. P. Donaldson and M. A. Haggstrom. Abingdon: Routledge.

Levy, M., and G. Stockwell. 2006. *CALL dimensions: Options and issues in computer-assisted language learning.* Mahwah, NJ: Lawrence Erlbaum Associates.

Lightbrown, P. M., and N. Spada. 1993. *How languages are learned.* New York: Oxford University Press.

Lin, C.-H., and M. Warschauer. 2011. Integrative versus instrumental orientation among online language learners. *Linguagens e Diálogos* 2 (1): 58–86.

Little, D. 2004. Constructing a theory of learner autonomy: Some steps along the way. In *Future perspectives in foreign language education*, edited by K. Mäkinen, P. Kaikkonen, and V. Kohonen. Oulu: Faculty of Education in Oulu University.

———. 2007. Language learner autonomy: Some fundamental considerations revisited. *Innovation in Language Learning and Teaching* 1 (1): 14–29.

Lomicka, L. 2006. Understanding the other: Intercultural exchange and CMC. In *Calling on CALL: From theory and research to new directions in foreign language teaching*, edited by L. Ducate and N. Arnold. CALICO Monograph Series 5. San Marcos, TX: CALICO.

Lomicka, L., and J. Cooke-Plagwitz, eds. 2004. *The Heinle professional series in language instruction, Vol. 1, Teaching with technology*. Boston: Heinle.

Long, M. H. 1981. Input, interaction and second language acquisition. In *Native language and foreign language acquisition*, edited by H. Winitz. New York: Annals of the New York Academy of Science.

———. 1991. Focus on form: A design feature in language teaching methodology. In *Foreign language research in cross-cultural perspective*, edited by Claire Kramsch and Ralph Ginsberg. Amsterdam: Benjamins.

Long, M. H., and P. Robinson. 1998. Focus on form: Theory, research, and practice. In *Focus on form in classroom second language acquisition*, edited by C. Doughty and J. Williams. Cambridge: Cambridge University Press.

MacWhinney, B. 1997. Implicit or explicit processes. *Studies in Second Language Acquisition* 19:277–81.

Magnan, S. 2007. Reconsidering communicative language teaching for national goals. *Modern Language Journal* 91 (2): 249–52.

Maher, M. W., B. Sommer, C. Acredolo, and H. R. Matthews. 2005. What are the relevant costs of online education? In *On becoming a productive university: Strategies for reducing costs and increasing quality in higher education*, edited by J. E. Groccia and J. E. Miller. Bolton, MA: Anker.

Marton, F., and S. Booth. 1997. *Learning and awareness*. Mahwah, NJ: Lawrence Erlbaum Associates.

Mazer, J. P., R. E. Murphy, and C. J. Simmonds. 2007. I'll see you on "Facebook": The effects of computer-mediated teacher self-disclosure on student motivation, affective learning, and classroom climate. *Communication Education* 56 (1): 1–17.

McGinnis, S. 1994. The less common alternative: A report from the Task Force for Teacher Training in the Less Commonly Taught Languages. *ADFL Bulletin* 25 (2): 17–22.

McLaughlin, B. 1987. *Theories of second language learning*. London: Edward Arnold.

McLuhan, M. 1964. *Understanding media: The extension of man*. New York: Signet.

Meskill, C. 2005. Triadic scaffolds: Tools for teaching English language learners with computers. *Language Learning & Technology* 9 (1): 46–59. http://llt.msu.edu/vol9num1/meskill/default.html.

Montrul, S. 2004. Subject and object expression in Spanish heritage speakers: A case of morpho-syntactic convergence. *Bilingualism: Language and Cognition* 7 (2): 125–42.

Moore, J. 2004. *A synthesis of Sloan-C effective practices*. http://www.sloan-c.org/effective/.

Murphy, L. 2008. Supporting learner autonomy: Developing practice through production of courses for distance learners of French, German and Spanish. *Language Teaching Research* 12 (1): 83–102.

Murray, G. L. 1999. Autonomy and language learning in a simulated environment. *System* 27:295–308.

Murray, J., D. Morgenstern, and G. Furstenberg. 1989. The Athena Language Learning project: Design issues for the next generation of computer based language-learning tools. In *Modern technology in foreign language education: Applications and projects*, edited by W. F. Smith. Lincolnwood, IL: National Textbook.

Nagata, N. 1993. Intelligent computer feedback for second language instruction. *Modern Language Journal* 77:330–38.

———. 1995. An effective application of natural language processing in second language instruction. *CALICO Journal* 13 (1): 47–67.

———. 1996. Computer vs. workbook instruction in second language acquisition. *CALICO Journal* 14 (1): 53–75.

———. 2002. An application of natural language processing to Web-based language learning. *CALICO Journal* 19 (3): 583–99.

———. 2010. Some design issues for an online Japanese textbook. *CALICO Journal* 27:460–76.

Nation, P. 2001. *Learning vocabulary in another language.* Cambridge: Cambridge University Press.

Nation, P., and R. Waring. 1997. Vocabulary size, text coverage, and word lists. In *Vocabulary: Description, acquisition, pedagogy*, edited by N. Schmitt N and M. McCarthy. New York: Cambridge University Press.

National Center for Educational Statistics. 2006. Enrollment in degree-granting institutions: Total enrollment. http://nces.ed.gov/pro grams/projections/sec2b.asp.

National Science Foundation. 2008. *Fostering learning in the networked world: The cyberlearning opportunity and challenge.* www.nsf .gov/publications/pub_summ.jsp?ods_key=nsf08204.

Nieves, K. A. 1996. The development of a technology-based class in beginning Spanish: Experiences with using EXITO. PhD diss., George Mason University.

O'Dowd, R. 2003. Understanding "the other side": Intercultural learning in a Spanish-English e-mail exchange. *Language Learning and Technology* 7 (2): 118–44.

———. 2005. Negotiating sociocultural and institutional contexts: The case of Spanish–American Telecollaboration. *Language and Intercultural Communication* 5 (1): 40–56.

———. 2006. *Telecollaboration and the development of intercultural communicative competence.* Munich: Langenscheidt ELT GmbH.

———. 2007. *Online intercultural exchange. An introduction for foreign language teachers.* Language for Intercultural Communication and Education 15.

———. 2010. Online foreign language interaction: Moving from the periphery to the core of foreign language education. *Language Technology* 31:57–71.

O'Dowd, R., and M. Ritter. 2006. Understanding and working with "failed communication" in telecollaborative exchanges. *CALICO Journal* 23 (3): 623–42.

O'Rourke, B. 2005. Form-focused interaction in online tandem learning. *CALICO Journal* 22 (3): 433–66.

O'Rourke, B., and K. Schwienhorst. 2003. Talking text: Reflections on reflection in computer-mediated communication. In *Learner autonomy in foreign language teaching: Teacher, learner, curriculum, assessment*, edited by D. Little, J. Ridley, and E. Ushioda. Dublin: Authentik.

Osuna, M. M., and C. Meskill. 1998. Using the World Wide Web to integrate Spanish language and culture: A pilot study. *Language Learning & Technology* 1 (2): 71–92. http://llt.msu.edu/vol 1num2/article4/default.html.

Payne, S. 2004. Making the most of synchronous and asynchronous discussion in foreign language instruction. In *The Heinle professional series in language instruction, Vol. 1, Teaching with technology*, edited by L. Lomicka and J. Cooke-Plagwitz. Boston: Heinle.

Payne, S., and P. J. Whitney. 2002. Developing L2 oral proficiency through synchronous CMC: Output, working memory and interlanguage development. *CALICO Journal* 20 (1): 7–32.

Pedersen, K. M. 1987. Research on CALL. In *Modern media in foreign language education: Theory and implementation*, edited by W. Smith. Lincolnwood, IL: National Textbook.

Pellettieri, J. 2000. Negotiation in cyberspace: The role of chatting in the development of grammatical competence. In *Network-based language teaching: Concepts and practice*, edited by M. Warschauer and R. Kern. New York: Cambridge University Press.

Peterson, M. 2006. Learner interaction management in an avatar and chat-based virtual world. *Computer Assisted Language Learning* 19:79–103.

———. 2010. Computerized games and simulations in computer-assisted language learning: A meta-analysis of research. *Simulation and Gaming* 41:72–93.

———. 2011. Digital gaming and second language development: Japanese learners interactions in a MMORPG. *Digital Culture and Education* 3 (1): 56–73. www.digitalcultureandeducation.com /cms/wp-content/uploads/2011/04/dce1048_peterson_2011.pdf.

Phillips, J. 1984. Practical implications of recent research in reading. *Foreign Language Annals* 17 (4): 285–96.

Pica, T. 1994. Research on negotiation: What does it reveal about second-language learning conditions, processes, and outcomes? *Language Learning* 44:493–527.

Pica, T., R. Kanagy, and J. Falodun. 1993. Choosing and using communication tasks for second language instruction. In *Tasks and language learning: Integrating theory and practice*, edited by G. Crookes and S. M. Gass. Clevedon, UK: Multilingual Matters.

Piirainen-Marsh, A., and L. Tainio. 2009. Other-repetition as a resource for participation in the activity of playing a video game. *Modern Language Journal* 93:153–69.

Pinker, S. 1995. *The language instinct*. New York: William Morrow/Harper Perennial. Orig. pub. 1994.

Porto, L. 2007. Learning diaries in the English as a foreign language classroom: A tool for accessing learners' perceptions of lessons and developing learner autonomy and reflection. *Foreign Language Annals* 40 (4): 672–95.

Prensky, M. 2000. *Digital game-based learning*. New York: McGraw-Hill.

Purushotma, R., S. L. Thorne, and J. Wheatley. 2008. 10 key principles for designing video games for foreign language learning. Paper produced for Open Language and Learning Games Project, Massachusetts Institute of Technology Education Arcade. http://knol.google.com/k/10-key-principles-for-designing-video-games-for-foreign-language-learning#.

Quinn, R. 1990. Our progress in integrating modern methods and computer-controlled learning for successful language study. *Hispania* 73 (1): 297–311.

Ranalli, J. 2008. Learning English with *The Sims*: Exploiting authentic computer simulation games for L2 learning. *Computer Assisted Language Learning* 21:441–55.

Read, J., and P. Nation. 2009. Introduction: Meara's contribution to research in lexical processing. In *Lexical processing in second language learners*, edited by T. Fitzpatrick and A Barfield. Bristol: Multilingual Matters.

Reeves, B., and C. Nass. 1996. *The media equation: How people treat computers, television, and new media like real people and places.* Stanford, CA, and New York: CSLI Publications and Cambridge University Press.

Reinders, H., and M. Thomas, eds. 2010. *Task-based language learning and teaching with technology.* London: Continuum International.

Reinders, H., and S. Wattana. 2011. Learn English or die: The effects of digital games on interaction and willingness to communicate in a foreign language. *Digital Culture and Education* 3 (1): 3–29. www.digitalcultureandeducation.com/cms/wp-content /uploads/2011/04/dce1049_reinders_2011.pdf.

Reinders, H., and C. White. 2011. Special issue commentary: Learner autonomy and new learning environments. *Language Learning & Technology* 15 (3): 1–3.

Reinhardt, J. 2011. Games to teach: Developing digital game-mediated foreign language literaries. http://games2teach.wordpress.com /publications/.

Reinhardt, J., and V. Zander. 2011. Social networking in an intensive English program classroom: Insights from language socialization. *CALICO Journal* 28 (2): 326–44.

Reynard, R. 2007. Instructional strategies for blogging. *Campus Technology*, May 9. www.campustechnology/article.aspx? aid=47775.

Rheingold, H. 2000. *The virtual community.* Cambridge, MA: MIT Press. www.rheingold.com/vc/book/3.html.

Rideout, V. J., U. G. Foehr, and R. F. Roberts. 2010. Generation m2: Media in the lives of 8- to 18-year-olds. www.kff.org/entmedia /upload/8010.pdf.

Robb, T. N. 2006. Helping teachers to help themselves. In *Teacher education in CALL*, edited by P. Hubbard and M. Levy. Language Learning & Language Teaching Series 14. Philadelphia: John Benjamin.

Roblyer, M. D. 1988. The effectiveness of microcomputers in education: A review of research from 1980–87. *T.H.E. Journal* 16 (2): 85–89.

Rovai, A. P. 2002. Sense of community, perceived cognitive learning, and persistence in asynchronous learning networks. *Internet and Higher Education* 5:319–32.

Russell, T. L. 2001. *The no significant difference phenomenon*, 5th ed. Chicago: International Distance Education Certification Center.

Salaberry, R. 1996. A theoretical foundation for the development of pedagogical tasks in computer mediated communication. *CALICO Journal* 14 (1): 5–34.

———. 1997. The role of input and output practice in second language acquisition. *Canadian Modern Language Review/La Revue canadiene des langues vivantes* 53 (2): 422–51.

———. 2001. The use of technology for second language learning and teaching: A retrospective. *Modern Language Journal* 85 (1): 39–56.

Salen, K. 2007. *The ecology of games: Connecting youth, games, and learning.* Cambridge, MA: MIT Press.

Sauro, S. 2009. Strategic use of modality during synchronous CMC. *CALICO Journal* 27 (1): 101–17.

———. 2011. SCMC for SLA: A research synthesis. *CALICO Journal* 28 (2): 1–23. https://calico.org/memberBrowsephp?action=article &id=867.

Schaumann, C., and A. Green. 2004. Enhancing the study of literature with the Web. In *The Heinle professional series in language instruction, Vol. 1, Teaching with technology*, edited by L. Lomicka and J. Cooke-Plagwitz. Boston: Heinle.

Schmidt, R. W. 1990. The role of consciousness in second language acquisition. *Applied Linguistics* 11 (2): 219–58.

Schmidt, R. W., and S. N. Frota. 1986. Developing basic conversational ability in a second language: A case study of an adult learner of Portuguese. In *Talking to learn: Conversation in second language acquisition*, edited by R. R. Day. Rowley, MA: Newbury House.

Schulze, M. 2001. Human language technologies in computer-assisted language learning. In *ICT and language learning: A European perspective*, edited by A. Chambers and G. Davies. Lisse: Sets and Zeitlinger.

Schwienhorst, K. 2008. *Learner Autonomy and CALL Environments*. New York: Routledge.

Scida, E., and R. E. Saury. 2006. Hybrid courses and their impact on student and classroom performance: A case study at the University of Virginia. *CALICO Journal* 23 (3): 517–31.

Selber, S. A. 2004. *Multiliteracies for a digital age*. Carbondale: Southern Illinois University Press.

Skehan, P. 1989. *Individual differences in second-language learning*. London: Arnold.

Smith, Bryan. 2003. Computer-mediated negotiated interaction: An expanded model. *Modern Language Journal* 87 (1): 38–54.

———. 2009. The relationship between scrolling, negotiation and self-initiated self-repair in an SCMC environment. *CALICO Journal* 26 (2): 231–45.

Soares, D. 2010. Second language pragmatic socialization in World of Warcraft. Doctoral diss., University of California, Davis.

Soo, K., and Y. Ngeow. 1998. Effective English as a second language (ESL) instruction with interactive multimedia: The MCALL project. *Journal of Educational Multimedia and Hypermedia* 7 (1): 71–89.

Sørensen, B. H., and B. Meyer. 2007. Serious games in language learning and teaching: A theoretical perspective. In *Proceedings of the 2007 Digital Games Research Association Conference*. Tokyo: Digital Games Research Association.

Sotillo, S. M. 2000. Discourse functions and syntactic complexity in synchronous and asynchronous communication. *Language Learning & Technology* 4 (1): 82–119. http://llt.msu.edu/vol4num1/sotillo/default.html.

Squire, K. 2006. From content to context: Videogames as designed experience. *Educational Researcher* 35:19–29.

Squire, K., and H. Jenkins. 2004. Harnessing the power of games in education. *Insight* 3:5–33.

Steinkuehler, C. A. 2004. Learning in massively multiplayer online games. In *Proceedings of the Sixth International Conference of the Learning Sciences*, edited by Y. B. Kafai, W. A. Sandoval, N. Enyedy, A. S. Nixon, and F. Herrera. Mahwah, NJ: Lawrence Erlbaum Associates.

———. 2006. Why game culture studies now? *Games and Culture* 1:97–102.

Stryker, S. B., and B. L. Leaver, eds. 1997. *Content-based instruction in foreign language education: Models and methods.* Washington, DC: Georgetown University Press.

Stutzman, F. 2006. An evaluation of identity-sharing behavior in social networking communities. *iDMAa journal* 3 (1). www.units.muo hio.edu/codeconference/papers/papers/stutzman_track5.pdf.

Swaffar, J. 1998. Networking language learning: Introduction. In *Language learning online: Theory and practice in the ESL and L2 computer classroom*, edited by J. Swaffar, S. Romano, P. Markley, and K. Arens. Austin: Labyrinth.

Swain, M. 1985. Communicative competence: Some roles of comprehensible input and comprehensible output in its development. In *Input in second language acquisition*, edited by C. Madden and S. M. Gass. Rowley, MA: Newbury House.

———. 2000. The output hypothesis and beyond: Mediating acquisition through collaborative dialogue. In *Sociocultural theory and second language learning*, edited by J. P. Lantolf. Oxford: Oxford University Press.

Sykes, J. M. 2009. Learner requests in Spanish: Examining the potential of multiuser virtual environments for L2 pragmatic acquisition. In *The next generation: Social networking and online collaboration*, edited by L. Lomicka and G. Lord. CALICO Monograph Series 8. San Marcos, TX: CALICO.

———. 2011. Multi-user virtual environments: User-driven design and implementation for language learning. In *Teaching through multiuser virtual environments: Applying dynamic elements to the modern classroom*, edited by G. Vincenti and J. Braman. Hershey, PA: Information Science Reference.

Sykes, J. M., and A. D. Cohen. 2009. Learner perception and strategies for pragmatic acquisition: A glimpse into online learning materials. In *Language and linguistics: Emerging trends*, edited by C. Dreyer. Hauppauge, NY: Nova Science Publishers.

Sykes, J. M., J. Reinhardt, and S. L. Thorne. 2010. Multiplayer digital games as sites for research and practice. In *Directions and prospects for educational linguistics,* edited by F. Hult. New York: Springer.

Sykes, J., A. Oskoz, and S. L. Thorne. 2008. Web 2.0, synthetic immersive environments, and mobile resources for language education. *CALICO Journal* 25:528–46.

Terrell, T. D., M. Andrade, J. Egasse, and M. Muñoz. 2002. *Dos mundos.* New York: McGraw-Hill.

Thomas, M., and H. Reinders. 2010. *Task-based language learning and teaching with technology.* London: Continuum International.

Thompson, I., and D. Hiple. 2005. Preface. In *Selected papers from the 2004 NFLRC symposium: Distance education, distributed learning and language instruction (NetWork#44),* edited by I. Thompson and D. Hiple. Honolulu: National Foreign Language Resource Center, University of Hawaii. http://nflrc.hawaii.edu /NetWorks/NW44.

Thorne, S. L. 2003. Artifacts and cultures-of-use in intercultural communication. *Language Learning and Technology* 7:38–67. http://llt .msu.edu/vol7num2/thorne/.

———. 2006. Pedagogical and praxeological lessons from internet-mediated intercultural foreign language education research. In *Internet-mediated intercultural foreign language education research,* edited by J. Belz and S. Thorne. Boston: Thompson Heinle.

———. 2008. Transcultural communication in open internet environments and massively multiplayer online games. In *Mediating discourse online,* edited by S. Magnan. Amsterdam: John Benjamins.

Thorne, S. L., and R. Black. 2007. Language and literacy development in computer-mediated contexts and communities. *Annual Review of Applied Linguistics* 27:133–60.

Thorne, S. L., R. Black, and J. Sykes. 2009. Second language use, socialization, and learning in internet interest communities and online gaming. *Modern Language Journal* 93:802–21.

Thorne, S. L., and J. S. Payne. 2005. Evolutionary trajectories, internet-mediated expression, and language education. *CALICO Journal* 22 (3): 371–97.

Truly Global Industry. 2008. Digital world, digital life: Snapshots of our online behavior and perspectives around the world. www.tns global.com/_assets/files/TNS_Market_Research_Digital_World_Digital_Life.pdf.

Turing, A. 1950. Computing machinery and intelligence. *Mind*, new series 59 (236): 433–60. http://cogprints.org/499/00/turing.html.

Underwood, J. 1984. *Linguistics, computers, and the language teacher*. Rowley, MA: Newbury House.

———. 1989. On the edge: Intelligent CALL in the 1990s. *Computers and the Humanities* 23 (1): 71–84.

US Department of Education, Office of Educational Technology. 2010. *Transforming American education: Learning powered by technology.* www2.ed.gov/about/offices/list/os/technology/netp.pdf.

Ushida, E. 2007. Robo-Sensei Personal Japanese Tutor, version 1.0. *CALICO Journal* 24 (2): 408–20.

Van de Pol, J. 2001. *Spanish without walls: Using technology to teach language anywhere.* http://ittimes.ucdavis.edu/mar2001/blake.html.

van Dijk, J. A. G. M. 2005. *The deepening divide: Inequality in the information society.* London: Sage.

VanPatten, B. 1996. *Input processing and grammar instruction: Theory and research*. Norwood, NJ: Ablex.

Varonis, E. M., and S. M. Gass. 1985. Non-native/non-native conversations: A model for negotiation of meaning. *Applied Linguistics* 6 (1): 71–90.

Vogel, T. 2001. Learning out of control: Some thoughts on the World Wide Web in learning and teaching foreign languages. In *ICT and language learning: A European perspective*, edited by A. Chambers and G. Davies. Lisse: Swets and Zeitlinger.

Vygotsky, L. 1986. *Thought and language*. Cambridge, MA: MIT Press. Orig. pub. 1962.

Walczynski, S. 2002. Applying the job characteristics model to Mallard Web-based classes. PhD diss., Illinois State University.

Ware, P. D., and C. Kramsch, C. 2005. Toward an intercultural stance: Teaching German and English through telecollaboration. *Modern Language Journal* 89 (2): 190–205.

Warschauer, M. 1995. *Virtual connections*. Honolulu: Second Language Teaching and Curriculum Center, University of Hawai' at Manoa.

———. 1996. Comparing face-to-face and electronic discussion in the second language classroom. *CALICO Journal* 13 (2): 7–26.

———. 1997a. Comparing face-to-face and electronic discussion in the second language classroom. *CALICO Journal* 13 (2–3): 7–26.

———. 1997b. Computer-mediated collaborative learning. *Modern Language Journal* 81 (4): 470–81.

———. 1999. *Electronic literacies: Language, culture, and power in online education*. Mahwah, NJ: Lawrence Erlbaum Associates.

———. 2002. Reconceptualizing the digital divide. *First Monday* 7 (7). http://firstmonday.org/issues/issue7_7/warschauer/index.html.

———. 2004. Technological change and the future of CALL. In *New perspectives on CALL for second and foreign language classrooms*, edited by S. Fotos and C. Brown. Mahwah, NJ: Lawrence Erlbaum Associates.

Warschauer, M., and I. De Florio-Hansen. 2003. Multilingualism, identity, and the internet. In *Multiple identity and multilingualism*, edited by A. Hu and I. De Florio-Hansen. Tübingen: Stauffenburg.

Warschauer, M., M. Knobel, and L. Stone. 2004. Technology and equity in schooling: Deconstructing the digital divide. *Educational Policy* 18 (4): 562–88.

Warschauer, M., L. Turbee, and B. Roberts. 1996. Computer learning networks and student empowerment. *System* 24:1–14.

Weizenbaum, J. 1966. ELIZA: A computer program for the study of natural language communication between man and machine. *Communications of the ACM* 9 (1): 35–36. http://i5.nyu.edu/~mm64/x52.9265/january1966.html.

White, C. 2006. Distance learning of foreign languages. *Language teaching: The international research resource for language professionals* 39 (4): 247–64.

Wildner-Bassett, M. E. 2005. CMC as written conversation: A critical social-constructivist view of multiple identities and cultural positioning in the L2/C2 classroom. *CALICO Journal* 22 (3): 635–56.

Wiley, T. 2007. Heritage and community languages in the national language debate: Beyond xenophobia and national security as bases for U.S. policy. *Modern Language Journal* 91 (2): 252–55.

Willis, D., and J. Willis. 2009. Task-based language teaching: Some questions and answers. *Language Teacher* 33 (3): 3–8.

Winke, P., and D. MacGregor. 2001. Review of *Hot Potatoes*. *Language Learning & Technology* 5 (2): 28–33. http://llt.msu.edu/vol 5num2/review3/default.htm.

Yagüe, A. 2007. "La tostadora se ha vuelto asesina y el ordenador no me puede ver . . .": A proprósito de la internet y la enseñanza del ELE. *Glosas didácticas* 16. www.um.es/glosasdidacticas/gd16 /todogd16.pdf.

Yanguas, I. 2010. Oral computer-mediated interaction between L2 learners: It's about time. *Language Learning & Technology* 14:72–79.

Yee, N., and J. Bailenson. 2007. The Proteus effect: The effect of transformed self-representation on behavior. *Human Communication Research* 33:271–90.

Young, J. 2002. Hybrid teaching seeks to end the divide between traditional and online instruction. *Chronicle of Higher Education* 48 (28): A33. http://chronicle.com/free/v48/i28/28a03301.htm.

Zhao, Y., M. J. Alvarez-Torres, B. Smith, and H. S. Tan. 2005. The non-neutrality of technology: A theoretical analysis and empirical study of computer-mediated communication technologies. In *Research in technology and second language learning: Developments and directions*, edited by Y. Zhao. Greenwich, CT: Information Age.

Zheng, D., M. F. Young, M. Wagner, and B. Brewer. 2009. Negotiation for action: English language learning in game-based virtual worlds. *Modern Language Journal* 93 (4): 489–511.

INDEX